The Power of Mindfulness Meditation

Finding Balance in the Midst of Chaos:
The Application of Mindfulness and
Vipassana Meditation for Personal Transformation

Peter Strong, Ph.D.

Outskirts Press, Inc.
Denver, Colorado

The Path of Mindfulness Meditation
Finding Balance in the Midst of Chaos: The Application of Mindfulness and Vipassana Meditation for Personal Transformation

Outskirts Press, Inc.
http://www.outskirtspress.com

ISBN: 978-1-4327-3688-0

Library of Congress Control Number: 2010921097

Outskirts Press and the "OP" logo are trademarks belonging to Outskirts Press, Inc.

PRINTED IN THE UNITED STATES OF AMERICA

CONTENTS

INTRODUCTION

The psyche is a remarkably complex and dynamic system that continually processess huge quantities of sensory information, and makes hundreds of unconscious decisions throughout the day, all designed to maintain balance and health. In the same way that physiological homeostasis maintains balance and well-being in the body, psychological homeostasis maintains stability and well-being in the mind. This whole dynamic process is imbued with an innate intelligence that leads towards the resolution of instability and the promotion of stability and well-being. In the ancient language of Pali, in which the Buddha's teachings were first recorded, this innate and intuitive wisdom-intelligence that leads to stability and well-being is called *satipanna*, which means "mindfulness-based wisdom-intelligence." This inner guiding principle exists in all of us, but in order to do its job of healing and restoring balance, it must have freedom to operate, and this is where the problems start.

Mental suffering, called *dukkha*, arises when the mind is not free to change under the direction of *satipanna* to resolve instability and inner conflict. The primary obstacles that take away psychological freedom, and prevent dynamic and intelligent change, are the conditioned habitual reactions that become firmly established in the mind. Habitual reactivity distorts our perceptions and makes the mind dull and inflexible. It is this inflexibility that inhibits inner transformation, as we become stuck in patterns of emotional reactivity, negative thinking and dysfunctional inner beliefs. Habitual reactivity limits our freedom to be fully present and fully engaged, and this inhibits creativity and intelligent action, which are essential for inner healing. Through ignorance and unawareness, we become prisoners of our habitual reactions and we become victims of out cognitive and emotional reactivity. Without freedom at the psychological level we cannot grow as spiritual beings, and without spiritual freedom we can never be truly happy.

During his awakening 2,500 years ago, the Buddha realized that reactivity depends on two key factors. These are *avijja*, or the ignorance that makes reactivity habitual, and *tanha*, which is the emotional force of unconscious addiction that compels us to react. The Buddha recognized that the path to freedom from reactivity and *dukkha* must involve removing the underlying roots of *avijja* and *tanha*. However, this transformation cannot be achieved by the thinking mind alone, because the thinking process tends to be corrupted by reactive conditioning. What is required is a totally different way of relating to experience that is not corrupted by reactivity. This non-reactive awareness is called mindfulness, or *sati*, in Pali.

The essential teachings of the Buddha are based on the cultivation of mindfulness in daily life and in a form of mindfulness meditation called *vipassana*, or insight meditation. The application of mindfulness is at the very heart of the Buddhist path of personal and spiritual transformation, and *sati* becomes our refuge and guiding principle in all our activities. It is through cultivating a deep awareness and presence in our living experience that we discover what is skillful and wholesome and what leads to happiness. The primary focus of The Path of Mindfulness and *vipassana* meditation is to overcome our patterns of habitual reactivity and free the mind so that we can engage fully and intelligently with life. Through mindfulness, we can restore the sensitivity and flexibility that allows the psyche to effectively heal from within, through the holistic action of our innate intelligence. Mindfulness also purifies our outward actions by restoring the same sensitivity and non-reactivity that allows us to discover what is most skillful in the moment and what produces the greatest benefit and well-being for others.

Mindfulness meditation is not an escape from suffering, but a passionate engagement with our inner pain through the focused application of mindfulness. When we relate with mindfulness, we cultivate a unique relationship, based on openness and compassion, in which we are fully present for our inner suffering. This pure objective knowing, the perfection of presence, is called *satisampajanna*, which is free from the reactions of greed, hatred and delusion. This means being completely open to whatever we are experiencing, pleasant or painful, with a mind that is willing to listen and investigate the deeper, intuitive dimension of experience. As we develop along The Path of Mindfulness, these three factors of *sati*, *satisampajanna*, and *satipanna* develop and exert their healing effects with each and every encounter with *dukkha*. Mindfulness, *sati*, allows us to be present and to overcome the patterns of habitual reactivity. *Satisampajanna* establishes the right kind of relationship with whatever arises in our experience, and *satipanna* purifies, transforms and heals. Throughout this book, these three dimensions of mindfulness are examined many times, in many different contexts. They are central to The Path of Mindfulness and mindfulness meditation.

Perhaps one of the most direct consequences of cultivating mindfulness is that we begin to penetrate the structure of our experience. We stop the conditioned reactivity that keeps us stuck at the superficial level of perception and begin a journey of discovery into the much richer dimension of our experience that was previously obscured by our superficial reactivity. Mindfulness is a movement from the superficial to the depth of experience; from the gross to the subtle; from the abstract to the real. In effect mindfulness is the movement away from ignorance and towards the truth of experience as it is, and this movement is universally transformative and liberating.

As we cultivate a relationship based on mindfulness and *satisampajanna*, we experience a fundamental shift from *becoming* the contents of the reactive mind to being the *knowing* of the contents of the mind. This has profound implications, and is the direct experience of freedom from the conditioned and the endless cycle of birth and death that compels us to re-live our habitual reactivity and suffering. To respond to the experience of the present moment with sensitivity and receptivity is the underlying theme in all the teachings of the Buddha. Above all, the Buddha invites us to discover for ourselves what leads to the resolution of *dukkha* through the direct investigation of our experience. This is The Path of Mindfulness, called *satipatthana*, in Pali. *Satipatthana* is a path, not a technique, and it is a life-long path. It is a journey that brings freedom with every step. This journey is about restoring our innate intelligence, the natural intelligence that heals and frees all that it touches, both within our broken minds and hearts and in our equally broken society.

The Buddha first taught about the power of mindfulness over 2,500 years ago, and his teachings continue to have great relevance in modern times. In the last 50 years there has been a resurgence of interest in mindfulness and mindfulness meditation throughout the world, including Europe and North America, where you will now find many centers that teach mindfulness meditation. Mindfulness has also found a place in many schools of psychotherapy for stress management or as a skillful way of working with emotional afflictions such as Mindfulness-Based Cognitive Therapy. Mindfulness is central to successful therapy, because it allows the client to tune in to the deeper structure of his or her emotional reactivity, and discover exactly what needs to change to facilitate inner healing.

This book briefly describes one form of mindfulness-based psychotherapy, which I have called Mindfulness Meditation Therapy. This can be defined as the direct application of mindfulness to facilitate the transformation of emotional suffering. In this approach, we make emotional suffering the primary object of meditation, and use mindfulness to create the ideal environment to bring about transformation and healing. Mindfulness training teaches us to recognize our patterns of habitual reactivity, which is an essential pre-requisite for transformation. Mindfulness Meditation Therapy allows us to respond to the emotional content that powers our reactions by creating a therapeutic relationship based on full presence, spaciousness and compassion. In this therapeutic space, repressed emotions are able to unfold and differentiate, often into a particular form of imagery called experiential imagery.

In Mindfulness Meditation Therapy, there is a particular focus on experiential imagery, because the mind thinks in pictures, not words, and emotions are encoded in the detailed sub-modalities of our inner imagery. Through mindfulness, we can uncover this inner imagery at the core of our emotional afflictions, and mindfulness creates the ideal therapeutic space in which this imagery can unfold and change, under the direction of *satipanna*. As the imagery changes, it brings about a resolution of emotional suffering, because the two are directly connected.

The *Dhamma* as taught by the Buddha can be found in many traditions. You do not have to be a Buddhist to practice the teachings of the Buddha, only be willing to open your heart and mind to investigate the truth of things as they are. Buddhism is a complex living religion with many different schools and traditions, but the underlying principles are actually very simple. The central message of the Buddha is to awaken to experience and be fully present for what unfolds. When we are fully awake, then we are also free, and we are no longer compelled to react according to habit and conditioning, but have choice in how best respond to life. When there is freedom and choice there is the possibility of intelligent and compassionate action in the world. We tend to complicate this simple message and chain ourselves to dogma, conventions, beliefs and practices. We attach to the wisdom of others, not realizing that the only wisdom that has any reality is in our own heart. Through The Path of Mindfulness, we discover the true compassion and wisdom that lies within, and this is the same wisdom and compassion that will purify our world. Just as suffering is universal, so the *Dhamma* is equally universal. When we take our firt step on The Path of Mindfulness, the whole of humanity takes one step with us towards freedom.

May the words in this book be of benefit to you and inspire you on your path towards greater freedom and happiness for all through the practice of mindfulness.

1 THE STRUCTURE OF EXPERIENCE

Each moment of our life is defined by what we experience. Each moment of experience is a unique composition of physical form and mental reactions. This is called *nama-rupa*, in Pali, which literally means "name and form." From the Buddhist perspective, each moment of existence is a complex of five fundamental components called *khandhas*, which literally means "heaps," or "aggregates." *Rupa khandha* consists of the actual external form of a physical object, such as the physical shape of a statue of the Buddha, which is called a "Buddha-rupa." However, *rupa* also includes the physiological and neurochemical processes of the sense organs of the body and brain that are required to perceive form. You need a body and a brain to see a Buddha-rupa, or a person or any other object, just as much as the actual physical presence of the object itself. The subjective mental component (*nama*) of our experience consists of four mental *khandhas* that arise in response to sensory contact. These are perception and memory (*sanna*), feeling (*vedana*), the cognitive reaction of thinking (*sankhara*) and sense consciousness (*vinnana*).

Everything that is experienced is formed by the interplay of these five aggregates in a continual flux of coming together, existing for a short while and then dissolving. Every mind moment, or *citta*, is like water that temporarily freezes into a rigid ice formation for an instant before it melts, only to refreeze a moment later into a different combination of the five aggregates. This view of existence as having no fixed essence is in contrast to our conventional view of mind as something that exists independent of contents. We imagine that we have a mind that thinks and experiences, but actually the mind *is the process of thinking* as it unfolds from moment to moment. This lack of essence is described by the term *anatta*, literally "not self." This insight does not mean that we do not exist or do not have a personality, but that there is nothing substantial in that personality, simply because it is continually changing. There is nothing that you can grab hold of and say, "This is who I am." The reality is that your notion of your self is an illusion. It is nothing more than a linguistic label, an abstract fabrication, and the closer you examine the reality of self, the more you see that it has no definable form. In fact, it is not only our mind that changes from one moment to the next; the body (*rupa*) is also continually changing so you cannot even define yourself by reference to your body. The form of the body that you claim to be who you are will be totally different from one year to the next and if you look closely you will discover that it is actually different from one minute to the next.

It is also a common mistake to try and define our self as equal to our consciousness. We think of our self as the entity that is conscious and we believe that this consciousness exists independently. Many take this a step further and believe that this consciousness forms a soul that can reincarnate or that can unite with some kind of higher universal consciousness. However, if you investigate the reality of your own experience, you will discover that consciousness arises due to conditions and these conditions change from minute to minute. When you see a pretty flower, your consciousness is defined by the visual sensations, combined with memories, preferences and beliefs, creating an awareness of beauty. A moment later, you see a beetle eating the flower and your consciousness changes to the awareness of disgust. Which of those states of consciousness defines you? If you argue that you are all states of consciousness, then you become something that cannot be defined at all. Therefore, the term *anatta* simply means that you cannot be defined or reduced to a single entity and that your true identity is as the process of living itself.

The Path of Mindfulness and *vipassana* meditation is one in which we reverse-engineer moment-to-moment experience and investigate these five aggregates and de-construct the blind attachment and identification with each. Through illuminating our attachment to the five *khandhas* with mindfulness, we begin to discover freedom from reactivity and the suffering created by habitual reactivity. Therefore, it is well worth becoming familiar with each one in more detail.

RUPA

All experiences have an objective physical component (*rupa*) in addition to the subjective mental component (*nama*). In short, you need a brain and a body to have conscious experience and the body is, therefore, an integral part of mental and particularly emotional experience. It is not surprising that the state of the body affects the state of the mind and of course, the state of the mind can profoundly affect the health of the body.

Mindfulness practice involves developing an acute awareness of physical sensations in the body as well as the awareness of physical activities, and this is collectively known as *kayanupassana*, the mindful-contemplation of the body. This is one of the four primary domains of mindfulness practice and the foundation for spiritual development, as taught by the Buddha. We tend to be so engrossed in thinking that we do not pay attention to our bodies, which is unfortunate, because the body is a powerful teacher. Through mindfulness practice, we can begin to access this teaching and become conscious of the way we hold emotional energy in our bodies. This is a very powerful method of working with deep-seated emotions, because it provides a path to access the non-verbal and deeper structure of the emotional complex than can be accessed through thinking alone.

SANNA

Sanna is the *khandha* of perception and memory, in which the mind recognizes and labels things according to past experience. When we see a cup, we do not simply perceive the original objective phenomenon, but we react to the visual data with a primary mental reaction that is conditioned by our past experience. We recognize and label the object as a cup. In fact, such labels are completely artificial, linguistic tools that we acquire through learning. There is no "cup" in the absolute sense and the label "cup" is added on to this objective reality as a primary subjective reaction. Another person may look at the same object and see a bowl rather than a cup. It all depends on our particular conditioning and the accepted conventions that we learn from family, culture and society. On a conventional level there is nothing wrong with calling a cup a cup, as long as we know that the label is not the object it represents. Unfortunately, the mind has a very strong tendency to create abstract representations such as word-labels and we tend to blindly attach to these labels and ignore the actual objective reality. The complex and dynamic reality of what we observe becomes reduced to a superficial representation.

Perception is conditioned by our inner beliefs and inner models of reality, which we create as a way of organizing sensory experience. Some of these beliefs are formed very early during our childhood and become core beliefs that shape the rest of our lives. We absorb the beliefs of our parents and influential people, including friends, ethnic and religious leaders and politicians and, of course, commercial advertising. All of these influences color our perception and give us a distorted picture of reality. If we are not mindful, we tend to identify with these distorted beliefs as real and true and lose sight of the reality of the present moment, which is always unique and beyond labels. We become limited by our blind reactivity, which makes us blindly believe the surface appearance of things. This attachment to superficial representations is the essence of delusion, called *moha* in Pali, which along with greed (*lobha*) and aversion (*dosa*), describe the three principle groups of habitual reactivity that create suffering. We think we see what is before us, but actually what we experience is our belief, our inner representation *about* the object; we do not actually see the object as it is. We don't see the truth of reality, but our *reaction* to reality.

This distortion and perversion of perception through blind attachment to our inner representations, labels and beliefs is called *sanna vipallasa*. When we attach to these delusions, we create the conditions in which reactivity and suffering proliferate. Problems occur when we are unable to break free from our habitual way of seeing things, because we are unable to adapt to the needs of present reality. When we attach to our labels and beliefs, we turn our back on the path of discovering truth and retreat into a world of half-truths, generalizations and misunderstandings. Many people spend their entire lives living in a world of illusion, created by their own perceptual reactivity, or through blind attachment to the beliefs of others. Krishnamurti spoke often on the subject of perception and the importance of freeing the mind from the perversions that come from attachment to labels and beliefs, as in the following passage:

> Perception without the word, which is without thought, is one of the strangest phenomena. Then the perception is much more acute, not only with the brain, but also with all the senses. Such perception is not the fragmentary perception of the intellect, nor the affairs of the emotions. It can be called a total perception, and it is part of meditation. Perception without the perceiver in meditation is to commune with the height and depth of the immense.

When we react to what we observe with labels, inner representations and beliefs, we inadvertently create division between an observer and the observed, because what we experience is not the observed, but the reactions of the observer. This subject-object duality lies at the core of all violence, experienced as inner conflict, as well as conflict in our external relationships. When we label a person as good or bad, it has the effect of closing the mind and heart to the complex reality and totality of the other person. We lose sight of reality and begins perpetuating delusion upon delusion, lie upon lie. Soon, the person we label as bad becomes our enemy. This makes it easier to justify reactions of hatred, aggression and violence. Violence depends on ignorance and delusion in equal portion. When we understand the corrupting influence of ignorance and delusion on *sanna* and the effects that this has on people and society, then we can understand just how important The Path of Mindfulness and meditation is for the world. Fundamentally, The Path of Mindfulness is the fight against ignorance and delusion, and this has direct beneficial consequences for all.

Perception without the perceiver means that there is no attachment to our subjective mental reactivity to the object perceived, but simply the direct experiencing of things as they are, and this is the function of mindfulness. Krishnamurti used the term *choiceless awareness* to describe this direct perception that is independent of the perceiver. There is, therefore, a fundamental difference between "fragmentary perception," based on the past, and "total perception," which is experience without any interference from the past. Choiceless awareness is another term for mindfulness, and non-reactive perception, which is called *satisampajanna*, or "clear knowing through mindfulness," in Pali. This clear seeing, or pure knowing is seeing the observed, without the reactions of the observer. When there is no reactivity, there is no separation between the observer and the observed, the knower and the known. What remains is simply "observing" and "knowing," or the pure awareness of things as they actually exist in the present.

The purpose of mindfulness practice and meditation is to develop *satisampajanna* so that perception is always fresh and grounded in the direct knowing of the present. With a mind that is free and open and non-reactive, we gain access to a much richer sensory reality than can be provided by our conditioned reactivity. To see a mountain in this way is to see true beauty in its highest form, which is beyond our ideas of beauty. To see a person, without the reactions of an observer, the ego, is to see him without prejudice and division. The same applies to our inner perceptions and when you can look at your mind with freshness, with what Suzuki Roshi called "beginners mind," then you open up to a tremendous depth and breadth of experience that makes transformation possible and that will enriche both the psychological and spiritual dimensions of our Being.

Overcoming the limitations of reactive perception is partcularly important when we relate to our emotions and when we look at reactions themselves. When we experience an emotion, we tend to label it as happiness, anger, depression, joy or sorrow and identify with these labels. The labels, which are reactions based on inner beliefs are sperficial illusions. They are the product of reactive thinking *about* the emotion and are not the same as the emotion itself. The label is not the same as the actual experience of happiness, anger or depression. Therefore, the perception of emotion, based on reactive *sanna* generates a pseudo-reality known as a *sankhara*, which is conditioned by ignorance (*avijja*). These *sankharas* are the superficial representations of our experience. When we blindly attach to these *sankharas*, we become blind to the ac-

6

tual reality of the inner structure of the emotion and this has the effect of freezing the emotional reaction in place.

If you look closely at any emotion, such as anger, you will soon discover that "anger" is not a single state of consciousness, but a dynamic and unfolding process consisting of a collection of many different feelings, thoughts, beliefs and memories that have simply been aggregated together into a *sankhara* and labelled as "anger" or "fear." This is an extremely important point, because it is almost impossible to transform something as abstract as "anger" or "fear," because it *does not exist in reality*. Transformation of an emotional conflict depends, therefore, on letting go of the label and engaging with the actual structural contents of the emotion as it unfolds in the form of specific feelings, thoughts and memories. We cannot easily change core beliefs, but we can change present experience, and if you change present experience, the beliefs will change in response.   Eventually, as you develop mindfulness, you will find that you become less and less dependent on labels and beliefs, and eventually you transcend the belief-making process altogether. Then your perception will be purified and you will be free to fully experience the vibrant and living reality of truth, of *Dhamma*, and it is the truth that liberates, not our efforts to manipulate and control the mind. The Path of Mindfulness is in many ways a process of stripping away the layers of reactive perception. Mindfulness is the universal movement from the superficial to the real; from the abstract outer appearance of things, including our emotions, to the actual inner structure of our experience. Or, put simply the movement from delusion to truth.

VEDANA

Descartes proclaimed "I think, therefore I am," but it might be more accurate to say, "I *feel*, therefore I am." Feeling energy is the power that gives both meaning and value to our experience and provides the motivation that leads to all actions of body, speech and mind. With perception comes feeling and all experience has an associated feeling tone or felt-sense called *vedana*, in Pali. *Vedana* is the undifferentiated feeling energy associated with sensory experience, and this energy occurs in three flavors. Experience can have a positive felt-sense (*sukhavedana*), which is pleasant, light and open in quality, or it can have a negative felt-sense (*dukkhavedana*), which is painful, dark and oppressive in quality. In addition, perception may be accompanied by a neutral felt-sense (*upekkhavedana*), which is neither pleasant nor painful, but is none the less compelling in giving meaning to experience. All three forms of *vedana* have positive and negative aspects associated with them.

The positive aspect of *sukhavedana* is that it is life affirming and provides positive energy that directs us towards a state of happiness and well-being. The negative aspect of *sukhavedana* is that it can lead to blind attachment and the compulsive emotional reactions of wanting and craving, called *tanha*, which is the primary force that leads to suffering. The positive side of *dukkhavedana* is that it is a signal that something is out of balance. Just like physical pain, unpleasant feelings can allow us to uncover the inner blind attachments that are the source of mental pain. The negative side of *dukkhavedana* is that it can lead to emotional reactions of aversion, which has the effect of repressing the underlying attachments. Repression amplifies instability and conflict and causes more emotional pain, more *dukkha*. The positive aspect of *upekkhavedana* is the feeling quality, or felt-sense, that accompanies inner balance, stability and well-being. It is the felt-sense of equilibrium in the psyche. The negative side of *upekkhavedana* is ignorance (*avijja*) and delusion (*moha*), which are associated with blind attachment and identification with inner beliefs. *Upekkhavedana* can accompany blind faith, unquestioned obedience and a general absence of awareness as well as apathy and a lack of presence and engagement with reality.

Besides being pleasant, painful or neutral, *vedana* also comes in a range of different intensities, ranging from very mild feelings, such as the feeling we have when we remember what day of the week it is, to the very intense *vedana* associated with anger or fear and other emotional reactions. Generally, the mind does not attach to experiences that have weak *vedana* and these will tend to fall away, without leaving a trace in the subconscious mind. If *vedana* is strong, then the mind will tend to become attached and fixated on these experiences and they will leave a deep imprint in the mind

8

as a memory that can influence future perceptions and reactivity. When *vedana* is very strong, it converts into *tanha*, the compulsive forceful energy that leads to attachment (*upadana*), and attachment forms the foundation for mental reactivity in the form of greed (*lobha*), aversion (*dosa*) and delusion (*moha*). Ignorance of this conversion of *vedana* into *tanha* creates instability and conflict in the mind, and this subtle shift from feeling to emotional reactivity based on blind attachment, creates the conditions for mental conflict, disharmony and suffering, that we call *dukkha*.

The optimum state of being is, therefore, one in which there is no clinging to pleasant, unpleasant or neutral feelings, but rather a complete freedom to fully engage with all our feelings, without any compulsion to react. We need to be free to engage with pleasant feelings, without becoming greedy. We need to completely engage with painful feelings, without aversion. We need to recognize neutral feelings and avoid indifference. Feelings are very seductive, whether pleasant, painful or neutral, and The Path of Mindfulness practice and meditation (*vipassana*) involves cultivating a very refined sensitivity and awareness to the movements of *vedana* and the relationship between *vedana* and *tanha* and how this leads to *dukkha*.

Focusing on the feeling tone of experience is extremely important in mindfulness practice and meditation and is called *vedanupassana*: the mindful relationship and engagement with feelings as they arise from moment to moment. During meditation, the practitioner deliberately seeks out areas of unresolved emotional conflict and chooses to work on them with mindfulness. However, this kind of work does not involve analysis or thinking, but cultivating a direct and open relationship with the more subtle and intuitive feeling level of the emotion. Through mindfulness, one begins to undo the reactive habits in which *vedana* converts into *tanha* and this has the effect of allowing *tanha* to change back into *vedana*. Transformation at the intuitive feeling level is much easier than trying to change emotional reactions powered by *tanha*, and with mindfulness, we introduce the element of freedom and choice and this provides the right conditions for change. Put simply, it is blind reactivity that sustains emotional suffering and it is mindfulness that provides an antidote to blind reactivity allowing the resolution of suffering, under the guidance of *satipanna*.

The open and non-reactive relationship with the feeling level of an emotion allows us to make conscious the complexity and multiple layers of feeling that lie at the heart of an emotional complex like guilt, anger or fear. The freedom that is inherent in mindfulness allows experiential unfolding, and this is how the psyche heals itself. What may start off as an unpleasant felt-sense associated with anger may change to a feeling of panic, which then changes to sadness, which may in turn change into another type of feeling. It is the conscious awareness of these subtle changes in *vedana* that arise during mindfulness meditation that leads to transformation. The process that leads to the resolution of *dukkha*, or inner mental conflict, needs this kind of freedom of movement between the different levels of *vedana* in conscious awareness. Mindfulness cultivates this inner freedom as well as providing the all-important conscious awareness that is essential fro change to occur.

The exact path of experiential unfolding that leads to the resolution of inner conflict can never be understood or analyzed, because it is an experiential process that unfolds at a much deeper intuitive level. This is where mindfulness is essential, because the mindful-relationship is free from prejudice and preconceptions, and it is this quality of awareness that allows feelings to change at the experiential level. More often than not, resolution of trapped *vedana* energy requires nothing more than simply making contact with the feeling in a way that is non-threatening and non-reactive. This simple act of being fully present is, by itself, remarkably healing, and this is not limited to the mind, but also applies to our personal relationships.

Another important feature of *vedana* is that it can be used as a measure of inner change. If transformation is happening during *vipassana* meditation, then this will be accompanied by a shift in the quality of *vedana* from *dukkhavedana* to *sukhavedana* and eventually to *upekkhavedana*, after resolution of emotional conflict and when balance is restored. The shifts in feeling tone allow us to align with those inner processes that lead to the maximum resolution of *dukkha*, and help us let go of those processes that do not. It should, however, be remembered that the transformational process is not linear and it is quite possible that feelings may intensify before they dissipate. In general though, even if a painful feeling becomes temporarily more intense, there is also a sense that what is happening *needs* to happen. For example, focusing on the painful felt-sense of anxiety may bring up a traumatic childhood memory that evokes even stronger *dukkhavedana*, yet the experience of this memory with mindfulness is also accompanied by a sense of release.

The net direction of transformation should be towards the resolution of *dukkha* and the restoration of inner balance that can be verified at the subtle feeling level. This is change at the deepest level, rather than through trying to manipulate feeling through thinking or rationalization. It is a good practice to revisit the emotion and see for yourself if it has resolved or not. Eventually, through repeated practice with this truthful attention to feeling, you will discover that something quite fundamental has changed at the experiential level. In this way we use the intuitive feeling level of our experience to guide us towards the resolution of *dukkha* and the core attachments that sustain *dukkha*, and release the mind from the shackles that prevent us from finding real peace and happiness. In mindfulness practice and meditation the feeling tone of experience guides us from the condition of bondage to the state of freedom, and this can be quite clearly felt in the body as well as in the mind. When we pay attention to *vedana* in this way, we learn to dance with this feeling energy with great sensitivity, and use the subtle changes in feeling as our guide on the path to freedom.

SANKHARA

Sankhara refers to anything, physical or mental, that is formed dependent on conditions. The word *sankhara* is composed of the prefix *sam*, meaning "together," and *kara*, which means, "doing or "making." *Sankhara* refers to anything constructed out of parts, including material objects, such as a mountain or a house, the most common use of the term is in relation to our experience and activities. In each moment of existence, a person expresses himself through body (*kayasankhara*), speech (*vacisankhara*) and mind (*cittasankhara*) in the form of particular actions, patterns of speech and thoughts. In reality they all arise together as an integrated whole. An emotional reaction like anger will involve an angry facial expression in combination with an angry voice and angry thoughts, which are all necessary to create the emotional state of anger. If you take away angry expression or talk with a slow and gentle voice tone or if you have peaceful thoughts, then you will not be able to sustain the emotional *sankhara* of anger. In this way, the term *sankhara* conveys the bringing together of all these elements into a particular formation. Anger is one particular synthesis of body, specch and mind, whereas gladness will involve a completely different assembly of patterns of body, speech and mind. Each moment of experience involves the arising and passing away of these formations, like the individual frames of a movie that appear on the movie screen in front of us.

The *cittasankharas* are thought-feeling complexes that bring together *sanna* and *vedana* in reaction to present sensory experience and this is the most common use of the term *sankhara*. In this context, *sankhara* is usually translated as the conditioned mental formations that arise in the mind as thoughts, emotions and beliefs. *Sankharas* are the reactive mental formations that influence all aspects of expression through body, speech and mind. As the Buddha said,

> All that we are is the result of what we have thought.
> The mind is everything. What we think we become.

In the same way that physical actions and speaking are largely automatic and performed without much conscious awareness, thoughts, beliefs and emotions also arise without much conscious awareness as they are happening. In other words, there is a degree of ignorance (*avijja*) that accompanies each *cittasankhara*. This is not ignorance as lack of knowledge, but ignorance as lack of *knowing*, of not being aware of what is happening while it is happening. Hence, in the teachings on Dependent Origination (*paticcasamuppada*), *avijja* is the first of twelve links, and the condition for the arising of *sankhara* and the subsequent reactive process that results in habitual reactivity and suffering.

12

Avijja paccaya sankhara.
Sankharas arise out of ignorance.

Paccaya means "the necessary condition for," which in this case is *sankhara*. When there is ignorance of what is happening in the present, the mind generates thoughts, beliefs and emotions based on habitual conditioning. The *sankharas* from the past influence the *sankharas* being formed in the present and present *sankharas* become the conditions for future *sankharas*. This is *kamma* (Skt. *karma*), the fundamental law of cause and effect, or reactivity. When *avijja* is dominant, then what manifests in the present will be largely influenced by reactivity based on the past and this leads to actions that don't quite fit the needs of the present, that are unskillful and unwholesome (*akusala kamma*). The Path of Mindfulness is fundamentally about removing this ignorance so that we do not become inadvertently attached to the *sankharas* that arise, and the habitual reactivity that follows. When we are free from domination by *sankharas*, by the superficial appearances and reactions, then we will have a clear perception of the present, and we will have a much better chance of responding with skillful and wholesome actions (*kusala kamma*) based on wisdom and compassion.

All *sankharas* are essentially superficial, incomplete and distorted representations of the truth and are, therefore, unsatisfactory. Attachment and blind acceptance of the superficial keeps us locked in a world of delusion, and causes conflict and unskillful actions that tend to create suffering. The combination of unsatisfactoriness and conflict between truth and delusion are the two sides of *dukkha*. Life is a dynamic process requiring fresh solutions in each new moment, and this means that we must let go of the superficial in order to discover truth. Hence, the Buddha proclaimed that attachment to *sankharas* is a fundamental cause of suffering, as in the following statement:

Sabbe sankhara dukkha.
All conditioned mental formations are unsatisfactory.

What arise in the mind as a thought, belief or even an emotional reaction, are simply superficial surface representations. The reality behind these representations remains hidden. To take the surface representation as true, keeps us locked in ignorance and prevents the movement of intelligence, and this prevents beneficial change. We are deluded into seeing things as black or white, good or bad, right or wrong. Attachment to any *sankhara* tends to create the illusion of boundaries, which do not actually exist in the real world. Blind attachment to beliefs or any representation of the world is a breeding ground for ignorance, and takes us further and further away from the truth. To quote William Blake,

> The man who never alters his opinion is like standing
> water, and breeds reptiles of the mind.

Attachment and identification with these "reptiles of the mind," the *sankharas*, creates friction and conflict, because any representation or belief is never quite in harmony with life as it actually is in the present. Life is never completely black or white, good or bad, right or wrong, but an ever-changing process moving between all the manifestations between these extremes. Because of this, *sankharas* are unsatisfactory, and this mismatch between the *sankharas* and reality gives rise to suffering (*dukkha*).

The next major problem with the *sankharas* is that they are very seductive, and we inadvertently become attached to them and blindly identify with them as "me" or "mine." If the thought "I am depressed," arises in the mind, we tend to blindly attach to this *sankhara* and then we *become* the thought "I am depressed." If sadness arises, we become the sadness. If anger arises, we become the anger. This is the endless wandering mind of *samsara*, the habitual reactivity that makes us slaves to whatever arises in the mind. The Path of Mindfulness is very focused on overcoming this automatic process of habitual reactivity that takes away our freedom and happiness, by training us to wake up and recognize what is happening as it is happening. Then we will have a moment of choice about whether we want to feel sad or depressed, and in that brief moment of choice there is freedom and the possibility of change. If there were no *avijja*, then there would be no attachment and no becoming, and whatever arises would simply dissolve away like a ripple on the surface of a pond.

Perhaps the single most important insight of the Buddha is the observation that all *sankharas* are inherently unstable and are subject to change,

> *Sabbe sankhara anicca.*
> All formations are impermanent.

This is the law of *anicca*, which is a central concept in Buddhism. All things fabricated, without exception, will change and finally dissolve back into their parts. Existence is simply a dance in the arising and pasing away of form, and it is by awakening to this that we find spiritual and psychological freedom. All things born must die, and it is the ignorance of this truth as a living reality, which is at the root of all our suffering. However, *anicca* is more than just a reflection on the impermanence of life, but an understanding that life and existence is a dynamic *process* that thrives on change. *Sankharas* are like the individual frames of a movie: they need to change in rapid succession to make a movie. Suffering arises when we attach to the individual frames, which leaves us with meaningless snapshots of life, instead of the full experience of the movie. Through the practice of mindfulness, we begin to align and harmonize with life as a dynamic process, without the constraints of attachment and clinging to *sankharas*. This is the condition of freedom that allows our innate intelligence and wisdom (*satipanna*) to arise and direct the psyche to make the subtle changes that lead towards stability and well-being. Without mindfulness, change becomes chaotic and creates disorder and dis-equillibrium.

The mind that is ignorant of its own reactivity is bound by that reactivity (*sankhata citta*) and suffers accordingly; the mind that is unconditioned (*asankhata citta*) and free from blind attachment to *sankharas* does not suffer. There will still be pain, because that is an unavoidable part of living, but there will not be the suffering that we add to the pain through our subjective reactivity. The purpose of mindfulness work in daily practice and in *vipassana* meditation is to reduce the blind identification with the conditioned contents of the mind and "switch" to the unconditioned state of being. Actually, any mind moment (*citta*) contains both the conditioned element and the unconditioned element in close and inseparable unity. The conditioned element consists of the contents (*sankharas*) in the form of thoughts and emotions. However, there is also the unconditioned element, the *asankhata dhatu*, that is not the contents, but the *knowing* of the contents, and this pure knowing arises spontaneously whenever there is mindfulness (*sati*) of contents.

In each moment of non-reactive knowing, the mind is not attached or identified with the thoughts or emotional reactions that arise, but simply *knows* them as they are. In this pure knowing, called *satisampajanna*, things are allowed to exist in freedom, and they will respond to this freedom by changing in an intelligent and beneficial way. This is the state of perfect alignment with *anicca*, where we move in unity with the arising and passing away of phenomena, and this is an essential component of awakening and liberation that leads to the cessation of suffering.

If we take the analogy of the ocean, the fish are the contents (*sankharas*) and the ocean is the formless element (*asankhata dhatu*) of pure knowing. The fish come and go according to conditions, but the ocean remains unchanged. Do you want to be a fish or do you want to be the ocean? In the Buddhist Path of Mindfulness, we choose to be the ocean, but this does not, in any way, mean rejecting the contents of the mind. In fact, when there is *satisampajanna*, we are free to engage with the world of form and the *sankharas*, with complete freedom and complete presence, that are denied when the mind is reactive. There is a Pali chant,

> *Anicca vata sankhara*
> *Upada vaya dhammino*
> *Upakituva nirujihanti*
> *Tesang vupasama sukho*

> All condfitioned things are impermanent.
> Their nature is to arise and pass away.
> To live in harmony with this truth
> Brings unsurpassable happiness.

The blind identification and attachment to the superficial formations of *sankharas* is like sitting on the rim of a spinning wheel, which is very unstable and stressful, the very ingredients of *dukkha*. Taking refuge in the unconditioned, the *asankhata*, is like sitting at the still center of the spinning wheel, a place that is stable and does not generate *dukkha*. The beauty of taking refuge in the still center is that it allows you complete and free access to all the *sankharas* on the rim, but allows you to retain balance in relation to them, without further reactivity. This is the "unsurpassable happiness" of the still center, in which the mind is no longer pushed around by changing conditions and no longer a victim of change. This is the goal of the Buddhist path of spiritual development, and which has tremendous significance for all of us: to transcend the unsatisfactory world of conditioned phenomena and abide in the Noble Stillness of full engagement, free from compulsion and habitual reactivity. From this place, we can discover the true wonder of authentic living, in which there is an alive and passionate engagement with everything.

VINNANA

This is the aggregate of sense consciousness that arises whenever the sense organs make contact with an object. As the Buddha said,

> Conditioned through the eye, the visible object, light
> and attention, eye-consciousness arises.

And this same statement is applied to the consciousness that arises through contact with sound, smell, taste and touch. Similarly, all mental objects are accompanied by consciousness as they arise in the brain, which is regarded as the sixth sense organ.

> Conditioned through the subconscious mind, the mind-
> object and attention, mind-consciousness arises.

Consciousness always arises in association with particular sense objects or mental objects and is therefore conditioned.

Many people like to believe in the concept of a soul, or a form of universal consciousness that exists separately from our body. From the Buddhist perspective this can never be more than abstract speculation that cannot be directly known. Whenever a person thinks they know the truth, what they are really experiencing is the delusional form of a *sankhara*. For the Buddha, the only thing that we can known is what is in the immediate here and now of our experience, and we must start there if we are to move beyond the superficial level of *sankhara*. If there is a God, then this can only be discovered by opening the mind and heart to the intuitive level of experience, and not by inventing an idea or image of God or by blindly following religious leaders and traditions.

2 THE REACTIVE MIND

In a public talk given in 1996, J. Krishnamurti made the following comments about the nature of habitual reactivity:

> Without freedom from the past, there is no freedom at all, because the mind is never new, fresh, innocent. It is only the fresh, innocent mind that is free. Freedom has nothing to do with age, it has nothing to do with experience; and it seems to me that the very essence of freedom lies in understanding the whole mechanism of habit; both conscious and unconscious. It is not a question of ending habit, but of seeing totally the structure of habit. You have to observe how habits are formed and how, by denying or resisting one habit, another habit is created. What matters is to be totally conscious of habit; for then, as you will see for yourself there is no longer the formation of habit. To resist habit, to fight it, to deny it, only gives continuity to habit. When you fight a particular habit you give life to that habit, and then the very fighting of it becomes a further habit. But if you are simply aware of the whole structure of habit without resistance, then you will find there is freedom from habit and in that freedom, a new thing takes place.

The mind is a remarkably creative instrument that is able to adapt to an extraordinary variety of changing conditions. This is testimony to the innate intelligence that we already possess and that we seek to further develop through The Path of Mindfulness.

However, although the mind has such a remarkable capacity for creativity, it also has a strong tendency to create habitual reactions, as a default mechanism for coping with the complex demands of life. We learn from our parents, family and friends, as well as from our culture, and we unconsciously acquire patterns of thinking and feeling that coalesce into attitudes and beliefs. In effect, we learn patterns of habitual reactivity and these patterns form our personality, called *sakkayaditthi* in Pali.

The Self is a vast network of inter-related habitual reactions that define what we think, act and feel, and greatly influence the possible outcomes of body, speech and mind. Reactivity depends on ignorance and the state of being unaware (*avijja*) of what is happening in the mind. Reactivity also depends on delusion (*moha*), which causes us to blindly believe and identify with the reactions that arise. Both of these factors lead to blind attachment (*upadana*) that keeps us repeating the same mental reactions over and over again. *Upadana* causes us to *become* the anger, worry, fear, guilt or other mental states that arise. As long as we remain ignorant of these underlying attachments and remain blindly identified with our reactivity, then it becomes self-reinforcing and habitual and will dominate our lives.

Attachment is in turn powered by the energetic and compulsive force known as *tanha*, which compels the mind to attach to reactive patterns of thinking and behavior. The combination of ignorance, attachment and compulsion perpetuates habitual reactivity and the endless cycle of becoming, which is called *samsara* in Pali. In the words of the great Tibetan master, Kalu Rinpoche,

> Our present circumstances are like those of someone who has been bound in chains and locked in a dark prison cell. The cell is samsara and we are bound up and confined in it by our own ignorance.

Like a recurring nightmare, conditioned habitual reactivity forces us to re-experience reactions of anxiety, fear, worry, grief, sadness, disappointment, frustration and anger over and over again. The mind that is dominated by reactivity and *samsara* can never fully engage with life as it is, because this continual reactivity actually takes us away from the full experience of life in the here and now. The Path of Mindfulness is concerned with awakening to our habitual reactivity and overcoming it, not through force, but by developing a conscious relationship with each of the many reactions that arise that creates a space around the reaction in which there is a sense of choice and freedom. This special kind of non-reactive relationship is the essence of mindfulness.

One of the fundamental problems of habitual reactivity is that it introduces a degree of inflexibility in the mind. On one level, habit gives us a sense of order and control, but this comes at a price, because each time we blindly identify with a habit, we lose a little more of our freedom. We become limited by our reactivity and our habits, and that makes us less able to adapt and respond with intelligence to new conditions. Like a train passenger, we are taken to our destination without any say on the route taken, because the route is fixed by the train tracks. In the same way, the mind reacts according to the tracks laid down by past conditioning. This is not to say that we lack free will, but free will depends entirely on conscious awareness, and if this is lacking and *avijja* is dominant, then there is no free will. Habitual reactivity is a powerful force that *limits* the possible outcomes in the present. It limits our responsiveness to the demands of life by keeping us chained to our habits and chained to our past.

Besides limiting our responsiveness, habitual reactivity also leads to a form of sensory distortion. Like daydreaming or sleepwalking, we perform activities as if on autopilot. Instead of seeing reality as it is, we see only the shadows of our past projected onto the present and our conscious perception is limited by our subjective reactivity. The combination of ignorance and the limitations imposed by conditioned reactivity corrupts and distorts the mind, making it inflexible and rigid. The principle corruptions or perversions, called *vipallasa*, are of perception (*sanna vipallasa*), mind (*citta vipallasa*) and the distortion of inner beliefs (*ditthi vipallasa*). We see what we are conditioned to see and we believe what we are conditioned to believe.

Reactivity distorts perception and what we experience is not actual reality, but the product of our conditioned reaction to reality. Distorted perception leads to distorted beliefs, which can have a very negative effect if they become core beliefs. The greatest of these is the attachment to "me" and "mine," in which we blindly identify with the surface appearance of our thoughts and emotions as real and true reflections of ourself. Instead of seeing an emotion, such as anger, as an objective mental phenomenon, we tend to *be-*

come the anger and we take it very personally as "my anger." When this happens, we lose perspective and become the victim of the emotional reaction or negative thought patterns that arise out of habit. This is the nature of attachment and identification at work in the mind and it is based on the fundamental reaction of delusion (*moha*), which causes us to blindly attach to the contents of the mind.

Besides distorting our experience of the world and limiting the range of possible responses, habitual reactivity has yet another detrimental effect: it decreases the quality and depth of our experience. When we react, what we see is restricted to the content of the reaction, and we become blind to the complex and dynamic nature of reality as it is. Instead of seeing the totality of a person as he or she really is, we see our label, our belief and the story we tell ourselves about that person. In the world of knowledge, we attach to our views and opinions and remain blind to the full range of interpretations and become unable to hear the views of other people. In the world of our emotional reactions, we don't see the reality of the detailed inner structure of the emotion, but only see the superficial outward appearance of things.

Instead of fully enjoying present experience as it is, in all its richness, we react according to our internal expectations and ideals. The effect of reactivity is to take us away from the full experience of the present, leaving us with a fragment that is superficial and unsatisfying. Habitual ractivity is in effect a form of sensory deprivation, and this separation from the living present leaves us with an existential emptiness that is a great source of suffering. People who are rective by nature are seldom happy, and are usually very negative and fearful, because they are unable to fully participate in the experience of living in the present.

REACTIVE DISPLACEMENT

One of the most detrimental consequences of any mental reaction is that it diverts attention away from the experience of the present. This is the principle of Reactive Displacement, in which our present experience is dominated by our reactions to sense objects, rather than the direct experience of the objects themselves. The moment a reaction takes hold, your attention is diverted from the present to an experience dictated by the reaction. You find yourself thinking *about* the sunset, rather than experiencing the sunset directly as it is. You see a person and react with a thought *about* him. This means that your attention is dominated by the thought and not by the reality of the person. We become distracted away from the experience of the present. You perceive a reaction of fear and react with worry *about* what you fear. The worry prevents you directly experiencing the feeling of fear. In effect you project your beliefs and reactions onto the present and you remain ignorant of the present. Reactive displacement takes you away from the richness of the living present as it unfolds before you and replaces it with a limited experience conditioned by the past, which is dead and unchanging.

Another more serious effect of the reactive displacement produced by secondary reactivity is that it diverts attention away from primary reactions. This has an unfortunate consequence, because conscious awareness is absolutely essential for the transformation of a primary reaction, or any other reactive pattern. Hidden from view, reactions become fixed in the mind and will not change. If, for example, you react to a primary reaction of fear with a secondary reaction of worrying, then you are effectively prevented from experiencing the primary reaction of fear, because consciousness is distracted into thinking about the fear, or worrying. The experience of the thoughts about the fear, which you have when you indulge in worrying, are not the same as the direct experience of the original feeling of fear. In the absence of direct awareness, the primary fear reaction becomes frozen in place, trapping any associated negative feeling energy with it. As a consequence, the fear is effectively repressed and pushed out of consciousness and becomes imprisoned in the deep recesses of the mind, where it remains uncared for and where it will continue to fester and generate *dukkha*.

This indirect repression can create deep-seated emotional complexes that become the inner "demons" that come back to haunt us over and over again. The effect of this feedback loop between the primary and secondary reactions is to produce a self-sustaining system that sustains the cycle of suffering. It may well be that just a few minutes of direct awareness focused on the original primary experience of fear might have been enough to allow it to resolve, but the secondary reactivity of worrying prevents this resolution from happening.

The Path of Mindfulness is a path of stopping reactive displacement so that we can experience reality in the here and now and regain the richness of experience that is lost to reactivity. Knowledge is power and opening the mind to see the totality of experience in the here and now is an absolute pre-requisite for beneficial change and spiritual transformation. Mindfulness allows us to regain access to the primary reactions so that we can bring about healing and transformation at the core level of our psyche. But above all, mindfulness is the direct antidote to the proliferation of reactivity that amplifies and sustains suffering. Through the practice of mindfulness the mind becomes flexibile and malleable and this prevents reactivity from becoming frozen into recurring patterns. This is the path of awakening that is central to the teachings of the Buddha and cultivated through The Path of Mindfulness.

THE CORE REACTIONS

In the Buddhist tradition, mental reactions in the form of fixed patterns of thinking, dysfunctional beliefs and emotional reactions are called *kilesas*. The *kilesas* include all the varieties of conditioned mental reactions that perpetuate conflict, stress and suffering (*dukkha*), and the habitual round of becoming that is *samsara*. They are the prison bars created through ignorance and delusion that dominate the mind and prevent us from responding with wisdom and compassion to the needs of the present and attachment to the defilements robs us of our freedom and happiness. The *kilesas* not only perpetuate suffering in our own life, but they inevitably reduce our ability to respond with wisdom and compassion to the needs of others and even to the needs of our environment.

The word *kilesa* comes from the verb *kilisati*, which means to stick, like mud sticking to your shoes. The *kilesas* cause the mind to become stuck in habitual patterns of reacting that condition and limit our ability to respond to the needs of the present. A mind that is dominated with reactivity becomes dull and inflexible and unable to respond effectively or intelligently. Just as trudging through mud is exhausting and unpleasant, continual reactivity drains us of our spiritual energy and leaves us fatigued and despondent. Depression can be viewed as a chronic state of habitual reactivity and one of the symptoms of depression is lethargy and lack of vitality.

There are, of course, many forms of mental afflictions, but all the *kilesas* are manifestations of three root defilements (*mula kilesas*), which are often described as the three poisons, or the three fires, of greed (*lobha*), hatred (*dosa*) and delusion (*moha*). Traditionally in Buddhist art, the pig is the animal chosen to represent *lobha*, which is an obvious symbol of greediness. Most people are attracted towards the things they like and easily become obsessed with wanting to acquire objects, status or some form of experience. Closely following *lobha* is aversion (*dosa*), which is represented by the snake, an animal that is apt to strike out in anger when provoked. *Dosa* includes reactions of dislike, anger and hatred as well as disappointment and frustration when we do not get what we want. The third root *kilesa* is delusion (*moha*), which is represented by the rooster, presumably because a rooster spends all of its time strutting around under the delusion that it is king and believes that he alone is responsible for making the sun rise in the morning, through his raucous crowing. Delusion causes us to become blindly attached to reactions and all the manifestations of *lobha* and *dosa* and this makes reactions habitual, creating the hell realm of habitual reactivity that is *samsara*. As the Buddha repeatedly stated, ignorance is the root of all evils, because in the unaware mind suffering becomes mechanical and will continue indefinitely. The three core reactions occur in close proximity, mutually reinforcing each other. Whenever there is wanting, there will also be some form of aversion to anything that oposes gratification and both forms of reactivity thrive on the milk of ignorance and delusion.

Lobha

Lobha, the first root *kilesa*, refers to subjective habitual reactions based on wanting to acquire and control. We want to acquire an object or an experience and we want to manipulate our environment so that we get what we want and hold on to what we have acquired. It is useful to think of *lobha* in energetic terms as the force of attraction, rather like the pull of gravity, or the force that attracts

25

iron to a magnet. It tends to pull us off balance and creteates a state of energetic instability in the mind. We are seduced by the promise of pleasure and happiness, like the songs of the Sirens, the bird-women of Greek mythology who lured sailors to their death on the rocks of reality. Other terms often used to describe wanting are *raga* and *kamacchanda*, the reactions of lust and sensual indulgence, respectively.

The energetic force of *lobha* is not necessarily a problem if accompanied by awareness and the freedom to choose. However, when it is accompanied by unawareness (*avijja*) or delusion (*moha*) then the energy of wanting becomes the force of compulsion and reactivity, called *tanha*, literally "thirst" and this produces great instability in the mind, which results in mental suffering as well as compelling us into unskillful actions. The force of *tanha*, leads to compulsive attachment and identification (*upadana*) with the object of desire, whether it is an external object or a mental thought or feeling. Such blind attachment limits and restricts happiness by tying us to certain conditions that have to be met before we can be happy. This inevitably leads to conflict, as those conditions seldom exist in the real world. This inner conflict is the experience of *dukkha*. Ultimately, the most important thing is whether we have freedom to choose how to respond in life, or whether we are compelled to react out of habit and unawareness. The former leads to happiness, stability and well-being, while the latter leads to suffering, instability and existential dis-ease. Ultimately, reactivity based on *lobha* creates instability in the mind, and leaves us dependent on external conditions for providing our happiness. This is unsustainable, because we cannot control external conditions and we cannot prevent conditions from changing. The world becomes unsatisfying and we become fearful and despondent or angry. A tremendous amount of energy is wasted in trying to make the world conform to our expectations and in trying to control what is beyond our control. Of course the primary result of this conflict is mental suffering, *dukkha*.

There is nothing inherently wrong with sensory enjoyment and the Buddhist path of awakening is not about removing sources of pleasure, but simply learning to remove the element of ignorance and delusion that causes us to cling. When we are free of clinging then we are able to fully enjoy all forms of sensory experience, without the addiction and compulsion, which inevitably lead to suffering. The Path of Mindfulness aims to restore freedom and choice, so that we can respond to our natural needs and desires, without becoming blindly attached, compulsive and reactive.

Dosa

Closely associated with *lobha* are the reactions of aversion and hatred. This is the second root *kilesa* and hindrance to psychological and spiritual freedom. *Dosa* and *lobha* are actually different sides of the same coin and wherever there is *lobha* there will also be some form of *dosa* in close proximity. The common theme that powers both *lobha* and *dosa* is *tanha*, or the force of compulsive attachment. When we become strongly attached to our expectations and ideals, then we will become equally strongly attached to reactions of disappointment and frustration created by the dichotomy of having or not having, gain and loss, success and failure.

Dosa describes the energy of repulsion, as when the same poles of two magnets are brought together. It has the effect of pushing us off balance, just as *lobha* pulls us off balance. The effect is the same, which is to create instability in the mind that leads to *dukkha*. In its active form, the energy of aversion can lead to violence and aggression as we try to get rid of the things we don't like. *Dosa* includes the emotional reactions of anger, hatred and ill will (*vyapada*) that clouds the mind, and lead to unskillful actions. In its passive form, *dosa* reactions take the form of frustration and disappointment and all kinds of negative thinking that collectively contract the mind and heart. *Dosa* reactions readily proliferate into secondary reactions of pessimism, apathy, cynicism, negativity and fear. People consumed with *dosa* are unable to fully engage in life, because their minds are closed by negativity and their hearts are contracted by fear. The reactions of hatred are closely associated with fear, because the world is seen to be threatening, unsafe and unreliable.

The Path of Mindfulness involves learning to relate to fear and anger and all the reactions based on *dosa* with an open mind that does not react with further aversion, but provides a healing space in which these negative emotions can change and resolve themselves. As with *lobha*, the best way to control reactions of fear and hatred is to surround them with non-reactive space, which is exactly what happens when you relate to such emotions with mindfulness. The challenge is to train yourself in the fine art of recognizing *dosa* in all its many forms just as you must learn to recognize all the varieties of reactions based on *lobha*. Your enemy is not the reactions of greed and hatred themselves, but the *ignorance* of these reactions as they arise in the present. The Path of Mindfulness is about becoming aware of all the movements of reactivity in the mind and to respond with equanimity and objectivity, rather than indulging in further blind reactivity.

Moha

The third major component of all mental reactions is the force of ignorance (*avijja*). *Moha* is closely related to *avijja*, but *moha* has a slightly different flavour, referring to the delusional characteristic of *avijja*. This is where we blindly accept the superficial appearance of things as somehow complete, genuine and true. *Moha* is the psychological glue that keeps us bound to the individual reactions of *lobha* and *dosa* and that perpetuates the wheel of *samsara*. Whereas *avijja* is simply an absence of awareness, the mental sleepwalking that sustains habitual reactivity, *moha* is the conscious expression of *avijja* in which we falsely believe in the superficial appearance of things as they present themselves in our experience. When *avijja* is dominant we blindly react with frustration when things don't go our way, because we are ignorant of what is happening. When there is *moha*, we are aware of the reaction, but are deluded into believing that the reaction is true and that there are no other possibilities. We go through life reacting with frustration, worry, fear or anger when things don't go according to our expectations and we blindly accept these emotional reactions as normal.

In reality, all reactions are learned and there is absolutely no law that dictates how we should react. The blind acceptance of learned reactions is the essence of delusion (*moha*) and fuels the whole process of reactivity. We inadvertently take these subjective reactions as reality and follow them blindly and without question. If someone insults us, we react by becoming angry; if we lose something we become upset; if things don't go according to our expectations we become irritated. These are examples of delusion-based reactions, because there is actually no law that compels you to feel angry, upset or irritated. These reactions are learned through personal and cultural conditioning and have no real substance. Whenever we react, we are operating from some level of *moha*, and the effect of this is that we are fooled into believing whatever arises in the mind. We are seduced into reacting, and when this happens we lose our choice and freedom, our mind becomes agitated and we suffer. We become victims to the changing conditions of pleasure and pain, gain and loss, praise and criticism, success and failure and have very little feedom to choose what feelings we will have.

In society, the delusional reactivity of *moha* fuels all forms of prejudice, fanaticism and fundamentalism. Ignorance and delusion perpetuates cruelty and violence and the worst aspects of human nature. Wars begin with the blind attachment to beliefs about what is right and what is wrong, who is good and who is bad. Attachment to ideals may seem important, but when that attachment is based on ignorance and delusion then it quickly becomes a force of evil, rather than a force for good. During war it is surprisingly easy to kill someone you don't know and have labelled as the "enemy." We become so brainwashed by our beliefs and concepts that we believe the label to be true instead of being nothing more than a superficial untruth. The distortion of perception and thinking by *moha* is the foundation for unwholesome and unskillful speech and action.

Ignorance is the way of the coward, someone who prefers not to face up to truth and the hard work of investigating the nature of reality. Humans have a great propensity for ignorance and will readily accept the superficial constructs of their mind, rather than open to the uncertainties of reality and truth. For this reason, ignorance is described as one of the seven *anusayas*, or underlying negative inclinations of the human mind. The other six are sensual greed, ill will, craving for existence, attachment to blind beliefs, conceit and sceptical doubt. These inclinations are themes that arise over and over again in all human beings and feed suffering and *samsara*.

3 THE FORCE OF BLIND ATTACHMENT

Habitual reactivity corrupts the mind by limiting our responsiveness to the unfolding drama of life. Reactivity makes the mind dull and mechanical and unresponsive, and underlies most of our emotional suffering. There are two fundamental driving forces behind our patterns of habitual reactivity that we must fully understand, because almost all of our efforts will be directed at overcoming these two factors. Habitual reactivity depends on the force of ignorance, called *avijja*, and the compulsive drive that causes us to attach to habitual reactions, called *tanha*, in Pali. The Pali term for attachment is *upadana*.

Upadana depends on the strength of *tanha*. If *tanha* is weak, then attachment will be weak, and the resulting reactions will be transitory, like bubbles rising to the surface of a pond. The stronger the *tanha*, the greater the attachment, and when *tanha* is very strong then the resulting habitual reactivity is likely to dominate our mind, our speech and our actions. Therefore, it is important to understand *tanha* in more detail. The Buddha described three different classes of *tanha*:

> There are these three cravings. Which three? Craving
> for sensuality, craving for becoming, craving for non-
> becoming. These are the three cravings.

Essentially, the energy of *tanha* is the blind and compulsive force that drives the ego. The thirst to acquire and control sensual experience is called *kamatanha*. The force to acquire and control desirable states of existence (*bhava*) is called *bhavatanha*, and the force that pushes us to get rid of states that we do not like is called *vibhavatanha*.

Kamatanha is the most familiar form of the compulsive energy of *tanha* and describes the compulsive wanting, craving and longing for sense objects. This includes craving for pleasant objects that we see, pleasant sounds that we hear, pleasant smells, tastes, and bodily sensations. These are the five physical sense objects that we perceive through the sense organs. However, in Buddhist philosophy, the mind is also considered as a sense organ, and its sense objects are memories, thoughts, ideas, beliefs and fantasies, to which we can also develop intense craving and attachment.

When ignorance is dominant in the mind, we are at great risk of becoming addicted to sense objects, and this addiction begins to take hold of us and define our personality. Whether we become addicted to food, alcohol, sex or work and achievement, addiction imprisons the spirit and contracts the mind, and we run the risk of being consumed by our addictions. In the practice of mindfulness, we make a deliberate effort to monitor the compulsive feeling energy of *kamatanha* as it arises in real-time. In the act of recognizing the impulse to react, we introduce a moment of freedom and choice, and through cultivating this inner freedom we are able to break free from the downward pull of craving. We choose to awaken to our craving and respond to the underlying emotional impulses with mindfulness. If the impulse is observed, rather than acted on, then it has a chance to unfold and change and diffuse, and mindfulness creates this all-important inner therapeutic space.

However, there is much more to *tanha* than just craving and desire. This is just one manifestation of the compulsive-obsessive energy of *tanha*. At a deeper level of understanding, we begin to appreciate that this same energy is the force that drives our habitual reactivity. It is the force that compels us to feel upset, angry, depressed or worried. We don't choose to feel these emotions, we are *compelled* to experience them; we are compelled to *become* the emotions, the negative thoughts or beliefs that arise in the mind. This force to become the reactions, the *sankharas* that arise out of our conditioning, is called *bhavatanha*. The word *bhava* means state of being, and so *bhavatanha* describes the compulsive and habitual drive that causes us to react repeatedly, re-creating states of mind such as anger or anxiety over and over again. It is the force of *becoming*. An anger reaction arises and we *become* the anger; disappointment arises and we are seduced into feeling disappointment; worry arises and we *become* worried. Over and over again, we are tricked by the habitual reactions that arise, and out of delusion, we fall right into their web, where we become entangled and suffer.

Besides this compulsive force that compels us to become the products of our reactions, the energy of *tanha* can also manifest as a destructive force of aversion to becoming. This negative force is called *vibhavatanha*. *Vi* means "without," and *vibhavatanha* decribes the compulsive drive to anhilate undesirable states through suppression and repression. This is the force of *non-becoming*, the forceful resistance to our habitual reactivity. However, this resistance is not based on choice or wisdom, it is not the response of wanting to make things better, but simply blind aversion-reactivity based on conditioning. *Vibhavatanha* creates inner warfare in the mind, creating division and conflict by setting one part against another. Such inner violence and conflict feeds negative emotional reactivity and leads to immense suffering.

Both *tanha* and *upadana* are blind forces that operate in the mind, manipulating and pressuring the mind to react; they depend entirely on ignorance (*avijja*), the powerful force of unawareness and not knowing. *Avijja* sustains reactivity by keeping it hidden from consciousness, effectively shielding the inner suffering from the innate transformational wisdom of *satipanna*, that we all possess. We become slaves to our conditioned reactivity, and this perpetuates craving, attachment and suffering. It is not surprising that in Buddhist philosophy, ignorance is considered the root cause of all suffering for both the individual and for the world at large. All the unwholesome actions of greed, hatred and delusion emerge from the dark slime of ignorance. As Buddhadasa, one of the great twentieth-century Thai Buddhist teachers said,

> All troubles arise from attachment, which has ignorance as its mother.

By ignorance, we do not mean the lack of knowledge, but not seeing what is happening in each unfolding moment of our present experience, and this unawareness is what allows reactivity to take hold. No one would say that it is wrong to be attached to your friends and family, your country or your beliefs, and the Buddha did not mean for us to stop caring about these things. What concerned the Buddha was whether we have the *freedom* to engage with these parts of our living experience. What he observed is that most of our attachments are reactive in nature and conditioned by *avijja*, and this reactivity inhibits our ability to fully engage with life and the things we hold dear to us. For this reason *upadana* is best translated as *blind attachment* or reactive attachment, in which ignorance (*avijja*) combines with the compulsive-obsessive energy of *tanha*. When *avijja* is dominant, we are not fully present for our experience, let alone the experience of others, and this actually creates a separation from the things we love. Our actions are dominated by habitual reactivity, like a machine on autopilot, with little real freedom or choice in how we relate to life. This is the state of sleep and mindlessness that propagates the endless round of habitual reactivity and becoming that is called *samsara*.

The fundamental nature of *upadana* is bondage and fixation on form. Each blind attachment is a chain that binds us and restricts our freedom. *Upadana* restricts, constrains and limits us so that we become *reactive*, rather than *responsive*. To be responsive, means that we are free to choose our actions, and have the flexibility to respond to life situations with intelligence. This means that we are able to respond to life in a way that reduces suffering and increases inner stability and happiness. The psyche, if allowed, will always move towards a position of greatest stability, both internally in the mind and externally in our personal relationships. This is the nature of spiritual freedom, in which intuitive intelligence (*satipanna*) is able to operate, without the constraints of compulsive reactivity. Every moment is unique and requires a fresh response, and to be truly free means that we have the freedom to adapt and respond appropriately to each moment of existence and this requires freedom from blind attachment.

There are four kinds of *upadana* described by the Buddha: *kamupadana*, attachment to sensory experiences; *ditthupadana*, attachment to views, opinions and beliefs; *silabbatupadana*, attachment to conventions, rules, authority and tradition; and *attavadupadana*, the unconscious identification with the subjective reactions of "me" and "mine."

Essentially, all forms of *upadana* lead to becoming, called *bhava* in Pali. We are in effect forced through ignorance and reactivity to *become* the products of our reactivity. We react with greed when we see something we want and we *become* the greed. If we are blindly attached to a reaction of anger when we don't get our way, we *become* the anger, and that emotion will dominate our

34

consciousness. We learn to react with disappointment when something goes wrong and we *become* disappointed, according to our conditioning. When we have a belief to which we are strongly attached, we *become* the belief and it dominates our perception. If we are strongly attached to a certain conventional way of doing things, then we *become* limited by that convention. We lose our freedom and choice as we are compelled to become whatever arises in the mind. In reality, we do not have to react with greed, anger or disappointment and there is no law that dictates how we should react. We react in these ways out of ignorance and conditioning and attahment to these particular forms of subjective reactivity.

The purpose of mindfulness practice and The Path of Mindfulness is to regain our freedom from the endless rounds of becoming (*bhava*); the endless rounds of birth and death, that characterizes *samsara* and *dukkha*. When we are free from the compulsion to become, then we are free to experience the full wonder and complexity of life *as it is* and this leads to skillful and wholesome responsiveness, that will be in harmony with the path that leads towards the resolution of suffering and the the blossoming of our true essence.

ATTACHMENT TO SENSORY EXPERIENCE

The first variety of *upadana* is called *kamupadana*, the attachment to sensory experience. The most obvious source of sensory experience comes from the physical sensations of sight, sound, taste, smell and touch. However, the mind itself is regarded as the sixth sense organ, and thoughts, beliefs and emotions are sense objects to which we can become very attached.

We tend to attach to sensory experiences that are pleasant, whether in the form of a pleasant sight or sound or in the form of a stimulating thought. Good food, music and things of beauty all create pleasant feelings and states of consciousness to which we naturally become attached. We become attached to our possessions, our friends and family, because they make us feel good. We become attached to symbols of wealth, power and respect from others, because they lead to pleasant sensations. We create a world in which we become dependent on having these things around us to maintain our happiness. Even painful emotions such as anger can be addictive, because they are stimulating and make us feel alive. However, the happiness that come from the pursuit of sensory experience depend on the conditions that create them, which presents a problem, because conditions change. Consequently, compulsive attachment to sensory experience will almost always result in disappointment and we are left feeling empty and grieving for what we have lost. As it says in the Dhammapada,

> Those who are infatuated with lust fall back into the stream as does a spider into the web spun by itself. The wise, cutting off the bond of craving, walk on resolutely, leaving all ills behind.

We have to find a balance in which we can enjoy sensory pleasures, without becoming dependent on them. This is the principle teaching of the Middle Way (*majjhima patipada*), in which we refrain from blind indulgence in sensory pleasure, nor in blindly reject it, either. Instead, we choose to develop balance and equanimity in relation to sensual pleasure. The problem is never in the sensual experiences themselves, but in the way we become blindly attach to them and become inadvertently dependent on something that is inherently not dependable. Equanimity (*upekkha*) is one of the most important qualities that we develop through mindfulness practice and *upekkha* is the principle vehicle for developing balanced engagement in life, so that we can enjoy sensory experiences to the full, without becoming dependent or addicted.

Needless to say, developing mindfulness of all these various manifestations of *kamupadana* is a primary focus of practice. However, the path of breaking these bonds is not an action of willpower and aversion to sense pleasure. The only effective way to break free from the grip of *kamupadana* is through awakening to the energetic force of *tanha* and the underlying *vedana* that fuels the compulsive attachments. It is is in the space of awakened mindfulness, where there is freedom and non-reactivity, that the bonds of *kamupadana* are broken quite effortlessly. Mindfulness counteracts *avijja* and *tanha* by no longer feeding them through indulgence in habitual reactivity. In the spacious dimension of mindful-awareness, we allow craving and the force of becoming to simply burn itself out. With the dissolution of *tanha*, the bonds of *upadana* will loosen, restoring freedom and wisdom-intelligence. Mindfulness is learning to be fully present for the emotional impulses of wanting and hating as they arise, and residing in that place of pure knowing, which is the essence of Buddha mind.

ATTACHMENT TO BELIEFS

The second major form of clinging and blind fixation, which causes all kinds of conflict and suffering, is *ditthupadana*, attachment to views, opinions and beliefs. The human mind is, as far as we know, unique in the animal kingdom for its ability to generate internal beliefs and conceptual models of the world, and it is through these internal models that we organize our memories and perceptions.

It should be made absolutely clear that beliefs are not in themselves a problem; the problem is only in how we relate to our beliefs and opinions. If we can maintain objectivity and equanimity (*upekkha*), then beliefs become tools that help us better understand and cope with life. If, however, we are negligent and become blindly attached to our beliefs, then they will limit our perception and limit responsiveness, leading to unskill actions.

All beliefs, by their very nature are superficial representations of the truth and are ultimately unsatisfactory representations of reality. Beliefs, views and opinions are like a carpenter's tools. Each tool has a specific use, which is limited to the specific task for which it was designed. Clinging to a belief is like trying to construct a house using only a hammer. The carpenter needs to use all the tools available to him, and we need to keep our minds open so that we can find the right belief for the right occasion. Clinging to beliefs as if they were true and perfect is one of the chief causes of *dukkha*, because it inevitably leads to conflict between our beliefs and reality. To quote Krishnamurti,

> Man has built in himself images as a fence of security -
> religious, political, personal. These manifest as sym-

bols, ideas, and beliefs. The burden of these images dominates man's thinking, his relationships and his daily life. These images are the causes of our problems for they divide man from man. His perception of life is shaped by the concepts already established in his mind.

Humans have a very strong propensity to codify life and reduce experience into a set of internal representations in the form of symbols and ideas. Every aspect of life is influenced by these internal beliefs, views and opinions, yet most are acquired without conscious choice. They are absorbed unconsciously from parents, family, friends and culture, and we unconsciously become attached to them. We blindly attach to beliefs and ideas, which in turn distort our perception, thinking, feelings and actions.

It is a good practice to investigate our beliefs and focus on the force of attachment that keeps us in bondage to them. If there is *tanha* associated with the belief, then we need to focus mindfulness on that feeling energy. There is a fine line between compulsion and passion. The first is based on *avijja*, while the second is imbued with genuine presence and engagement with life, which is the expression of *panna*. Beliefs should be brought into the light of mindfulness so that they can adapt to the truth of the present, under the influence of *panna*, rather than *avijja*. We need to make space for the truth, which is always bigger and more complex than our beliefs and other superficial representations of reality.

Ultimately, we must understand what constitutes Right Belief (*sammaditthi*) and what constitutes Wrong Belief (*micchaditthi*). From the Buddhist perspective, right beliefs are simply those views that lead to Right Action. Right Action is defined as any response in the present that is guided by wisdom-intelligence, or *panna* and that leads to freedom and the resolution of *dukkha*. Whether *dukkha* exists internally in your mind, or externally in your relationship to family, society and the world, Right Action should lead to the state of greatest stability and happiness. Right beliefs are always in harmony with the Four Noble Truths, which means awakening to suffering and awakening to what leads to the resolution of suffering and the promotion of well-being. The basic question to ask yourself is do your beliefs lead to more happiness or more suffering? If they lead to more suffering then they are wrong beliefs. The intelligent awareness of this principle should guide us in everything we do, whether we are relating to our internal world or with our external world.

Taking this argument further, we need to understand that there can be no absolute beliefs, because conditions are always changing, and a belief is essentially static and unable to reflect change. *Sammaditthi* is not a static entity, but something to be discovered and re-discovered from moment to moment, as a direct response to the specific conditions of the present. If you try to impose beliefs onto reality, then you will create fragmentation and conflict, because no belief can adequately match the needs of the present. Therefore, in order to be open and flexible enough to perceive *sammaditthi*, mindfulness becomes extremely important, because mindfulness is opening to the reality of the present, without the intervention of the ego and habitual subjective reactivity.

Language and labels

We see a river and label it "river" and think we know the object that is before us. However, in reality, all we really see is our label, our internal model of "river," which is an abstract and constructed representation of the actual thing. What we experience through our concepts is a superficial surface representation of the actual, a particular fabrication that is called a *sankhara*. We have a very strong tendency to become attached to our perceptions, labels and *sankharas*, as if they are actually true, when in reality they are simply projections of our own mind. When there is a lack of awareness, we tend to blindly attach to our labels and concepts, and these preconceptions and *sankharas* become a barrier that effectively separates us from the truth. As Merry Browne expressed it,

> Preconceived notions are the locks on the door to wisdom.

We try to impose our labels and concepts on life in an attempt to control the world by reducing it to definable entities that we take to be permanent and unchanging. In reality, life is a dynamic process of continual change and flows like a river. We think we know what

39

a river is, but actually a river is impossible to define, except as an abstract and generalized concept. One day the river is full and flows rapidly; the next day, it is nothing more than a trickle. We say it is the same river, but what exactly is the same?

We have labels for everything, and we impose these labels and inner constructs on people; on our inner experience of ourselves; and on the world at large. All these labels may be true at the superficial and abstract linguistic level of accepted beliefs and conventions, but unfortunately we tend to go a step further and believe these labels to be the reality they represent. This is the primary reaction of delusion (*moha*) that lies at the heart of much of our suffering. We must be very careful not to fall under the spell of the *sankharas* of our own preconceptions and prejudices, because this spell denies access to the actual reality and truth of existence.

In its most violent manifestation, we can be brainwashed by our beliefs into killing someone we label as "enemy." If you let go of the belief and genuinely seek to understand and know the reality behind the concept of "enemy," you would find it almost impossible to kill another person. Prejudice, hatred and mistrust are all fuelled by ignorance and attachment to the labels we impose on others.

In the same way, we also do great injustice when we impose labels and preconceptions on ourselves. Nowhere is this more problematic than when we blindly attach to the superficial inner experience of suffering. We convince ourselves that we are anxious, afraid, depressed or that we have no self-confidence and then attach to there beliefs. We stay stuck at the superficial level of the *sankharas* instead of taking the opportunity to fully investigate what is beneath the surface of the label "anxiety" or "depression." We have to reveal the inner deep structure of our suffering in order for it to heal, and this happens when we iluminate the emotional complex, or *sankhara*, with mindfulness and investigate the reality and truth of what is there.

Mindfulness is, therefore, a journey beyond labels, beyond our concepts and representations and all superficial *sankharas*, to discover and uncover the reality beneath. This is a path that leads to transformation and healing both in the heart and in our world. Ignorance, *avijja*, is the path to suffering and *dukkha*; mindfulness, *sati*, is the path to wisdom, compassion and happiness, both internally and externally.

Expectations

Blind attachment to beliefs inevitably generates expectations and demands. Any statement with "should" or "shouldn't" in it, is based on an expectation formed through blind attachment to an ideal, and because of the force of ignorance, it is very easy to become convinced that our expectations are right. The self-righteousness attitude of the ego drives us to expend significant energy in trying to control the world according to our expectations of what should be and shouldn't be. Our computer should work, and when it doesn't we react by becoming frustrated. We should be treated with respect, and become upset when we are treated unkindly. If he loves me, then he should behave differently. If our expectations are fulfilled, we will have a brief moment of happiness, but more often than not, our expectations are not fulfilled and we suffer. We have very little control over external events and, as Mark Twain said,

Climate is what we expect, weather is what we get.

Expectations are like cats, they have a tendency to scratch! We must take great care not to become blindly attached to ideals and expectations, because this will result in a very unhappy existence, filled with endless disappointments and frustrations. There is nothing wrong with expectations in themselves, as long as we do not become blindly attached to them. If we can retain freedom and balance in relatioin to our expectations, then we will not suffer if they are not fulfilled.

Not only are we faced with the problem of attachment to expectations, but also with attachment to our habitual subjective reactions to expectations when they are not fulfilled. Things are as they are and usually fall short of our expectations, because they are not under our control. However, this does not mean that we have to react with disappointment, anger or any other manifestation of suffering. These emotional reactions are nothing more than subjective

41

fabrications that we add on to objective experience through ignorance and conditioning.

Not getting what we expect may produce a painful feeling, but suffering is an entirely subjective creation that we add on as a conditioned negative reaction to the pain. This is analogous to burning your hand by grabbing hold of a red-hot coal and then plunging your painful hand into boiling water. Attachment to an expectation produces one level of suffering, but attachment to the subjective reactions of greed, hatred and delusion when expectations are not fulfilled, amplifies *dukkha* many fold. The blind attachment (*upadana*) to all these subjective reactions is one major aspect of attachment to self, or *attavadupadana*.

All expectations have a compulsive forcefulness behind them and we must learn to develop a balanced relationship with this energy so that it does not dominate our mind. In the practice of mindfulness, we focus on this impulsive energy by directing attention to the feeling level behind our thinking, rather than indulging in the contents and story. In order to transform compulsion, you need to establish a relationship that is not itself based on the compulsion to control. This means letting go of thinking and analyzing, and opening to the deeper intuitive level of the psyche. Transformation is seldom about what you do, but much more about how you relate to experience, and the relationship of pure knowing, or *satisampajanna*, is the primary force that transforms *dukkha*. Mindfulness transforms compulsion by opening up a space around the emotion that is non-reactive and non-clinging and allows intelligent change.

Expectations are essentially an impulse to control through outward projection, but beneath these impulses there may be feelings of powerlessness, helplessness and fear. To gain freedom form the compulsiveness of expectations, we need to explore these more subtle feelings in depth and create the conditions that allow their transformation. When change occurs at this subtle level, then the forcefulness of our attachment to our expectations, demands and the need to control will also change. Mindfulness is the art of listening to experience at the intuitive and subtle level and creating a therapeutic space in which these often unheard and unseen forces can emerge into consciousness. It is when these subtle aspects of *dukkha* emerge into the light of consciousness that they can undergo self-transformation and resolution.

Causal beliefs

One of the noticeable characteristics of the ego is that it seeks causal links between what is felt internally and what happens externally, and if it doesn't find any links, it makes them up. Just as we can become attached to an ideal or a belief about how things should be, we can also become attached to beliefs about cause and effect.

The mind is designed to search for patterns through which it can organize experience, and this has been very important for humans as a species. However, as always, this mental faculty must be accompanied by flexibility and freedom so that we do not become victims of delusion. If there is an absence of awareness and *avijja* is dominant, then this extraordinary ability to find connections becomes reduced to an unskillful and harmful process of superstitious thinking that leads to unfounded assumptions and generalizations.

One particular manifestation of delusional attachment to causal beliefs occurs when we blindly link subjective emotional reactivity to external objective reality in "because" statements. We blindly accept that we feel happy *because* something went right, and that we feel upset *because* something went wrong. We feel uplifted *because* he was kind, and we feel angry *because* he treated us badly. We feel at ease *because* we have money in the bank, or we become worried *because* we don't have enough money to pay the bills. We become anxious *because* we have to take an exam, and then we become relaxed *because* the exam has finished. Throughout the day, we continually make these causal connections between external conditions and how we respond and feel internally. However, if you really think about it, there is no law that dictates that you must react with a particular emotion in one situation and with another emotion in a different situation. These causal connections are learned through conditioning and ignorance, and to identify with them as inevitable is a form of delusion (*moha*). The reality is that there is no *because* except that we make it so. When we can really understand this in depth, then we will have the confidence to see that we have choices about how we feel and that nothing is fixed.

In the absence of awareness, causal beliefs are like ropes that coil around us ever more tightly and keep us bound to the wheel of *samsara*. However, if we choose to become aware of each reactive impulse, and respond to it with mindfulness, then it is possible to develop more functional responses that do not create suffering. This is one of the principle aims of mindfulness practice: to develop the wisdom (*panna*) to dissolve illusory beliefs and restore freedom.

Through the practice of mindfulness, we learn to recognize the mental hooks that keep us bound to habitual reactivity. This simple act of recognition, when well cultivated throughout the day is a very powerful and empowering practice that helps break habitual reactivity. Mindfulness and reactivity are mutually exclusive, and when you are mindful of a reaction, then in that moment, the causal link, founded on ignorance and delusion, is replaced with freedom and choice to discover a better way of responding.

The more you develop awareness of your *because* statements, the more freedom you will have and the less you will be caught out. You may still be poor, but you do not have to compound this fact with the suffering caused by your conditioned emotional reactivity. Someone may offend you, but if you respond with mindfulness, you break the link that compels you to feel hurt. A project may fail, but you approach the failure with mindfulness then you will be less likely to be sucked into reacting with disappointment. With continued mindfulness practice, we can cultivate a non-reactive relationship with experience in which there is the spaciousness of pure knowing that we call *satisampajanna*. From this state of awareness, we can fully experience life, but without being compelled to react out of habit. This relaxed, yet dynamic relationship with experience allows us to break free from our attachment to causal beliefs and empowers us with the freedom of choice about how we want to feel. We begin to take responsibility for our own happiness.

ATTACHMENT TO CONVENTIONS

The third kind of *upadana* describes attachment to conventions and is called *silabbatupadana*. Conventions are learned from family, friends, community, religious groups, politicians and others. We learn certain ways of doing things and conventional ways of behaving through unconscious conditioning, rather than through conscious choice. There is nothing inherently wrong with conventions or traditions as long as we are fully aware of them and that we don't become slaves to conventions.

We must maintain balance and freedom to respond wisely and in a way that is guided by *Dhamma* and the path that leads to freedom and the resolution of suffering. All too often, we see examples of the negative effects of blind conformity to tradition and the dictates of authority. Such blind conformity leads to division and conflict and a dulling of our intuitive intelligence. It is very easy to become blindly attached to the teachings offered by charismatic leaders, including spiritual teachers, because they seem to have the authority that we feel lacking in ourselves. This tendency to follow authority is a particular problem for the spiritual seeker, because a spiritual path requires letting go of the familiar so that we can discover a totally new way of being. Simply attaching to another set of conventions and practices is not liberation, but simply a movement within the same world of conventions.

In particular, we must avoid becoming dependent on others for providing the answers to our problems, because it is only when we can face *dukkha* directly, by ourselves, that we can discover the inner path that leads to transformation and freedom. The Buddha was very insistent on encouraging us to take responsibility for our own spiritual journey, as the only reliable path, as in the following passage from the *Kalama Sutta*:

> Do not go by revelation or tradition,
> do not go by rumor, or the sacred scriptures,
> do not go by hearsay or mere logic,
> do not go by bias towards a notion or by another person's seeming ability and
> do not go by the idea "He is our Teacher."

But when you know that a thing is good, that it is not blameable, that it is praised by the wise and when practiced and observed that it leads to happiness, then follow that thing.

We must not blindly follow tradition or the rituals, conventions and practices of religions, whether taught by a teacher or learned from books. It is so easy to be seduced by the majesty of historical traditions, ancient rituals and the inspired historical creations of art and architecture. There is the mistaken assumption that if a tradition or practice has been around for thousands of years then it must be superior; but ignorance has been around much longer than that.

Krishnamurti spoke often of the dangers of blind conformity and urged us to trust nothing accept the alive awareness of the present as in the following passage:

To carry the past over to the present, to translate the movement of the present in terms of the past destroys the living beauty of the present. There is nothing sacred in tradition, however ancient or modern.

The Buddha taught the Middle Way (*majjhima patipada*), which means the perfection of non-attachment as well as non-aversion.

The Middle Way has a positive message, which is that we can passionately engage with all traditions, practices, rituals and teachings, as long as we maintain conscious choice and freedom from delusion and compulsive attachment. This, of course, requires the cultivation of mindfulness and an openness of mind that seeks to learn from moment to moment. To engage in a truly spiritual path requires that you open to the reality of your own experience and discover the truth for yourself, not as an abstract concept, but in the concrete experience of the here and now. Zen master Suzuki Roshi called this the attitude of "beginner's mind," the mind that is forever open to discover the truth of each moment of life, as it unfolds.

The term *sila* in *silabbataupadana* means virtue and morality, and another important dimension of *silabbataupadana* is the problem that results from blind attachment to moral beliefs and rules about right and wrong. The Buddha urged us not to blindly follow commandments, but to use them as skillful signposts to help us awaken to *Dhamma*. True *sila* can arise only if we remain open to discover what is the appropriate moral action in each present moment. Each new moment is unique and what is required in response to each new moment will also be unique. If there is a difficult moral decision to be made, then we should respond to this emotional conflict with mindfulness, rather than following the rules set for us by some external authority.

Through mindfulness and the investigation of experience as it unfolds in the present, intuitive intelligence (*satipanna*) naturally arises. This natural intelligence allows us to see the totality of the situation and maintain a balanced perspective, which is essential for right action. Without mindfulness, ignorance and reactivity take over, and when this is coupled with strongly held beliefs and practices, the resulting actions are likely to cause more suffering than good. Moral rules are useful guides, but there can never be one rule to fit all occasions. Such rules of conduct should be taken as aspirations designed to inspire and guide us towards wholesome action (*kusalakamma*). But, ultimately the actual form that action takes has to be discovered in each new moment of life. This requires a great sensitivity and openness of mind and heart that we seek to cultivate through mindfulness. It is only when the mind is free of the past, free of conditioning and the reactive patterns of the ego, that we can discover true morality, and this is the purpose of the path of liberation through mindfulness. In the end, true morality is the *kusalakamma* that leads to the greatest resolution of *dukkha* and the greatest happiness and well-being for self and others. How can you know what that action will be unless you are completely open to experience the truth of the present moment?

ATTACHMENT TO SELF

The fourth variety of *upadana* is *attavadupadana*, the attachment to ego-identity (*atta*) or simply attaching to manifestations of "me" and "mine," called *atta* and *attaniya*, in Pali. In the same way that we become blindly attached to sensory experiences, beliefs, or particular conventions and traditions, we also have an even stronger tendency to become attached to the habitual subjective reactions of the ego.

Through ignorance, we become slaves to the unwholesome reactions of greed, hatred and delusion that arise from blind conditioning. This unquestioned attachment to our subjective reactions is best described by the term *identification*. Identification is a particular form of attachment, in which we blindly attach to the conditioned reactions themselves. The ego arises in the very moment when we fall victim to blind attachment to the subjective reactions of "me" and "mine." As Bikkhu Buddhadasa said,

> In terms of the Four Noble Truths, suffering results from the feeling of me-and-mine; the cause of suffering is me-and-mine; the cessation of suffering, nibbana, is the cessation of me-and-mine; the Noble Eightfold Path is the method or means of eliminating me-and-mine.

Through the process of *attavadupadana*, we blindly identify with all the subjective reactions that arise from our past conditioning. This collection of habitual patterns of reactivity to which we become attached forms the very basis of personality, called *sakkayaditthi*. Where ignorance and unawareness exists, *upadana* thrives and we become bound to the patterns of our subjective reactivity and prisoners of our own personality.

Identification with self does not mean that we think about experiences as my thought or my feeling, but that we unwittingly identify with our subjective reactions of "me" and "mine." *Atta* and *attaniya* arise through blind identification with the habitual reactions that arise due to conditioning. We fall under their spell and essentially *become* the reactions of the mind. *Atta* is not an abstract concept of self or what we think about our self, but what actually happens in each present moment when we blindly react out of habit. When we say or think, "I am irritated; I am agitated; I am depressed; I am worried; I am angry; I am fearful," we are reacting in a way that creates *atta*. We inadvertently take the feeling of irritation or agitation or anxiety to be real and we give it a solidity and permanence through our blind identification. In other words, iden-

48

tification with our subjective reactions causes us to *become* the object of the reaction and this is *atta*.

Upadana leads to *bhava*, which means that attachment leads to becoming the thing to which we are attached. When we react with anger, we *become* the anger. When we react with worry, we *become* the worry. When we react with irritation, we *become* the irritation, and so on. If something doesn't go to plan, we will most likely react with disappointment, and we tend to unconsciously identify with this emotional reaction and become the disappointment. In that moment when we come under the spell of the reaction of disappointment, it will proliferate into all kinds of secondary reactivity. Perhaps the disappointment gives rise to anger or fear reactions, and through unconscious identification, we are dragged along by these thoughts and emotions and become the anger or fear. When we lose objectivity through identification with the thoughts, beliefs and emotions that arise, we lose control and become the story dictated by our conditioning. This is the world of *attavadupadana* and subjective reactivity that sustains *samsara* and the round of becoming from moment to moment, day to day and beyond.

Anatta

In reality the self is not a definable entity, but a process in continual flux, changing from moment to moment according to changing conditions. There is no fixed entity that we can call a self, or an ego, that is independent from conditioned habitual reactivity. In fact, without reactivity and the underlying ignorance that sustains habitual reactivity, *atta* cannot exist. The positive news is that once the attachment to reactivity ceases, the ego also ceases. What remains, when the mind is not reacting and the ego is no more is the goal of the journey: to awaken to the innate purity of a mind that is free of its contents; the Buddha mind of pure knowing.

The Path of Mindfulness is essentially the path of rediscovering our true identity as a dynamic and intelligent process of being, and this comes about when we are living in harmony with *anatta*. In its practical application, living in harmony with *anatta* means letting go of attachment and identification, and living as a dynamic changing process that is continuously engaged with existence as it unfolds. There is a very important saying in Buddhism,

> *Sabbe dhamma nalam abhinivesaya.*
> No *dhamma* whatsoever should be grasped at or clung to.

This one simple statement, if fully understood, and fully implemented in our daily lives, will lead to complete awakening and complete freedom from suffering.

Mind objects, such as thoughts, perceptions and emotions are called *dhammas*, with a small "*d*" to distinguish them from *Dhamma*, or the teachings about the truth of the nature of *dhammas*. When there is no more blind attachment to the world of conditioned phenomena, then there is harmonization with *anatta* and the mind is free.

Understanding the dangers of blind attachment and blind identification, and applying these insights to life can be very beneficial. However, the full realization of *anatta* means *living anatta* in each moment of our lives. This goes far beyond a belief system about non-self or a belief in the importance of non-attachment. You cannot create the state of *anatta* through thinking, because this is simply the conditioned ego trying to control life. Essentially, there is nothing to do other than be mindful in the present moment and awaken to whatever arises. This is the response of pure knowing, the awakening to the here and now, which is the essence of the practice of mindfulness. In the very moment when *sati* arises, *anatta* also arises and *atta* ceases to be. The teachings of the Buddha can be made incredibly complex, filling volumes with philosophical analysis, but the heartwood of the teaching is actually incredibly simple: establish mindfulness (*sati*) in the present moment and trust in the intuitive intelligence (*satipanna*) of that moment. In each moment of pure knowing, or *satisampajanna*, there is just the process of *knowing* and in that moment there is complete liberation from the confines of the conditioned personality. This is the taste of freedom that we wish to cultivate, and as we gain more experience of *anatta* through the practice of mindfulness, we will naturally gain more freedom and happiness. When *anatta* is present in every moment of our lives, then the ego is extinguished and we will have become fully liberated, a state referred to in Pali as *nibbana* (Skt. *nirvana*).

The ego continually reacts to the world, generating thoughts and emotions, like streams of bubbles rising from the bottom of a pond. One moment we are happy and the next moment we become sad. All these mental phenomena, or *dhammas*, will naturally fade away if allowed to do so, because it is their nature to arise and die. It is only because of our tendency to identification and attachment that we inadvertently keep these mind moments alive, and interfere with the natural cycle of arising and passing away.

For example, if you hold a grudge towards someone who hurt you, and blindly identify with your subjective emotional reaction of feeling hurt, then in that very moment the ego comes into existence. This identification fuels emotional reactivity by proliferating negative thinking and feelings of indignation at how badly you were treated. This is the ego in motion, compounding the problem through secondary reactivity. If on the other hand, you can respond to the feeling of hurt without attachment, but with mindfulness, then you stop feeding the reactive habit of aversion. The ego dies right there and then, in that very moment of non-identification, and it is in each of these unique moments of non-reactivity that true freedom comes about.

This is fundamentally different than trying to destroy the ego through effort and belief, which in reality is simply one part of the ego fighting another part of itself. It is the relationship of mindfulness that leads to transformation and freedom from reactivity, not our efforts to change anything. The only effort required, is to cultivate and sustain mindfulness, and allow change to happen naturally and spontaneously under the direction of our intuitive intelligence, or *satipanna*.

The less identified you are, the less you will suffer. Even intense emotional states, like depression and anger depend on identification to keep them alive. If you stop blindly identifying with the feelings and thoughts that arise through reactive conditioning, then even the most complex emotional states will subside in time. This does not necessarily mean that they will be gone forever, but simply that you no longer feed them and compound the problem.

51

Through the response of mindfulness, you create the right conditions in which emotional complexes will eventually change and resolve themselves. Reactivity can never do this, because reactivity inhibits change by confining consciousness to the inadequate reactions of the past. It is only when you apply mindfulness through *vipassana* meditation and allow *satipanna* to bring about transformation at a deeper level that deep-seated emotional reactions can resolve themselves.

Through the practice of mindfulness, we begin to transcend the whole reactive process and discover our true identity as the *knower* of experience, or more precisely, as the *knowing* of experience, as there is no "ego" who knows. This very direct and pure knowing is the essence of Buddha mind, which is non-reactive, non-fabricated and pur unconditioned awareness. To emphasise the point, the path of *anatta* means not identifying with any contents of the mind. Be fully engaged with perceptions, thoughts and feelings, but do not identify with them. This is the perfection of objective equanimity (*upekkha*), which is regarded as one of the most noble and sublime qualities that can be cultivated.

If your mind says "I am worried, because I don't have enough money to pay the rent," don't allow yourself to be seduced into worrying, but attend to the feeling level of worry with mindfulness. Worrying never changes anything, but simply adds suffering to an already difficult situation. We need something different, a response that creates a space around the emotion, and where we can relate to the emotion as an object to be cared for. It is in the silent mind that *satipanna* arises and operates fully to transform internal conflict and dissonance. If the thought arises "I am unhappy," don't fall for it, just respond with mindfulness to the underlying feeling and relate to it as an object for meditation. Thinking and analyzing won't cure the underlying suffering, but being truly present for a feeling in an open and caring way through mindfulness, will create the best conditions for transformation. If anger arises, because someone hurt your feelings, don't allow yourself to be seduced by negative thinking. This will simply fuel the anger and strengthen the anger reaction, which will hurt you more. It is a much better practice to attend to the feeling of anger with mindfulness and nonproliferation of reactive thinking, so that the anger has the opportunity to resolve itself.

There is nothing that will not benefit from the response of mindfulness as an alternative to blind reactivity, and this is what we mean by "*Sabbe dhamma nalam abhinivesaya.*" It is through the path of non-attachment and non-reactivity that we realize *anatta*, and can begin to engage fully and intelligently with the chaos of our daily lives.

4 PRIMARY AND SECONDARY REACTIVITY

After contact with physical objects through the physical sense organs, or contact with mental objects, such as thoughts, memories and feelings, the unaware mind tends to react according to past conditioning with either attraction (*lobha*), repulsion (*dosa*), or delusion (*moha*). When we see something we like, we react by wanting to possess it. When we see something disagreeable, then we react by pushing it away. In general, we become seduced by whatever arises and tend to unconsciously identify and attach to these subjective reactions, which is the nature of delusion. These initial and automatic reactions based on past conditioning are called *primary reactions*. Something doesn't go to plan and we become upset or angry, or disappointed. We see a snake and react with fear, or we see a beautiful sight and react with joy.

During mindfulness practice we try to cultivate an awareness of all these automatic reactions as soon as they arise, so that we don't become seduced into further reactivity. If we are not mindful, then the mind will start reacting to the primary reactions themselves and produce *secondary reactions*, such as the proliferation of ruminative thinking and worrying, and other forms of further emotional reactivity. We start to generalize and make false assumptions and become consumed by delusional beliefs. Most of all, this proliferation of thinking and emotional reactivity reinforces and feeds the primary reactions and this keeps them alive. Worry is a classic example of secondary reactivity. It serves no purpose other than to intensify an underlying fear and actually prevents the fear from being resolved. Preoccupation with negative thinking is unskillful and does not help resolve fear or any other core emotional complex, but simply feeds the inner demons and sustains ignorance.

Secondary reactivity has the effect of preventing the resolution of *dukkha* through the phenomenon of Reactive Displacement. Secondary reactivity effectively takes our attention away from the underlying primary reactions and this prevents their transformation and resolution. Secondary reactivity simply causes the repression of primary reactivity and prevents us from fully knowing what is there. This prevents us from uncovering the deep structure, the iceberg beneath the waterline, which is to sustain ignorance, or *avijja*. Consequently, it is very important to become attentive to all forms of secondary reactivity and ruminative thinking, which is a major activity in mindfulness practice.

THE FIVE HINDRANCES

The Buddha described five common classes of secondary reactivity, called the Five Hindrances (*nivarana*). These are sensual craving (*kamacchanda*); ill will (*vyapada*); sloth and torpor (*thina-middha*); agitation and worry (*uddhacca-kukkucca*); and doubt (*vicikiccha*). They are called "hindrances" because they sustain *dukkha* and mental instability and keep us in bondage to habitual reactivity and *samsara*. The hindrances prevent us from seeing things clearly by distracting us away from the present into different reactive pathways. They prevent us from being fully present with the original suffering that needs our attention, and this perpetuates ignorance. Suffering will only resolve itself, if we can be fully present with our pain, or the pain of others. Without this complete presence brought about by mindfulness, the painful cycle of suffering will continue indefinitely.

Sensual craving is like water that is colored by a dye so that whatever is seen, is also colored. Ill will is like water that is boiling, so that nothing cn be seen in depth. Sloth and torpor is like water that is covered with waterweed that equally obscures seeing the deeper structure of experience. Agitation is like water that is whipped up by the wind. Doubt is like water that is muddy and prevents any possibility of insight, even if the other hindrances are removed. In each case, we are prevented from seeing into the depth of the water and are confined to the superficial level of perception, characterized by ignorance and delusion. Unable to see the full nature of reality, we are condemned to suffer.

During mindfulness meditation and mindfulness practice throughout the day, we must pay particular attention to these five types of secondary reactivity and learn to recognize them when they arise and also recognize the conditions that cause their arising. It is only through becoming mindful of secondary reactivity that we can overcome them. Once we have learned to recognize the hindrances, we learn to respond to them, not with aversion or further ego-directed reactivity, but with sustained mindfulness. We choose to form a caring and receptive relationship with our afflictions in which we create the right conditions of mindfulness that will allow the hindrances to recsolve themselves. The hindrances are not our enemy, they are the reality of the human condition and we must come to terms with this reality and work with it in a constructive manner. We can never rid the mind of the hindrances through the actions of the ego or any attempt to control the mind through willpower or coercion. These are simply other forms of secondary reactivity, and other manifestations of *nivarana*. The only effective way to purify the mind is to learn not to react to the hindrances or any other manifestation of the *kilesas*, but to respond to them with mindfulness and trust in the transformative power of a mindfulness-based relationship.

Sensual desire

One of the most obvious forms of secondary reactivity is the proliferation of craving for sensual stimulation, called *kamacchandha*. Preoccupation with sensory stimulation, whether originating from the physical senses, or from the pleasant sensations associated with thinking and fantasy, distracts us from being aware of the present moment. We become lost in the experience of our sensations, which leaves us unable to be fully present with either the experience of the external world or our inner experiences. Besides becoming lost in pleasant experiences, we also easily become lost in thinking and planning about how to get more. This can lead to obsession and the proliferation of craving that is called *tanha papanca*.

This hindrance can take on many forms. The ego always seeks pleasant experiences and will create distractions that take you away from your attempts to be mindful, especially if you are focusing on inner pain. The skillful response to this form of secondary reactivity is to focus mindfulness on the impulse that takes you away from your primary object of meditation. All reactions have an impulsive core, based on *tanha*, and through mindfulness training, we can learn to recognize this impulse before it takes control of the mind and compels us to react.

Ill will

This hindrance, called *vyapada* has the same effect as sensual desire in distracting us away from being fully present with our experience, and prevents us from fully experiencing the reality of our present expeience.

If you choose to meditate on some form of *dukkha*, such as anxiety or fear, then it is important to be aware of any secondary reactions of aversion that may arise. Aversion is a very powerful form of secondary reactivity that has the effect of distracting attention away from the primary experience. This inhibits change and keeps us confined to the superficial level of experience. In fact, the very act of resistance creates division between you as the ego-observer and the problem as something to be fixed. This division prevents you from uncovering the deep structure of your suffering, or any other form of experience, and if you cannot see the subtle internl structure of your emotions, then they will not change.

If you notice a feeling of revulsion or dislike for whatever you are experiencing, including painful emotions, then you must learn to recognize what is happening, and respond with "No. Not now. I choose to sit with my pain." It is likely that the secondary reactions of aversion will carry a strong energetic charge and this is a signal that you need to switch focus onto the *vyapada* itself. Work with that energy until it resolves itself, before returning to the primary object of your meditation. Again, after you have resolved the aversion to your inner pain you will probably also find that the original emotional suffering will have significantly changed.

Besides specific aversion to inner suffering, it is also possible to become consumed by hatred and thoughts of revenge directed against someone or some situation that caused you pain. Anger, thoughts of ill will and revenge are not skillful responses and often these negative thoughts will do more harm to you than to the perpetrator. As the Buddha said,

> Holding on to anger is like grasping a hot coal with the intent of throwing it at someone else; you are the one who gets burned.

If the hindrance of *vyapada* arises during meditation, then it essential that you respond to it with mindfulness and don't try to suppress it. Remembering that the whole purpose of mindfulness meditation is to resolve suffering and find the natural state of balance that lies within, you must attend to whatever arises, without prejudice. If the dominant feelings that arise are of anger and ill will, then you must make these emotions the primary object for *vipassana* meditation. In *vipassana*, we always attend to exactly what is present in the present moment and never ignore it in pursuit of something more pleasurable.

The mind is like a complex ecosystem or energy field, in which all our emotional complexes are interrelated. Every emotional state is linked to some aspect of sensual craving and aversion, which represent the way that we cling to internal beliefs and perceptions. The hindrances are often the symptoms of a much deeper conflict within the mind. More often than not, it is the hindrances of craving and aversion that prevent the tranformation of our inner pain and suffering. They get in the way and prevent us from bringing the healing power of mindfulness to the core *dukkha* within. Therefore, we must not allow ourself to become caught up in further reactivity, but use the present experience of the hindrances to guide us back to the source. In meditation and the practice of mindfulnes, we embrace the hindrances and use them as our teachers. Like any other experience, any other *sanhkhara* that arises, what we see is only the superficial surface structure. But, we can use this as a starting point to guide us to the reality beneath. Transformation and liberation are always a function of what we bring into conscious awareness and know fully. Mindfulness is the process of investigation in which we uncover the deep structure of each moment of experience, and this is immensely transformational and liberating.

Sloth and torpor

The next common hindrance and group of secondary habitual reactions is called *thina-middha*, which is most often translated as sloth and torpor. This hindrance encompasses all the forms of reactivity that cause the mind to contract and withdraw. This mental contraction manifests as apathy, indifference and inflexibility. *Thina-middha* is a hindrance to meditation and The Path of Mindfulness, because the mind needs to be fresh and alert and actively engaged with experience, in order to develop the inner wisdom that leads to purification and transformation.

Blind attachment (*upadana*) leads to the particular type of mental torpor and stiffness, called *thina*, which literally means to congeal and become hard. The mind that is dominated by blind attachment to beliefs, conventions and practices and to habitual patterns of reactivity becomes mechanical, inflexible and lacks the malleability necessary for transformation. *Thina* describes those reactions that lead to a loss of spontaneity, creativity and responsiveness. This hindrance feeds on *avijja*, the ignorance that dulls the mind and makes us blind to the richness of life. The mind consumed by *thina* exits in a state of psychological and spiritual sleep that is in fact a form of living death.

Mindfulness is the path of letting go of the constraints of ignorance and the chains of habitual conditioning and opening to the unfolding possibilities of the present. Through the cultivation of mindfulness, we begin to peel off the death mask of *thina*, so that we can develop full presence and engage fully with present experience as it unfolds. Mindfulness is the antidote to apathy and reactivity. It allows us to become responsive, rather than reactive, and empowered, rather than remaining the victim of habitual reactivity. Through mindfulness we emege from the stiff chrysalis of our conditioning and discover the freedom of authentic living in the immediate present. This alive wakefulness is the innate nature of the psyche, the vibrancy and aliveness that is obscured by the hindrances and habitual reactivity. The chief function of mindfulness practice is to remove the obstacles that prevent us from being our true enlightened self. This we do, not by trying to remove them by force, but through the much more refined approach of mindfulness, in which we allow them to dissolve away by not feeding them with attachment. Hindrances are made powerful by ignorance, clinging and resistance: they feed on these three forms of reactivity. If we simply stop feeding them, then they will wither away, quite naturally, under the warming rays of innate wisdom, *satipanna*.

Drowsiness and fatigue, or *middha* is the natural consequence of a closed and contracted mind. Attachment to subjective reactivity, beliefs and fixed ways of doing things consumes energy and leaves the mind stressed and exhausted. In partcular, we become fatigued from the continual frustration of not getting what we want and the immense effort of trying to make the world conform to our expectations. This is the stress of the ego trying to acquire and control experience. The ego is in a state of perpetual conflict, which is draining, produces mental fatigue and in its severe form, depression.

However, this hindrance has much to teach us, and we can make it the object for our meditation. By focusing with mindfulness on the emotional state of fatigue, we can access the blind fixations and *tanha* that lie beneath the surface. If we can release just a fraction of the energy that was previously trapped in the underlying patterns of blind attachments, then we will find that the drowsiness and fatigue will lift quite naturally.   Mindfulness has a profound effect in restoring the natural and healthy flow of energy in the psyche by releasing the energy that was previously frozen into patterns of habitual reactivity. As the flow of emotional energy is restored, we feel the rapture and joy of new life. This is the great happiness of non-attachment, of not clinging to anything as "me" or "mine," and this happens quite naturally when mindfulness is established and cultivated.

Mental Agitation and Worry

One of the hardest hindrances to work with is the complex of mental agitation and worry (*uddhacca-kukkucca*). This hindrance includes the universal problems of agitation, restlessness and distractedness (*uddhacca*), and the negative emotional reactivity of worrying (*kukkucca*). Both of these factors are strong reactive forces that create and sustain *dukkha*. When the mind is agitated, our attention is distracted away from the present experience into secondary reactivity. Worry and negative thinking simply take our attention *away* from the direct and full experience of our inner emotions and this feeds ignorance and prevents change. Therefore, it is essential to be very vigilant for this hindrance and not allow yourself to be seduced into worry or any form of reactive thinking that takes us away from our immediate experience.

If we choose to meditate on our fear, anxiety or depression, we must be able to create the right kind of relationship with our inner experience, based on stillness and careful investigation. Transformation requires the absence of reactivity combined with complete presence of mind, which is provided through mindfulness and inhibited by reactivity. No presence, no change; partial presence, partial change; complete presence, complete change. The Path of Mindfulness is the primary way through which we can cultivate complete presence.

Instead of fighting the tendency of the mind to become seduced into agitation and worry, we can learn to work skillfully and intelligently with this hindrance, in what can best be described as the dance of mindfulness. Mindfulness is about tuning in to your immediate experience so that you see what is arising as it is arising. The more aware you become of the natural impulses that lead to agitation, the easier it will be to pull the mind back, and the less time will be lost in daydreaming and worrying. Each time your mind wanders, and you bring it back, strengthens the beneficial habit of mindfulness and weakens the dysfunctional habit of reactivity. Over time, the faculty of mindfulness will develop into a powerful balancing force that will stabalize many aspects of life where concentration, non-reactivity and presence of mind are important.

Through the sustained practice of mindfulness of the hindrance of agitation and worry, you will develop a very real form of *samadhi* that will stabalize how you relate to all the ontents of the mind, pleasant or unpleasant. This in turn will further strengthen the faculty of mindulness. *Samadhi* is the opposite of agitation and worry and the best possible way to develop *samadhi* is to work with *uddhacca-kukkucca* and use it as a teaching platform. This transforms it from being a hindrance, into being a means for purifying the mind and cultivating freedom from all the hindrances. The objective of mindfulness practice and meditation is not to rid the mind of distractions and agitated thoughts, but to learn a new way of relating to these reactive thoughts such that we maintain balance and stability in the real world. Through mindfulness, we learn to neutralize the agitation and worry by simply creating lots of space around these thoughts. We don't avoid them, but actually turn towards them and observe them with great care and attention. With such vigilance, they can do us no harm and we are no longer at their mercy.

Mindfulness teaches us the art of how to avoid *becoming* the reactions of the mind and teaches us how to respond with pure *knowing* to each reaction, as an object to be known. Any factor that overcomes *avijja* will tend to reduce reactivity and suffering, and mindfulness is the pre-eminate antidote to *avijja*. This strengthens the perceptual shift from subjective reactivity to objective knowing, and little by little, we become more in tune with the *knowing* part of our experience, rather than becoming attached to the *known*. The process of not getting caught up in reactivity takes away the fuel that powers emotional reactions and when we stop feeding them, they will wither away and resolve themselves.

The mind may experience anxiety produced by habitual reactions to memories of the past or thoughts about the future. Worry, called *kukkucca* in Pail, is a form of secondary reactivity that intensifies and sustains the experience of anxiety in the present. The word "worry" has its roots in the Old English *wyrgan*, which literally means, "to strangle." Generally, this kind of reactive thinking does not resolve problems, but simply intensifies the mental anguish of *dukkha*. Negative thinking and worry simply intensifies the hindrance of *thina-middha* and makes the mind rigid, contracted and fearful, which leads to apathy and fatigue. During mindfulness meditation, we learn to recognize worry-thoughts as they arise and respond to them with mindfulness, and therby stop the proliferation of secondary reactivity.

However, stopping the proliferation of secondary reactivity is only the first step of the mindfulness response; the most important part is what follows. This is the response of opening our awareness and forming a relationship with the worry-thought based on mindfulness. Mindfulness is all about the quality of relationship and about increasing our ability to engage objectively with our experience and investigate the deeper structure of the emotion. The name for this special quality of non-reactive relationship is *satisampa-*

janna, or the pure knowing that accompanies mindfulness (*sati*). If we perceive worrry, then we choose to make the emotional complex of worry the very object for our meditation. Mindfulness meditation (*vipassana*) creates the space in which dissonant feeling-energy can unfold and reveal its inner structure in the form of more subtle feelings and other sensory modalities. As always, mindfulness allows the differentiation of experience from the gross and superficial to the detailed inner reality of what sustains the emotion. All emotions, including anxiety and depression have an inner structure. It is the seeing of this inner structure that makes change possible. In essence, through mindful-investigation, we overcome the basic ignorance of this inner structure. Through mindfulness we create the right conditions in which the underlying anxiety can spontaneously resolve itself through the action of intuitive intelligence (*satipanna*). It is always reassuring to see for ourselves how anxieties and worries respond to the attention we give them through mindfulness. When we respond to them with mindfulness and the natural compassion that comes with mindfulness, they respond by changing and healing and releasing energy back into the psyche.

Doubt

It is healthy to have doubt and skepticism to the extent that it encourages investigation and allows you to discover for yourself what is skillful and what leads towards the resolution of *dukkha*. Buddhism is very much a path of self-discovery and is not about blindly following dogma. However, there is another kind of doubt that is not healthy and leads to indecision and spiritual contraction. This is called *vicikiccha*, the spiritual paralysis that leads prevents change. Such skepticism is like a brick wall that closes the mind and heart and prevents the development of experiential wisdom. The greatest cause of doubt is ignorance, the unwillingness to open the mind and look and see what is actually there. Chronic doubters live behind a wall of beliefs that creates a smokescreen, and insulates them from reality. The Path of Mindfulness is not something that requires blind belief, but simply a willingness to let go of prejudices and really look closely at the world of experience; at the happiness and suffering in our lives and the lives of others; and discover how we contribute to the creation of both.

We may feel that we are not skilled enough to practice mindfulness or that we are not capable of facing our emotional pain, without being overwhelmed by our inner demons. We convince ourselves that we don't have the time to practice, or that we tried meditating for a month or two, but it just didn't lead anywhere, so we gave up. However, it is important to understand that these stories, like any other form of secondary reactivity, are simply superficial constructs, *sankharas* of the mind, and we should not fall victim to their spell.

The path for overcoming doubt, or any other negative reactions that arise during mindfulness practice, is not to blindly accept them, not to be seduced into inactivity, but to recognize that they have arisen and then attend to each with mindfulness. If you are plagued by insecurity and a lack of confidence, be mindful and know that these thoughts have arisen. Do not allow yourself to be seduced into believing them. Instead, make these emotional reactions of doubt and insecurity the very objects for *vipassana* meditation. Study the feeling tone in detail and establish a relationship with these feelings based on mindfulness, and allow them to change internally and resolve themselves.

The Path of Mindfulness teaches us not to accept the superficial appearance of what arises in the mind. With mindfulness, we greet each and every thought and emotion as a visiting guest, with respect, but also with caution. The most important thing is not to give in to the doubt and insecurity, because that will only further strengthen the reactivity. Similarly, we do not try to reject our doubts through rationalization and positive thinking, as that will also take our attention away from the most important thing, which is to attend to the underlying feeling energy that empowers insecurity. If there is doubt and insecurity, then these reactions must be acknowledged and attended to with genuine respect, kindness and compassion, but above all with a keen interest in investigating what is below the superficial appearance of the emotional hindrance.

The most effective path for the resolution of insecurity is to be open and mindful of the negative energy (*dukkhavedana*) that empowers the thought-emotion. In the open therapeutic space that is created by mindfulness any trapped negative energy will be free to transform itself, without interference from the ego. Reactivity simply locks *dukkhavedana* in place, and when you are feeling inadequate or overwhelmed the last thing you need to do is tighten up further. Through mindfulness of these reactions of self-doubt and insecurity, we create a space in which things can change and we can witness the release of *dukkhavedana* and the gradual resolution of insecurity. Working at this subtle level of change brings positive experiences and in the light of this experience, the negative hindrance of *vicikiccha* will fade away and be replaced by a growing faith and confidence, called *saddha*. As we experience the dissolution of suffering and the cause of suffering through the application of mindfulness, we directly experience a new possibility for living. However, the development of *saddha* should arise from our inner intuitive experience and not through blind attachment to beliefs and dogma. Faith has to come from within, from the heart and from the totality of the psyche if it is to be truly transformative.

In conclusion, the primary approach in meditation should be to treat each of the five hindrances as mental objects for mindful-investigation. The approach to the hindrances should be the same as for any other form of mental reactivity. We begin with vigilance to prevent further reactivity; we create a relationship based on receptivity and investigation; and finally we allow our innate intelligence (*satipanna*) to bring about resolution. These three factors are all part to the response of mindfulness.

5 DUKKHA: THE SUFFERING DUE TO REACTIVITY

The word *dukkha* is a compound of *du*, which means "bad, painful, hard to endure" and the suffix *kha*, which means "space," and so *dukkha* literally means "bad space." *Dukkha* is a very complex term with multiple meanings depending on the context, which is not unusual for many key terms used in Buddhism. However, the general meaning of *dukkha* conveys that which is unsatisfactory and associated with suffering.

The Buddha describes the First Noble Truth of *dukkha* in terms of the conditions of existence that provide the ground from which suffering can arise,

> And this, monks, is the Noble Truth of dukkha: birth is dukkha, and old age is dukkha, and disease is dukkha, and dying is dukkha, association with what is not dear is dukkha, separation from what is dear is dukkha, not getting what you want is dukkha - in short, the five aggregates of grasping are dukkha.

Although usually translated as suffering, *dukkha* refers to something much more specific than the conventional meaning of the word. From the Buddhist perspective, suffering refers to the mental anguish produced by our subjective reactions to objective events, rather than the event itself. The objective component of suffering is best described as "pain," which comes from the inevitable ups and downs of life. Birth and death, physical pain, sickness or the pain of growing old, are all examples of the inevitable objective physical pains of life, as are personal loss, disappointment, failure and abuse by others.

The objective ups and downs of life are classically described as the "eight worldly winds" of changing worldly phenomena (*lokadhamma*). These include the polarities of pleasure and pain, gain and loss, success and failure, praise and criticism. Conditions come and go; sometimes they go our way; more often they do not. The intensity of *dukkha* varies between people according to the nature of their subjective habitual reactivity. What is very upsetting to one

67

person may not affect another person; what makes one person angry may have no affect on another. Also, the intensity of suffering changes over time as our habits change. Clearly, the conditioned subjective reactivity is the main component of the mental anguish we call suffering and this is the true meaning of *dukkha* as taught by the Buddha. There is a popular saying that summarizes the difference very well:

Pain is inevitable; suffering is optional.

Suffering has been described as the process through which we complicate our pain. We prolong the pain or make it more intense through the stories we tell ourselves and through the beliefs that we create around our pain. We take the concrete reality of pain and turn it into a monster of abstraction and generalization. A blemish on the skin becomes skin cancer; a failure at work becomes the end of the world. The perpetuation of craving (*tanha papanca*), of beliefs (*ditthi papanca*) and the preoccupation with self and other (*mana papanca*) creates a complex superstructure of secondary reactivity around pain, and this is the origin of *dukkha*. Pain comes and goes as conditions change, whereas *dukkha* tends to persist, even if the external objective pain has gone, because of the inner demons that we have created through blind subjective reactivity.

Of course, what sustains our patterns of subjective habitual reactivity is the force of compulsive attachment called *tanha*, and this is why the Buddha summarized *dukkha* as being due to, "the five aggregates subject to clinging." These are the components from which our habitual reactivity is made: physical form, perception, feeling, mental formation, and consciousness.

Dukkha has an emotional form in the primary subjective emotional reactions of sorrow (*soka*), lamentation (*parideva*), anguish (*domanassa*) and despair (*upayasa*). We get caught up in our reactions of wanting things to be a certain way (*bhavatanha*), or in reactions of aversion to the things we don't like (*vibhavatanha*), and the consequence of this blind attachment is one or more of these painful emotions.

These negative emotional reactions represent negative feeling energy (*dukkhavedana*) that has become trapped and frozen in place in the subconscious recesses of the mind. If left untended, this repressed negative energy will crystallize into core emotional complexes. Hidden from view, these inner demons corrupt the actions of body, speech and mind, and have a serious long-term impact on our lives. This is why the Buddha placed such emphasis on *dukkha*, because the only effective way to discover happiness is through the resolution of the core emotional complexes of *soka*, *parideva*, *domanassa* and *upayasa*. It is by paying close attention, through mindfulness, that we can create the right conditions for the release of the trapped and repressed life energy that lies at the core of all emotional reactions.

THE VARIETIES OF DUKKHA

When the Buddha described *dukkha* he referred to three principle states of suffering (*dukkhata*) that arise in the mind whenever there is blind attachment to subjective reactivity. These are *dukkha-dukkhata*, the subjective secondary reactivity to physical and mental pain that amplifies suffering; *viparinama-dukkhata*, the subjective reactions of resistance to change and impermanence; *sankhara-dukkhata*, the anguish and stress produced by reactivity to memories, thoughts, beliefs, emotions or any other mental formation.

Suffering associated with pain

Pain is an inevitable part of life, of birth, growing, aging, sickness and death. However, we have a tendency to accentuate our pain through our reactions of resistance and the proliferation of negative thinking and craving. This suffering that we create through our subjective reactions to pain is called *dukkha-dukkhata*.

Life produces pain, both physical and mental, and this is a universal, experienced by all. Life is just as it is: neither good nor bad, satisfactory or unsatisfactory, and is not in itself suffering. Suffering arises through our blind subjective reactions to pain. There is clearly pain associated with death, illness and loss, as there is with failure or being treated unfairly. However, this pain is not *dukkha* as described by the Buddha. *Dukkha* is produced solely by the mind and comes from what we add on to experience, painful or otherwise, through our blind conditioned reactivity. One person reacts to disappointment with wise acceptance, while another person has a mental break down. Even with physical pain, the degree of suffering experienced is closely related to the emotional reaction of fear, and fear is created by the mind and depends on conditioning and previous experience. Fear amplifies pain and generates distress, but fear is a subjective reaction that we unconsciously add on to the actual experience of pain. In the words of Dan Millman, the inspirational writer and athlete,

> Pain is a relatively objective, physical phenomenon; suffering is our psychological resistance to what happens. Events may create physical pain, but they do not in themselves create suffering. Resistance creates suffering. Stress happens when your mind resists what is...The only problem in your life is your mind"s resistance to life as it unfolds.

When we follow *Dhamma* and The Path of Mindfulness, we choose to investigate how we create suffering by first learning to recognize our subjective mental reactions as they arise and choose not to react and not to create suffering. We then take this a step further and make *dukkha* the very object for contemplation with mindfulness. The general rule is that the more you open to things as they are, the less you will suffer and conversely, the more you react and close up, the more you will suffer. The choice between responsiveness and reactivity is a choice available for all of us to make in each and every moment of life. By opening our awareness and mindfulness to the patterns of our habitual reactivity, we can begin to uncover the attachments and trapped feeling energy that keeps us reacting over and over again. This is the essence of The Path of Mindfulness that leads to transformation and release from the subjective habitual reactivity that creates suffering in our minds, and in the world.

Suffering associated with change

The next level of suffering that we produce through subjective re-activity is called *viparinama-dukkhata*. This is the pain and disappointment that we create as a subjective reaction to the most fundamental law of all phenomena: the law of impermanence (*anicca*) and change. *Dukkha* is often translated as the "unsatisfactoriness" of physical and psychological phenomena, simply because all *sankharas* are subject to *anicca* and are inherently unstable and unreliable and cannot give lasting happiness. In fact, *dukkha* can equally be defined as the suffering that arises from the instability and unreliability of the phenomena to which we have become attached. In the words of the Buddha,

> *Sabbe sankhara anicca.*
> All formations are impermanent.

The Buddha's last words are said to have been on this very subject:

> Disciples, this I declare to you: All conditioned things
> are subject to disintegration - strive on untiringly for
> your liberation.

The Buddha summarized the fundamental problem of *dukkha* as the mental anguish that results from blind, compulsive attachment to the five *khandhas* that define our existence. All five *khandhas* of the body and material form (*rupa*), perceptions (*sanna*), feelings (*vedana*), reactive thinking (*sankhara*) and consciousness (*vinnana*), are inherently unstable and subject to change. In each moment of life, these five *khandhas* come together depending on conditions and exist for a brief moment, before they begin to dissolve. However, change is not the cause of *dukkha*; it is the resistance to the natural flow of change that brings about suffering. When we become blindly attached or identified with any of the five *khandhas*, we immediately create conflict between an unchanging ideal and the reality of change. For this reason *dukkha* can be translated as the mental anguish that results from reactive aversion to instability and *anicca*. It is amazing how much of the time we live in denial of this most basic fact, and how we live with

71

the delusional hope that things will not change. However, it is a characteristic of all phenomena that they are unstable and therefore cannot provide a reliable foundation for lasting happiness. It is the inability to live in harmony with this natural flow of life that generates the conflict, stress and the mental anguish of *dukkha*.

In the end, we cannot control life, but we can learn to live skillfully in relation to change and we can control our habitual reactivity to change. In mindfulness practice, we deliberately cultivate awareness of the reactions of resistance and aversion to change. We choose to form a relationship with the compulsive feelings of both aversion and the underlying fear around change. Through this practice we come to live in harmony with *anicca*, and this is the nature of authentic living, in which we embrace life as it is, without fear or regret. Another way of thinking about living in harmony with *anicca* is that we are training ourselves to live in harmony with death. As Carlos Castaneda said,

> Death is our eternal companion. It is always to our left, an arm's length behind us. Death is the only wise adviser that a warrior has.

Of course, the death of the body is inevitable and we must come to terms with this fact. The practice of mindfulness includes the contemplation of our death and the death of our friends, and we choose to engage with the feeling energy that surrounds the experience of aging and death. Death is a very skillful subject for contemplation and meditation. The objective of such contemplation is not to indilge in reactive thinking, but rather to pay close attention to any emotions and reactions that arise when you contemplate death. These should be known fully and embraced with mindfulness. Then your fears cannot hurt you. This is how we should approach all anxieties associated with change: greet them as teachers, embrace them, investigate them; in short, awaken to these thoughts and emotions and let them show you the way to peace.

When anything changes, something needs to die, whether in the form of an old belief, an attitude, an expectation or a feeling. We have to let go of the past, which means allowing any mental construct, any *sankhara*, to die and make way for something new.

Only when we can accept this natural flow of change that is *anicca*, will there be the freedom for new life to arise, and only then will we be living in harmony with the reality of existence as a flowing river of change. However, we must always remember that it is not you who lets go of the past; rather the letting go happens in response to mindfulness. Be mindful and let the old die so that the new may be born.

Suffering associated with mental formations

The next major source of *dukkha* is inherent in the mental formations and fabrications (*sankhara*) of the mind and is called *sankhara-dukkhata*. The mental aggregate of *sankhara* describes the process of subjective reactivity that produces thoughts, beliefs, emotions and anything synthesized under the influence of *avijja*, or unconscious conditioning.

Existence is a process, very much like a river, which is continually changing form from minute to minute. One minute the river appears as a collection of ripples and bubbles and swirling eddies only to change seamlessly into another collection of ripples and bubbles. If we were to take a snapshot of the river, then that particular formation of ripples and bubbles would be a *sankhara*. However, this *sankhara* has no basis in reality, because the river is continually changing. Therefore, any given *sankhara* cannot adequately represent the truth or reality of the river. All *sankharas* are, therefore inherently imperfect and unsatisfactory and are formed at the expense of the truth. As the Buddha said,

> *Avijja paccaya sankhara.*
> Ignorance is the necessary condition for the formation
> of *sankharas*.

The same principle applies to the *cittasankharas* of the mind. They are formed as part of a continuous process of living and do not have any inependent existence in reality. This is the teaching of *anatta*: that nothing has a separate existence independent of the dynamic changing process of existence.

If we become attached to mental constructs such as beliefs, expectations, perceptions, memories or emotions, then we are attaching to something that is imperfect and unsatisfactory and that is in effect an illusion. Attachment to *cittasankharas* leads to conflict between the static and imperfect *sankara* and the reality of existence as dynamic change, and this conflict is experienced as *dukkha*. In the same way that a grain of sand irritates the soft tissues of the eye, the rigid unchanging *sankharas* irritate the mind and cause pain. As the Buddha said,

> *Sabbe sankhara dukkha.*
> All conditioned formations are subject to suffering.

There is nothing inherently wrong with thoughts or mental representation, and this teaching is not an attack on thinking. However, we must fully accept that no *sankhara* can adequately represent reality: it will always be imperfect, inadequate and unsatisfactory. Therefore, we must not allow ourselves to become *blindly attached* to thoughts or anything that takes form in the mind. It is really quite simple: if there is no blind attachment to mental objects, then there will be no suffering. There may still be pain, but we will not create suffering.

In mindfulness practice, we learn to fully engage with reality as it is. With mindfulness, we can fully experience *sankharas* as they arise, but without being seduced by them. We receive them, but do not believe them, but see them for what they are: imperfect and unsatisfactory illusions. We do not dismiss them or react with aversion to *sankharas*, but simply stop proliferating the habitual emotional reactions of the ego that creates *dukkha*. To attach to any *sankhara* is to play Russian roulette with our happiness and the odds are not in our favor. The challenge is to meet all *sankharas* with mindfulness and equanimity (*upekkha*), which is the response of freedom, where we can choose how to act, based on intelligence rather than compulsion.

AWAKENING TO DUKKHA

In the beautiful and succinct words of the Thai meditation master, Ajahn Chah,

> There are two kinds of suffering: the suffering that leads to more suffering and the suffering that leads to the end of suffering. If you are not willing to face the second kind of suffering, you will surely continue to experience the first.

The message is clear: mindfulness practice and mindfulness meditation should be directed towards the resolution of suffering as you encounter it in your daily life. This is important to understand when you approach your practice of *vipassana* meditation, because meditation is not meant to be an escape from the suffering in your life, but rather a choice to directly engage with *dukkha* with mindfulness in order to create the best conditions possible for its resolution. To take this a step further, we should take up the challenge, and actively seek out *dukkha* wherever it exists and surround it with the healing energy of mindfulness. It is better to take the initiative, rather than wait for *dukkha* to attack you when you are least prepared.

We should search through every aspect of our mind and seek out any manifestation of inner conflict. Examine painful memories and past traumas, or the failures and disappointments from your past and investigate them with mindfulness in the present. Look at your fears and worries about the future and contemplate them with mindfulness. These are all examples of *dukkha* that result from some form of deep-seated attachment and secondary reactivity. If they remain hidden, they will continue to fester and create further suffering. The Path of Mindfulness, or *satipatthana* asks us to seek out each and every manifestation of *dukkha* and relate to it with mindfulness. This does not mean becoming caught up in thinking about past traumas or worrying about the future, because any such form of thinking is reactive by nature and like any reaction, it takes you away from the direct experience of the original emotion. What we are trying to cultivate is the art of listening and of being completely present for our painful emotions, and this occurs when the thinking mind is silent and mindfulness is established.

Examine your relationships with your partner, family, friends and colleagues. Look for *dukkha* in the form of conflicts, hurt feelings and bruised pride. Relationships are a great place for practice and will provide countless opportunities to develop mindfulness in relation to *dukkha*. There is no need to dwell on thinking or analysis, but simply surround the pain with mindfulness, and allow actions to arise from that still space of compassionate presence.

Look at how you relate to the world, to your possessions and expressions of wealth. Can you fully appreciate what you have, or do you become embroiled in wanting something different? Can you fully enjoy the richness of your present experience, or do you live in perpetual disappointment? Can you enjoy sensory enjoyment and pleasure, without becoming addicted? Do not blindly accept the habitual reactivity that generates *dukkha*, but respond to this reactivity with mindfulness. Learn to recognize your habitual emotional reactions in great detail and become an expert on the workings of your own mind.

The Path of Mindfulness and *vipassana* meditation is fundamentally one of learning a totally new way of relating to *dukkha*. In the unaware and unawakened mind, we blindly react to *dukkha* with wanting (*lobha*), with aversion (*dosa*), and with delusion (*moha*). This is the first kind of suffering described by Ajahn Chah, which simply perpetuates suffering and prevents its resolution. The alternative approach is to learn to respond to our suffering with mindfulness, which is non-reactive and provides the right conditions for beneficial change. This is not an easy path, and may involve more suffering before suffering comes to an end. However, every step on The Path of Mindfulness is a wise step that offers the possibility of release from suffering, whereas the path of reactivity and ignorance can only lead to more suffering.

The choice you face in each and every encounter with *dukkha* is between the opposing actions of *reactivity* or *responsiveness*. Reactivity is characterized by ignorance (*avijja*) and attachment (*upadana*), while responsiveness is characterized by mindfulness (*sati*) and wisdom (*panna*). Mindfulness (*sati*) leads to a higher quality relationship with *dukkha* that is spacious, intuitive, soft and pliable and allows us to see the subtle details of each manifestation of *dukkha*. This opens up a therapeutic space that both stops further reactivity and allows *dukkha* to transform itself. Mindfulness allows a creative and intuitive intereaction between the whole psyche and the experience of *dukkha*, which is quite different than relying on the ego to try and fix things through thinking. By forming a relationship based on mindfulness, we are learning to trust our intuitive intelligence (*satipanna*). We let this natural inner wisdom direct the show and guide us towards the resolution of *dukkha*. This is a very wise choice that we can make in every encounter with emotional suffering, whether originating internally, or in relation to the suffering of others.

The Buddha realized that each manifestation of *dukkha* also contains within it the path to its own resolution and eventual cessation. In effect, the arising of *dukkha* and the cessation of *dukkha* are inseparable; they are simply different sides of the same coin. The whole purpose of mindfulness practice and the form of mindfulness meditation called *vipassana* is to uncover this natural path. If you engage mindfully with *dukkha*, then your innate intuitive wisdom-intelligence (*satipanna)* will guide you towards the resolution of the core emotional complexes that generate suffering. In the spiritual freedom of a relationship based on mindfulness, and where *satipanna* operates freely, *dukkha* in all its forms will melt like snowflakes in the sunshine. Mindfulness is the warmth and light of the sunshine that heals everything it touches.

Dukkha is not the enemy; the enemy is *avijja*, because ignorance perpetuates reactivity and keeps us blind to the reality of what we are doing. This same blindness also prevents the natural process of resolution of *dukkha* by preventing the action of *satipanna*. The Path of Mindfulness is a steady journey of uncovering the dark places where *avijja* thrives and illuminating them with mindfulness so that the innate wisdom-intelligence of *satipanna* can arise and bring about healing and the resolution of *dukkha*.

6 MINDFULNESS: THE ANTIDOTE TO DUKKHA

Habitual reactivity is the fundamental driving force that sustains suffering, and at the heart of every reaction there is some form of blind attachment (*upadana*), fuelled by the compulsive force of *tanha*. But, there is an even more fundamental force that supports reactivity, attachment and compulsion and that is ignorance (*avijja*), the absence of awareness that allows reactivity to dominate the mind and to take away our freedom.

Besides the basic absence of awareness, there is another dimension to *avijja*, which is the blind and unquestioned acceptance of our reactivity. This is the form of ignorance called delusion, or *moha* that seduces us into becoming whatever arises in the mind. An anger reaction arises and we become the anger. Happiness arises and we become happy. Sadness arises and we become sad. Fear arises and we become afraid. *Avijja* prevents us from seeing reactions as they arise, which causes us to become attached to them, but *moha* makes us believe them once they have arisen. Both *avijja* and *moha* lead to the *identification* with the *sankharas* produced by subjective reactivity. It is this identification and attachment that imprisons the mind and condemns us to act in unskillful and unwholesome ways.

The Buddha investigated the fundamental problem of ignorance, delusion and attachment, and understood how individual suffering spreads outwards like a virus, causing suffering and violence in the family, the community and beyond. He saw that the only way to stop the spread of this disease is for the individual to awaken to his own habitual reactivity. As a person awakens and becomes fully conscious of each reaction as it arises, then in that very moment of awareness, he has choice and a brief moment of freedom from the compulsive force of the reaction. This opening allows wisdom-intelligence to arise, and this leads to the purification of thought and action. The primary tool for creating this opening and illuminating ignorance is mindfulness, or *sati* in Pali. The path for cultivating mindfulness is called *satipatthana*, The Path of Mindfulness, in which we establish mindfulness in relation to the four major components of our experience: body, feelings, mind, and the governing principles of mind, the *dhammas*.

The Buddha also saw the great potential of the individual for creating happiness and well-being through compassionate and intelligent action. He understood that these positive forces lie dormant in all of us, waiting to spring forth quite naturally when the mind and heart gain freedom from reactivity and ignorance. Therefore, the Path of Mindfulness is a path that develops freedom from ignorance and reactivity, while simultaneously cultivating the right conditions that allows the wholesome and good qualities of the individual to develop and flourish. Mindfulness provides the essential ground from which the noble qualities of wisdom-intelligence (*panna*), love (*metta*) and virtue (*sila*) can develop and transform our lives and the lives of those around us.

MINDFULNESS OF HABITUAL REACTIVITY

Suffering, or *dukkha*, refers specifically to the mental anguish created by our subjective emotional reactions to the stresses of life. Pain is an inevitable part of life, whereas suffering is created through our subjective reactions to pain. These, we learn from our parents, our culture and even from our religious teachers. Through cultural and parental conditioning, we unconsciously acquire patterns of reactivity that produce mental anguish and suffering, and then we spend the rest of our lives trying to free ourselves from these habits.

The challenge of The Path of Mindfulness is to undo the conditioned patterns of habitual emotional reactivity that create and proliferate suffering, both within and without. This begins when we awaken to reactive habits and learn a totally different way of relating to *dukkha*: a relationship based on mindfulness, rather than further reactivity.

The Path of Mindfulness develops the ability to recognize and respond to reactivity, in all its many forms, with complete presence of mind. The ability to recognize reactivity is a skill that has to be learned. Also, after mastering this skill, we also have to learn the right way to respond to reactivity, after we have detected it in ourselves.

Most of the time, we are not aware of our habitual reactions, and we blindly obey them as if under a hypnotic spell. We become angry or sad, frustrated or afraid when events happen, but never stop to question whether we need to react in these ways. In reality, we react out of habit, not choice, and we blindly accept this way of being out of habitual ignorance, not conscious awareness. Reactivity depends on this blind attachment, the combination of *upadana* and *avijja* and this is what we seek to counteract through the practice of mindfulness. Instead of blindly reacting to situations, we choose to treat each and every moment of experience, whether reactive or non-reactive, as a means of developing and strengthening the response of mindfulness. The beginning of The Path of Mindfulness is learning to say "No!" to reactivity and to respond instead, with the open heart of mindfulness.

Recognition is the first and most important step in the response to reactivity and stops the proliferation of further reactivity. It allows us to break the habit of reacting to situations and experiences and re-introduces freedom and choice. But mindfulness is more than simply recognizing reactions when they arise. Mindfulness is also a *response* to reactions, and that response is to form a relationship with each reaction, based on openness, receptivity, sensitivity and complete presence. It is only when we can establish this mindfulness-based relationship with our own afflictions and *kilesas* that they can transform and resolve themselves. The mindfulness response to reactivity must involve both aspects: Recognition and Relationship.

Mental reactions come with varying intensities, ranging from minor disappointments and irritations to core traumas and unresolved emotional issues. When we practice mindfulness, we choose to pay close attention to all these manifestations of *dukkha*, no matter how big or small. Nothing is left out, because our mission is to resolve *dukkha* and discover freedom from suffering, wherever it occurs. All *dukkha* arises from the same roots of ignorance and attachment, and all manifestations of *dukkha* are connected. When we heal one form of suffering, we strengthen our innate ability to respond to all suffering in a skillful way that facilitates resolution.

By choosing not to react to *dukkha*, but rather to respond with complete presence, openness and receptivity, we create a safe space in which *dukkha* can heal. It is when *dukkha* is allowed to unfold in full consciousness that it will begin the process of healing, under the direction of the innate intuitive intelligence of the psyche that we call *satipanna*. When we practice mindfulness, we choose to cultivate a relationship based on compassion and openness, in which we neither indulge in, nor react against pain or the secondary reactions to pain, but choose instead to respond to either with complete objectivity and presence of mind.

Stress

It is 8am and you wake up after a difficult night's sleep only to discover that the alarm didn't go off. This makes you very agitated as you realize that you will be late for work and your boss told you off for being late only last week. You tumble out of bed and rush down stairs for breakfast. No coffee. You become flustered at the prospect of starting the day without coffee, and you lose your temper with your partner for forgetting to turn on the coffee maker. Then you feel guilty about being angry, and that weighs heavily on your mind as you climb into your car. The car won't start. Now you are furious, because you recently paid a lot of money to have the car serviced. Being late, you hit rush hour and have to deal with all the frustrations of slow traffic, which increases your stress level to boiling point. Things are made even worse when a car cuts in front of you, and you explode with anger and yell at the driver. The driver turns out to be an old lady, and you feel embarrassed and guilty for your inappropriate reactions. Eventually you make it to the office, but there is nowhere to park, since you are late and you become even more dejected. Exhausted, you finally make it to the office, sit down at your work and begin a day doing a job that you don't enjoy in an environment that you hate and with people who do not seem to appreciate how hard you try. The boss says he wants to see you and panic sets in.

Does this sound familiar? For much of the time we live as slaves to the negative habitual emotional reactions of agitation, disappointment, frustration, anger, guilt, stress, anxiety and fear. The emotional suffering of *dukkha* is not caused by being late or the difficult drive to work. These may be a source of pain, but are not sufficient to cause mental suffering. *Dukkha* is always a product of the way we react to such events and these subjective *dukkha*-producing reactions are something that we have learned unconsciously.

We learn to react with anger and disappointment when things don't go our way in exactly the same way that we learn to be happy when our expectations are fulfilled. This is an important point, because although you cannot have complete control over external events, you can control how you react to them. If you remain attached to your reactions, then you will suffer as long as those attachments remain in place. The first phase of The Path of Mindfulness involves learning to recognize and respond with mindfulness to all these forms of emotional stress reactions as they arise throughout the day. Each stress reaction may be relatively small, but the combined effect can be very debilitating. You will benefit greatly if you train yourself to recognize these habitual stress reactions as soon as they arise, and then respond to each with mindfulness. This allows you to have choices and freedom is empowering. The first phase of mindfulness: active vigilance and recognition of reactivity, takes you away from being the victim and puts you back in the driving seat of your own happiness, rather than simply falling under the spell of your habitual reactivity and creating yet more suffering.

Emotional Trauma

Reactions of disappointment, frustration and the stresses of life are one thing, but there are much more intense challenges that we must encounter. These include the significant life changes, including sickness and death or the breakdown of a marriage, or a major conflict within the family. Another source of deep emotional trauma comes from the experience of significant personal loss, such as the loss of a home to fire or flood or earthquake. Those involved in war or violent conflict are faced with intense emotional traumas, which may remain unresolved and produce post-traumatic stress, nightmares and recurrent anxiety attacks for years after the event. Many people suffer equally devastating traumas as children, in the form of physical, emotional or sexual abuse.

Such traumatic life events can be a source of great emotional pain, and frequently, the mind will unconsciously produce secondary reactivity to this unresolved pain. The trauma becomes enclosed in a complex of habitual reactions that amplify and sustain the original pain, creating even more suffering. This secondary emotional reactivity is like pouring salt onto a wound, and simply makes the pain much worse and last much longer.

These unresolved traumas become the demons of the mind that come back over and over again to haunt us, and may take the form of recurrent fear, anger, depression, guilt, low self-esteem, or feelings of helplessness. These inner recurrent emotional complexes eat us from the inside and will paralyze the mind and spirit if left unresolved.

Such reactive emotional complexes require the greatest attention and compassion, which can be best provided by the therapeutic space of mindfulness. Mindfulness Meditation Therapy is a particularly good way of working with these deep-seated emotions, because it allows us to establish a non-reactive relationship with the trapped emotional feeling energy that lies beneath the surface. When you take away the secondary reactivity, then you create a therapeutic space in which that trapped energy can unfold and transform, experientially.

The inner demons usually begin to take shape in childhood when the mind is most vulnerable and least able to process intense emotions. Physical, sexual and emotional abuse, leave powerful imprints in the subconscious mind, because the child is unable to process and assimilate these traumas. Faced with inner unresolved conflicts, the child develops a complex of negative secondary reactivity such as reactions of guilt, low self-esteem, generalized anxiety, fearfulness and anger. These secondary reactions effectively prevent adequate processing of emotional conflict through the principle of Reactive Displacement, and the unresolved negative feeling energy becomes frozen in place, where it continues to fester and generate future suffering.

Therapeutic change proceeds through the transformation of the internal structure of an emotional complex, and this requires bringing the complex back into immediate present awareness. The whole structure has to change and for this reason, everything depends on the quality of the relationship that you establish with your core emotions. If the relationship is reactive, then nothing will change; if it is non-reactive, then change becomes a real possibility. The relationship with emotional pain must be primarily experiential, rather than analytical, because thinking is always biased and limited by past conditioning. Therefore, we choose to establish a relationship based on mindfulness with our emotional pain, and allow transformation to occur internally from the experience itself, which it will do if we remain mindful and resist secondary reactivity. Even the most painful and traumatic memories will resolve themselves given time, if we allow the natural innate intelligence of the psyche, called *satipanna* to operate freely.

Thinking and analyzing are a particularly subtle form of reactivity based on the past and are actually a form of distraction, like emotional reactions, that take us away from being fully present with our pain. This is not to say that psychological insights are not important, but they should arise out of a foundation of mindfulness, rather than out of reactive thinking. The conscious ego cannot heal the problems that it has created, and we must open to the deeper intuitive level of the psyche to find a deeper source of healing.

Specifically, during mindfulness meditation, we learn to sit with the feelings that surround the stress, traumatic memory or core emotional complex. Rather than indulging in thinking or analysis, we listen with care and attention, without trying to change anything or fix anything. This can be described as the art of not doing, rather than doing. As you develop the skill of listening with mindfulness, you create the right inner therapeutic space that allows the emotion to unfold and differentiate. It is the conscious awareness of these subtle changes that brings about transformation and resolution of suffering.

Over and over again, we return to this creative interface at the feeling level, taking small steps with each encounter. As you learn to relate with mindfulness to your inner pain, it will respond by changing internally under the guidance of your innate intelligence. It is this totality of change within the structure of the emotional complex, as well as in the way the psyche relates to *dukkha* that leads to transformation and liberation.

7 THE RELATIONSHIP OF PURE KNOWING

Sati directs our attention away from reactivity and back to the direct conscious experience of the present. It puts us face-to-face with our immediate experience. *Sati* brings us back into a relationship in which there is no reacting, but just the simple bare experiencing of things as they are. This direct perception, without the observer or subjective reactivity is called *satisampajanna*.

Sati is like switching on the light in a dark room, while *sampajanna* is the direct awareness of the contents of the room. *Sati* brings you into direct contact with things, while *satisampajanna* is what you see after you have made contact. The word *sampajanna* is made up of the prefix *sam*, which means "right, complete, entire" and the suffix *pajanna*, which means, "knowing with wisdom." *Sampajanna* is often translated as "clear comprehension," although this does not mean conceptual understanding, but rather the process of knowing things objectively in their true, original form, in the present moment of experience. Given the essential requirement for mindfulness, the two terms are most often combined together as *satisampajanna*, which means the pure knowing through mindfulness. In reality, you cannot have *sampajanna* without mindfulness, because mindfulness is required to be fully present. Each moment of contact with an object of experience through mindfulness brings a moment of *satisampajanna*. When we become distracted or reactive, it is *sati* that returns us to this state of pure awareness.

Ajahn Sumedho uses the term "intuitive awareness" to describe *satisampajanna*. "Intuitive" is a good term, because it indicates the deeper form of knowing that precedes the more superficial level of knowing that comes from thinking. Intuition is a form of inner wisdom that arises from opening to the entirety of an experience and not just the habitual reactions of the ego.

Satisampajanna can also be translated as *pure knowing*, in the sense that there is no subjective reactivity from a *knower* that gets in the way of seeing and experiencing things objectively. There is, in effect, no "you" who does the "knowing," as there would be when you think or react. When there is *satisampajanna*, there is no separation between the knower and the known, no observer who observes, but simply the direct conscious process of knowing and observing. *Satisampajanna* is the pure *knowing* of both the *known* and the *knower*.

Satisampajanna is awakening to the reality of the here and now, and this is the essence of The Path of Mindfulness and *vipassana* meditation. We learn to awaken us to whatever is in the field of our awareness and see it with objective equanimity (*upekkha*) and non-reactivity (*samadhi*). If our focus of awareness is on something external, then this means awakening to what we can see, hear, smell, taste or touch and know it *as it is*, without the distortion of perception, beliefs and other forms of subjective mental reactivity. If our focus of awareness is internal, then this means being able to fully know and engage with thoughts, feelings, emotions, beliefs, and all our mental reactions and *know* them objectively, without any further reactivity. Of course, there will always be subjective reactivity and, therefore, *satisampajanna* must include and embrace both objective and subjective reality; it embraces both the *known* and the *knower*.

Satisampajanna is the antidote to ignorance (*avijja*) and the whole cycle of *samsara*, which depends on ignorance. When there is *satisampajanna*, then in that state of spacious freedom *satipanna* also arises, and the mind is transformed from being a reactive machine, to being a finely tuned channel for intelligent action. When action arises from this intelligent ground of mindful knowing, it is purified. The psyche becomes in alignment with *Dhamma* and the path that leads to the resolution of *dukkha* and the promotion of happiness and well-being in the mind. This same alignment with *Dhamma* also naturally extends outwards to heal suffering in our external relationships, society and the world.

When we are mindful and not reacting, we open a space around the thought, emotion or external object of attention, and this space is both transformational and brings about healing. In meditation and The Path of Mindfulness, we actively cultivate this space of pure objectivity and natural healing.

The first property of this space is that it creates a safety zone in which we are much less likely to become overwhelmed by reactivity, which is in dramatic contrast to the contracted and cramped nature of the reactive mind. We discover that as *satisampajanna* develops, the compulsion to react naturally begins to wane and the mind begins to stabilize. This quality of stability and non-reactivity is called *samadhi*. Agitation arises when the mind is not grounded in the present, but is seduced into patterns of reactivity based on conditioning. When we settle into directly investigating present experience, with *satisampajanna*, then the mind naturally settles into a state on non-agitation, or *samadhi* in which sustained mindfulness becomes possible.

With the development of mindfulness, we become more and more attuned to the reality of our experience, as it exists in the present moment, both internally and externally. The first effect of opening our eyes is that we see more, and the quality of our experience is naturally enriched. In the famous words of Sir Isaac Newton,

> I have been as a child playing on the seashore, every now and then finding a brighter pebble, while all around me the great ocean of truth lay undiscovered.

The enrichment of experience that comes with mindfulness and *satisampajanna* is naturally very satisfying and nourishing and brings joy, rapture and bliss (*pitisukha*). This is the natural joy that arises when the mind lets go of old perceptions and allows experience to come alive. *Satisampajanna* changes experience from the dull monochromatic view of the contracted mind into vibrant full color. Truth naturally leads to greater fulfilment and a greater sense of authenticity and a feeling of being alive, whereas ignorance always leads to emptiness, inauthenticity and the death of the spiritual.

OPENING TO INTUITIVE INTELLIGENCE

The direct consequence of *satisampajanna* is that we become increasingly aware of subtlety and it is in this subtle realm that the shy voice of intuitive intelligence can be heard. The Pali term for this intuitive wisdom-intelligence is *satipanna*, "mindfulness wisdom," and this is the force that directs beneficial transformation.

Whatever the insight or intelligent action that results, it always leads in the direction of decreasing suffering and increasing happiness and well-being. *Satipanna* transforms instability into stability, both in the mind and in our personal relationships. *Satipanna* is not "wise knowledge," in the conventional sense of the word "wisdom," but refers to the dynamic fluidity of movement in the psyche that leads towards stability. Through *satisampajanna* we are able to access a much deeper dimension of our experience than is possible when we are reactive, and it is this unconstrained insight into the inner workings of reality that allows *satipanna* to arise.

Mindfulness and pure intuitive knowing has the effect of releasing the mind from its blind attachment to habitual reactions, beliefs and conventions. In this condition of freedom, the whole system of the psyche becomes fluid and responsive, and where there is freedom to change, *satipanna* will naturally guide the internal process of transformation towards the resolution of suffering. This requires a stillness, in which the mind is not lost in thinking and reacting, which is often referred to as the Noble Silence or the *creative void*. It is void, because it is empty of thinking and subjective reactivity, and creative, because it is not limited by past conditioning. Free of the corruptions of the past, this inner stillness is pure and untarnished, like gold, which is one of the noble metals. Mindfulness practice cultivates this *creative void*, the silent interval between thoughts, where true authenticity and true healing flourishes.

Anyone who meditates will soon become aware of the way one thought leads to another in a continuous stream of consciousness, sometimes referred to as the "monkey mind." It is the nature of consciousness to move in this way from one sense object to another, like a monkey swinging from one branch to another in search for food and stimulation.

During mindfulness meditation, called *vipassana* or insight meditation, we pay close attention to this natural tendency of the mind to wander. The purpose of mindfulness practice, in general, is to learn to become increasingly present for each new experience and resist the habitual tendency to react. With practice, we become more and more tuned in to the interval between thoughts, and as practice deepens, these intervals become longer. It is in this creative void that wisdom-intelligence flourishes and transformation takes place. This state of mind, that is not consumed by thinking is also called *sunnata*, a term which means "the state of emptiness." This is where the mind is free from the constraint of conditioned reactivity, and is free to change in the direction that leads to the maximum resolution of suffering and the greatest state of stability of mind and spirit.

If the thought "I am afraid" arises, the most likely reaction will be blind and obedient acceptance of this reaction, which is an example of an attachment to habitual subjective reactivity, called *attavadupadana*. We *become* the reaction. We may then indulge in speculative thinking and worrying about why we became afraid and generate imaginary scenarios that simply perpetuates and intensifies the problem. This is the secondary reactivity of *papanca* that leads to the proliferation of suffering. However, there is another possibility open to us, where we respond to the primary fear reaction with mindfulness and *satisampajanna*. When we do this, the fear becomes nothing more than an object that is experienced within the field of awareness of *satisampajanna*. With *satisampajanna* there is simply the direct knowing of "fear" with no further reaction. In the sustained mindful relationship of *satisampajanna*, we create the right conditions, the "creative void" in which the emotional knot of "fear" can and will unfold and become fluid again. As it unravels and differentiates, the whole field of both the fear as an object and the psyche that contains the object, changes in a way that will eventually lead to the resolution of the fear.

In other words, the more we see and the more we become conscious of the fine details of experience, the more likely it is that transformation will occur. The concept of sensory enrichment leading to transformation is a major part of *satisampajanna* and described by the term *gocara sampajanna*. *Gocara* literally means "field or domain," and *gocara sampajanna* means to know every aspect of whatever we are contemplating with mindfulness. The field of mindfulness includes the physical and material components of our experience; the feeling energy that permeates our experience; and all movements of thought, memories, emotions and other products of mental reactivity. Above all, the field of *gocara sampajanna* includes the clear knowing of *Dhamma*: the natural laws of experience, and knowing what actions are unwholesome and lead to the perpetuation of *dukkha*, and what actions are wholesome and lead to the resolution of *dukkha* and freedom.

When we comtemplate an object such as fear, we investigate every aspect of the object of "fear" as it manifests in our body and mind, and we contemplate it in such a way that leads to the resolution of the *dukkha* of "fear." Perhaps one of the most consistent messages throughout the teachings of the Buddha is that we should not blindly accept the superficial appearance of things, but investigate thoroughly the reality of what we experience, with mindfulness. When we do this, then what we blindly accepted as real, such as the emotion of "fear," is seen not to be a solid or real entity, but dissociates into a million pieces, like a mirror shattered by a rock. The reality is in the million pieces, and freedom from suffering is in the process of seeing these millions of individual pieces with clear and direct *satisampajanna*.

NON-DELUSION

Above all, *satisampajanna* is non-delusional awareness, called *asammoha sampajanna*, by which we mean the absence of blind acceptance, or identification with thoughts, beliefs, emotions or any *sankhara* produced by the reactive mind. *Satisampajanna* allows us to see a reaction as a reaction and learn not to identify with it, and not become entangled in it, or seduced into further reactivity. With *asammoha sampajanna* all *sankharas* are seen as illusions in the sense that they are only superficial snapshots that never represent the total story or truth, and should not to be attached to as "me" or "mine."

Being imperfect and unsatisfactory, we recognize that all *sankharas* are not to be relied upon. However, it would be a great mistake to then take the attitude that the contents and reactions of the mind are inferior and unworthy of our attention. This tendency towards aversion is such a common problem, and can prevent spiritual progress during our meditation. We must understand that mindfulness is the expression of *metta* and awakening, not self-judgement and the egocentric desire for control. The way of mindfulness is to choose to be fully present for all *sankharas*, and to relate to them all with care and openness of mind and heart. The mind is not your enemy; your thoughts and emotions are not your enemy. The only enemy is ignorance, because with ignorance comes bondage and suffering. When there is mindfulness clearly established, then no *sankhara* will have the power to dominate you: they simply become objects to be known with mindfulness.

Asammoha sampajanna, or knowing with non-delusion, also means to be in complete harmony with *anicca*, the truth of impermanence and change. Existence is a dynamic process in which parts come together into temporary structures, the *sankharas*, and then instantaneously begin to dissociate back into their component parts, which are free to reassemble into new *sankharas*, ad infinitum. At the psychological level of experience, thoughts, feelings and perceptions come together into moments of conscious experience that exist for a brief moment before changing into another *cittasankhara*. This is the natural order of life, of existence and experience that is the *Dhamma*. Understanding this at the conceptual level of insight is valuable, because it helps modulate our tendency to grasp things that we know are not under our control and that will not last. But, what is much more important than this conventional wisdom, is to *harmonize with anicca* in each living moment. Rather than resisting change, we embrace change with mindfulness and watch the whole unfolding show with great care and attention. When we form a relationship with *anicca* in which we live as a process instead of a series of disjointed *sankharas*, then we will be harnessing the great energy of the river of change. Living in harmony with *anicca* is another way of talking about freedom and liberation, because true liberation is the freedom to change. With mindfulness and *satisampajanna*, change becomes an intelligent process, under the direction of *satipanna* that always leads towards the resolution of *dukkha*. When *avijja* is dominant, then the process of change becomes chaotic, leading to instability and *dukkha*.

At another more basic level, *sampajanna* means that there is an understanding of the purpose and suitability of what you are doing, called *satthaka* and *sappaya sampajanna*, respectvely. At the practical level, this means doing things with care and attention. At a spiritual level it means that you fully comprehend what is skillful and wholesome (*kusala dhamma*) and what is unskillful and harmful (*akusala dhamma*). With *satisampajanna* you see quite clearly, at the experiential level whether your actions lead to happiness, stability and freedom, or whether they lead to unhappiness, instability and bondage. You gain direct insight into how your conditioned reactivity causes *dukkha*, and how freedom from conditioned reactivity leads to the resolution of *dukkha*.

For much of the time we are on autopilot and perform actions of body, speech and mind without ever questioning their purpose or suitability. For example, you may find yourself consumed by worrying about your marriage, or your health, or your financial circumstances, but at no time did you consciously choose to experience these mind states. There is no clear understanding of the purpose of worrying or the suitability of worrying as a means of promoting happiness; it just happens. When mindfulness is directed to the *cittasankhara* of a worry reaction, you begin to see that the proliferation of worrying only leads to more suffering. You understand that blind attachment to that *sankhara* leads to *dukkha*. If you continue to be mindful, you will also see that the more you illuminate the reaction with mindfulness, the less power it has to proliferate *dukkha*. With *satisampajanna*, wisdom-intelligence (*satipanna*) arises and you gain direct insight (*vipassana*) into how letting go of reactivity resolves *dukkha*. Seeing this directly, the psyche naturally moves from the condition of instability to a condition of stability and the mind lets go of the reactivity as a natural consequence of clear and direct insight.

You gain direct experience of a totally different state of being that is not continually creating conflict and suffering and this is nothing short of the realization of the Four Noble Truths in the here and now, which is the ultimate purpose of The Path of Mindfulness. Forming a relationship with the *dukkha* of worry is the First Noble Truth of awakening to *dukkha*. Awakening to the force of blind attachment to the habitual patterns of reactivity that cause the *dukkha* of worry is the Second Noble Truth. Directly experiencing the non-suffering that comes from non-attachment to these patterns of habitual reactivity is the Third Noble Truth, and The Path of Mindfulness that takes you to this new way of being is the Fourth Noble Truth.

SATISAMPAJANNA AS REFUGE

The word "Buddha" literally means "the awakened one," and this signifies the central importance of pure non-reactive, non-conditioned awareness in Buddhism. Taking refuge in *satisampajanna* means trusting in the pure direct knowing of experience in the here and now, and the wisdom-intelligence that comes from this pure knowing. The contents of experience as thoughts, feelings and beliefs come and go according to changing conditions, but the conscious knowing element, the Buddha mind, remains constant and is, therefore, much more reliable as a refuge.

The practice of *Dhamma* through mindfulness is a path in which we gradually let go of dependence on the reactive mind that creates thoughts, views, opinions and emotional reactions. What is left is the Original Mind, the Buddha Mind or *bodhicitta* that is the clear, luminous and unlimited spaciousness of unconditioned consciousness. Unlike the conditioned world of *form*, which is unstable and not dependable, *bodhicitta* is completely dependable, stable and beyond the transient world of *form*. From this ground of *bodhicitta* all becomes possible, and living becomes an adventure in which we fully engage with each moment of life with vitality and passion. This is the Buddha's vision of freedom, of being truly alive and truly authentic.

Taking refuge in *satisampajanna* is like being at the center of a hurricane, where it is completely still. You are free to fully engage with all the individual mental objects as they fly around the rim of the storm, but without clinging to them and becoming part of the debris. This still center of tranquility and stability is called *samadhi* and arises quite spontaneously whenever you establish mindfulness. This still center is not something that you create, but something that you discover and awaken to through *satisampajanna*, when you come into relationship with whatever you experience with mindfulness.

In the pure and direct knowing of things, there is nothing that can harm you, no matter how horrible it might be. Not even the most fearful wild beast or demons of the mind can pull you off balance, because as long as there is non-reactive attention, then you are able to move freely and respond wisely. If the beast attacks, mindful-awareness allows you to respond by stepping back. Even if the beast has horribly sharp teeth and claws, it cannot harm you as long as you remain vigilant and mindful. It is what you can't see that has the power to harm you, and your real enemy is not the beast, but ignorance and unawareness (*avijja*). *Satisampajanna* dispels ignorance through direct illumination of whatever you are experiencing, pleasant or unpleasant, internal or external. You can, in fact, dance with the beasts and demons of your mind when there is *satisampajanna*. You can engage with them and experience a completely different way of being in the world. In this dance of mindfulness, which is also a dance of compassion and wisdom-intelligence, the demons are finally given permission to change, which is what they have wanted to do all along.

As an inner demon transforms and resolves, it rewards you with a gift of the energy that was trapped in its tortured form. This release of energy is energizing, producing the natural rapture of *piti*, and eventually leads to a new state of stability and inner tranquility, called *passadhi*. Your inner demons can be either your enemies or your spiritual friends depending on whether you relate to them with aversion and ignorance, or mindfulness and wisdom. If you treat them with aversion, they will drain your energy and leave you fatigued and broken. If you respond to them with mindfulness and compassion, then they will bring passion and energy back into your life. They are not to be fought against or destroyed, but to be fully *known*. This is the wisdom of the Buddha's teaching, and the truth of the *Dhamma* that leads to freedom from suffering and the round of habitual reactivity that is *samsara*.

This "knowing mind" has no form in itself, but has an infinite capacity to know anything that does have form. It is a process that has no beginning and no end. The path of Buddhism and the cultivation of mindfulness is essentially to make this "pure knowing" the center of our Being, the refuge from which we can relate to all phenomena. One of the great insights of the Buddha was that our true original nature is not defined by the contents of our experience, but the experiencing itself, the pure conscious knowing of contents. To quote James Bugental,

When I begin to realize that my truest identity is as process and not as fixed substance, I am on the verge of a terrible emptiness and a miraculous freedom.

Through The Path of Mindfulness and awakening, we begin to uncover our Original Mind or *bodhicitta*, which is Pali for "awakened mind." Mindfulness is the mental process of bringing attention back to *bodhicitta*, through the "pure knowing" of our experience in the here and now. *Bodhicitta* cannot be created, but simply comes into existence whenever mindfulness is present. This state of being is to be known in each moment of experience, whether in deep meditation or in the chaos of daily living. *Satisampajanna* is the one sure refuge that can bring stability in the midst of happiness and sorrow and all the vicissitudes of life. It is the "miraculous freedom" that heals, transforms, liberates and leads to the full realization of compassion and wisdom.

Buddhism is a vast subject, but it is good to realize that the heart of the Buddha's teaching is quite simple and is about awakening to the objective reality of present experience. The heart of the path is the cultivation of mindfulness. If you make this your path, then you will be walking the same path as the Buddha, and awakening and transformation of mind and spirit will follow quite naturally for you, as it did for the Buddha. When you take refuge in mindfulness and *satisampajanna*, you are taking refuge in the Buddha and the *Dhamma*, and the *Sangha* of all other beings who also follow The Path of Mindfulness.

THE COMPASSIONATE FACE OF MINDFULNESS

On the Statue of Liberty is engraved the sonnet by Emma Lazarus, which includes the lines,

Give me your tired, your poor,
Your huddled masses yearning to breathe free,
The wretched refuse of your teeming shore.
Send these, the homeless, tempest-tost to me,
I lift my lamp beside the golden door!

You cannot be mindful without also developing compassion, because mindfulness is by definition, a non-judgmental relationship to *all* experience, and this includes suffering as well as happiness. The response of *sati* is an invitation to all, beginning with opening the door of awareness to the inner world of thoughts, feelings and reactions, followed by reaching outwards to every aspect of your world. With mindfulness you open to the truth of *dukkha* and welcome in "Your tired, your poor, your huddled masses yearning to be free." All await illumination by the lamp of mindfulness and when we, "lift our lamp beside the golden door," we embrace all suffering, internal or external with the compassionate embrace of mindfulness.

The Buddha described four beneficial qualities of mind, known as the four sublime abodes (*brahmaviharas*) that develop quite naturally when we cultivate mindfulness and wisdom, instead of reactivity and ignorance. These qualities of mindfulness are friendliness (*metta*), compassion (*karuna*), appreciative joy (*mudita*), and equanimity (*upekkha*). When true mindfulness (*sammasati*) is established, these qualities naturally express themselves in our relationship to our internal experiences as well as to the external experience of the world and other beings.

The first of these benevolent qualities, called *metta*, is most often translated as loving-kindness. This is the quality of relationship based on friendliness combined with complete openness and receptivity. All aspects of our experience, whether pleasant or unpleasant, beautiful or ugly are attended to with love in the same way that you would welcome a friend into your home. It is the attitude of reaching out and embracing, of holding and caressing experience, knowing that there is room for all. This is not naïve openness, but openness that comes from wisdom and understanding completely that nothing can hurt you more than your own reactivity and ignorance. With *metta* we open our mind and heart to receive our pain and suffering as well as our success and happiness. We open to the pain and suffering of others and we open to the success and happiness of others. We open our eyes, our mind, our spirit and our whole being to the experience of everything in life, without discrimination or prejudice.

The sublime abodes of *karuna* and *mudita* are manifestations of *metta* as it naturally reaches out to embrace suffering or happiness, respectively. Compassion (*karuna*) is opening the heart and mind to receive suffering wherever suffering exists, in self, in others or in the world. This compassion is always coupled with wisdom (*panna*), which means that *karuna* naturally leads to actions that reduce suffering and the cause of suffering in the here and now.

Mudita means opening to non-suffering, or happiness (*sukha*) in self and others. *Mudita* is essential, because in order to effect a movement from suffering to non-suffering, you must develop a clear understanding at the experiential level of non-suffering, just as you must develop an understanding of *dukkha*. Suffering and non-suffering are both part of the reality of existence and must be fully embraced if we are to become fully authentic human beings. When the mind truly opens to experience both *dukkha* and *sukha* completely, without discrimination, then the intuitive and innate wisdom-intelligence of *satipanna* will naturally guide the inner and outer actions that lead to the greatest benefit for self, others and for the world.

The fourth sublime quality of mindfulness is equanimity (*upekkha*), or balance of mind in the midst of the chaos of life. Equanimity is the perfection of non-reactivity, non-attachment and perfect objectivity. *Upekkha* provides the foundation for *metta*, *karuna* and *mudita* and is required for each of these to develop and mature. Compassion and the ability to engage positively with another, requires complete presence of mind, and you cannot be fully present with someone if you are caught up in reactivity. Just as *metta* reaches out to engage with experience, *upekkha* provides the steadiness of mind that allows you to receive experience, without becoming reactive, and this is essential for any kind of relationship, internal or external. *Upekkha* becomes absolutely essential when working with painful core emotions in oneself or in a personal relationship, because it allows us to remain objective and resist the compulsion to react and become overwhelmed by subjective emotional reactivity.

These four qualities of mindfulness work together to develop the highest form of presence in our relationships with self, in our relationships with other people and in our relationship with the world. The very core of The Path of Mindfulness is about learning to be fully present with your experience, with the positive intention to resolve suffering and to enhance happiness. The response of mindfulness should have these qualities of reaching out to fully embrace all experience, pleasant or painful, with the positive attitude of genuine interest and love. Every moment of mindfulness towards self or others is an expression of *metta, karuna, mudita* and *upekkha*. This happens naturally, because of the fundamental nature of mindfulness, rather than through our efforts to be kind, compassionate or objective. In fact, the best possible way of developing these noble virture is through the cultivation of mindfulness and *satisampajanna*.

The Path of Mindfulness, called *satipatthana*, is a truly living and passionate relationship and engagement with all experience and involves every aspect of our being. It is this quality of being that will ultimately resolve suffering and facilitate healing in the psyche and in the world. In fact, when we develop mindfulness, we are doing a great service that not only leads to our benefit, but also benefits the whole world. It is worthwhile reflecting on the true purpose of mindfulness practice before we begin each session of meditation, so that we keep our practice alive and fully in tune with the ultimate purpose of The Path of Mindfulness. We practice to reduce *dukkha* and the conditions that sustain *dukkha*. We practice to promote freedom and happiness in all aspects of life through the Noble Eightfold Path. This is the path of *Dhamma* that we choose to cultivate through The Path of Mindfulness.

8 INNATE WISDOM-INTELLIGENCE

The natural consequence of *satisampajanna* is that we become liberated from blind reactivity due to the simple fact that we cannot be both reactive and mindful at the same moment in time. This simple principle of Reciprocal Inhibition is the first and most significant change that interrupts the habit of reacting, and creartes a space in which transformation can occur. This freedom brings a fundamental shift in the mind, from habitual blind reactivity to present-centered and intelligent responsiveness, called *cetovimutti*. Released from reactivity, the psyche is free to heal itself, which it is more than capable of doing if given the freedom to operate. This essential freedom is brought about by mindfulness and allows our innate wisdom-intelligence, called *satipanna* to arise and direct beneficial change internally and externally. This is called *pannavimutti*, the liberation *satipanna*, so that it can heal and transform the psyche.

Panna (Skt. *Prajna*) is a very broad term that describes wisdom and intelligent insight. *Panna*, like many other concepts in Buddhism, consists of two quite different levels of understanding. The first is the conventional level of understanding, which we are all very familiar with in the form of ideas, beliefs and knowledge. This is the level of *sammuti sacca*, or relative truth. At the conventional level, wisdom takes the form of knowledge and psychological insights that help us resolve suffering and prevent the unskillful actions that produce suffering. However, this kind of conventional wisdom is still limited and conditioned, and what works in one situation may prove completely inadequate in a different situation. There is another level, called *paramattha sacca*, or absolute truth that cannot be reduced to thoughts or psychological insights, but comes from direct and immediate experience. This is the penetrating insight that arises whenever we open to the intuitive and experiential level of experience in each present moment. Conventional wisdom is comprised of what is known, whereas ultimate wisdom can only be known in the immediacy of the present moment: it is the *knowing* rather than the *known*. For this reason, *panna* depens on *satisampajanna*, which in turn depends on *sati*. Hence *sati* and *panna* are combined into *satipanna*, the intuitive intelligence that arises through mindfulness in the living present.

The great awakening of *satisampajanna* gives us access to a tremendous quantity and quality of knowledge. This sensory enrichment enhances the effectiveness of our actions as well as providing the subtle details of the internal structure of experience that facilitates transformation. You cannot change what you cannot see and this is why *satisampajanna* is so important, because it allows you to know clearly and precisely what is happening while it is happening.

Satipanna depends on this living insight into the structure of experience. When there is full presence and full conscious awareness, then our innate intelligence will direct beneficial change in a direction that leads to the resolution of *dukkha*. For example, if you find yourself too close to a fire, you will experience pain. If you refuse to turn your attention towards the pain and remain unaware (*avijja*), then the pain will persist as suffering. If your mind is open and free to be fully present with the pain, then you will intuitively know the right action to take and you move away from the fire. This is the intuitive intelligence of *satipanna* in action and it naturally leads to the resolution of *dukkha*. You do not have to think about what to do or try and analyze the situation. You simply respond with intelligent action based on *satisampajanna* and guided by *satipanna* that is perfectly aligned to the needs of the present.

As long as there is freedom to respond, then any action that results will be purified by *satipanna*. With *satisampajanna* as foundation, actions of body, speech and mind become more in tune with the needs of reality and they become more refined and more wholesome under the purifying action of *satipanna*. The ultimate purpose of mindfulness practice and meditation is to develop this skillfulness and intelligence in each unfolding moment so that we can fully engage and respond to life, rather than simply react out of habit, compulsion and ignorance.

Dukkha is the expression of emotional instability and suffering in the mind. If we resist this instability or remain ignorant, then *dukkha* will persist indefinitely. If we approach *dukkha* with mindfulness and establish an objective and non-reactive relationship with this instability, then we create a therapeutic space in which the unstable emotion will become malleable. The emotional complex looses its solidity and is seen as a dynamic movement of thoughts, memories and shades of feeling. With mindfulness, we let go of the superficial appearance of the complex and begin to see the reality and fine detail of what is actually there in its deep structure. When we become conscious of this richness of sensory experience, the psyche will naturally move under the direction of *satipanna* until it reaches a state of stability.

All emotional *sankharas* are inherently unstable and will automatically resolve into a more stable state under the direction of *satipanna*. All that is required is freedom to see the subtle reality and the truth of experience that lies below the labels, beliefs, thoughts and emotional reactions. It is not what we do that is as important as creating the freedom in which *satipanna* can operate unobstructed in the mind. Mindfulness practice and insight meditation (*vipassana*) is not the process of developing psychological insights that we then apply to solve our suffering, but the living process of allowing *satipanna* to operate in the present moment, allowing it to resolve *dukkha* directly. This is the psyche healing itself, which produces change at a much deeper level than can ever be attanined by the ego and the thinking mind.

Imagine a fantastic glass sculpture of an eagle, in which every detail and every feather is carved in immaculate detail. Now imagine that this delicate glass eagle is entombed in a huge block of dirty ice that must be removed. First, we try to free the eagle by chipping away the ice with an ice pick, which is the approach of the thinking mind and ego. This approach works well at the surface level and much ice is successfully removed. However, as we get closer to the eagle, the blows from the ice pick are more and more likely to damage the delicate glass sculpture. The tool of thinking becomes less and less skillful the closer we get to the truth; the ego becomes helpless.

The healing that is brought about by mindfulness and clear comprehension (*satisampajanna*) is analogous to opening the window and allowing the warm rays of the sun to shine onto the block of ice. The ice naturally melts, freeing the glass eagle and leaves it undamaged and in its full glory. Even as the ice melts, it has a cleansing effect as the water washes away the dirt. This is the nature of the transformational effect of the innate intelligence of *satipanna*. The illumination of pure knowing allows the psyche to heal itself and melt the frozen ice of our habitual reactivity and attachments. All that is needed is to allow *satipanna* the freedom to operate and it will do the rest, and this freedom is provided by the care and attention of mindfulness.

INTUITIVE WISDOM

We think that the ego is in control and makes all the important decisions in life, but if you look more closely you will see that most decision-making actually arises from intuitive thinking and not from the conscious ego. When you make a decision to accept a job, buy a house, or even what to have for dinner, you begin by accessing your intuitive felt-sense of what feels right. Thoughts and actions follow after this contact at the pre-conceptual intuitive feeling level. The ego claims to be in control, but actually the ego had very little to do with the decision making process.

Mindfulness not only frees the mind from the grip of compulsive habitual reactivity, but also opens awareness to the intuitive and creative dimension of the psyche. Mindfulness helps us expand our awareness and see more, as well as deepening awareness so that we penetrate beneath the superficial surface structure of experience. The practice of mindfulness allows us to access this deeper intuitive knowing, and from this place of inner freedom, intuitive intelligence flourishes. *Satipanna* is the intuitive intelligence that shines through when there is mindfulness that brings us back into contact with experience in the present. It arises in the fertile ground of *satisampajanna*.

When thoughts, actions and words arise under the direction of *satipanna*, they will be much more effective and in tune with reality and the needs of the present moment. It is not our intention to replace thinking with pure intuition, but to make this intuitive ground and creative space the foundation for skillful thinking and action. In fact intuition has been described as a kind of superior logic, a powerful and direct expression of intelligence. To quote Robert Graves,

Intuition is the supra-logic that cuts out all the routine processes of thought and leaps straight from the problem to the answer.

The intuitive mind works through the language of feelings (*vedana*), and sensitivity to these subtle intuitive feelings is the primary way to access the intuitive intelligence of *satipanna*. We can sense what needs to happen through monitoring the subtle changes in feeling-tone. *Satipanna* coupled with the sensitive mindfulness of *vedana* provides a powerful guide that will promote skillful thoughts and actions during daily life and ultimately such intelligent action will facilitate the resolution of *dukkha*, both internally, and externally in our relationships.

In mindfulness meditation, we deliberately use mindfulness to explore the feeling level of whatever we experience. This is particularly important when we encounter *dukkha* in the form of painful emotions. If you focus mindfully on an emotion like anger, you may find that the deeper felt-sense level of the emotion is more about feeling hurt than feeling angry. Following the felt-sense of feeling hurt may reveal an underlying sadness, and beneath that there may be a feeling of loneliness, and beneath the loneliness, a feeling of abandonment. Staying with the felt-sense of abandonment, you may notice that something shifts internally, and somehow the whole emotional complex, including the original anger becomes less intense and begins to lose its hold over you. This is a very common experience during *vipassana*, or insight meditation. By following the intuitive level of feelings under the natural direction of *satipanna*, we are taken through a sequence of subtle changes, and it is the conscious experience of these subtle changes in feeling that leads to the resolution of emotional suffering.

FREEDOM FROM ATTACHMENT TO SELF

Satipanna is the inner intuitive intelligence that guides the psyche towards freedom and inner balance. Freedom implies space, and when we can relate to our inner suffering with spaciousness, then we create a safe place for change. Wisdom and intelligence begin to unfold only when we let go of identification, attachment and delusion. There has to be a clear space that is free from the clutter of reactivity, free from domination by the ego (*atta*) and the blind beliefs and habitual patterns of our personality structure (*sakkayaditthi*). This does not imply that we should try to get rid of the contents of our personality, because the problem is never in the contents (*sankharas*) of the mind, but in how we relate to the contents. If we cling out of ignorance, then the contents will control us, but if we create and maintain a relationship based on *satisampajanna*, then we will be free from the control of the *sankharas*, and with this freedom arises an infinity of new possibilities. This is the essence of intuitive wisdom, or *satipanna*. The Buddha outlined this as follows:

> Whatever is material shape, past, future, present, subjective or objective, gross or subtle, mean or excellent, whether it is far or near, all material shape should be seen by perfect intuitive wisdom as it really is: "This is not mine, this I am not, this is not my self."

> Whatever is feeling, whatever is perception, whatever are habitual tendencies, whatever is consciousness, past, future, present, subjective or objective, gross or subtle, mean or excellent, whether it is far or near, all should be seen by perfect intuitive wisdom as it really is: "This is not mine, this I am not, this is not my self."

"Me" and "mine," or *atta* and *attaniya* in Pali, refers to the process of blind attachment (*upadana*) to the subjective reactions of the ego. When you become angry, there is no "you" who becomes angry, only the process of blind identification with the specific emotional reaction of anger. When you become upset, worried or sad, there is no "you" behind these reactions; you are simply the process manifesting these reactions in the present. What we refer to as our personality, or *sakkayaditthi*, is simply the accumulation of all these different subjective reactions to which we have become identified through ignorance. The teachings on *anatta*, or not self, which is perhaps the most central teaching in Buddhism, is about this very observation: that there is no "ego" or "self" that can be

106

found independent of these accumulated habitual reactions. Or, to reduce this statement further: When you react, ego exists; when you cease to react, ego ceases to exist. When *satipanna* is operating in the mind, then we no longer attach to the subjective reactions of *atta* and *attaniya* and these delusions cease to exist.

We do not create *satipanna*, it arises spontaneously when there is *satisampajanna*, and *satisampajanna* arises when there is *sati*. This is living in harmony with *anatta*, which is one of the most important living insights of the awakened mind. As the mind becomes free, we begin to see that who we are is something far beyond the contents of our experience and cannot be defined by any *sankharas* or anything created by the mind. Mindfulness is the path of non-attachment, or *anupadana*, and as we let go of the illusion of "me" and "mine," we become free to engage with all the contents of our experience with a new freedom that enriches experience and reveals a multitude of new possibilities. However, the wisdom of letting go cannot be created by the thinking mind deciding to let go, but happens when we open to the truth of experience through the relationship of mindfulness. Mindfulness is the direct antidote to both attachment and reativity and the *avijja* that spawns both. In the very moment when there is *sati* there will also be *anupadana*, without us thinking about it or trying to make ourselves free.

PSYCHOLOGICAL HOMEOSTASIS

The body is regulated by a complex series of responses called *homeostasis*, which literally means "same state," and which are designed to maintain physiological equilibrium, stability and health. The body adapts to instability, created by external or internal stress, by initiating self-correcting responses. Muscles and bones become stronger or weaker depending on how much they are used. If blood glucose level becomes elevated after a meal, then insulin is secreted to reduce it to the optimum level. The concentration of oxygen in the blood is carefully controlled, and homeostasis increases or decreases the rate of breathing in order to maintain the optimum level to meet the needs of the body during exercise or rest. There are countless examples of such self-correcting mechanisms at work in the body and all are guided by the principle of homeostasis, which directs change in an intelligent direction away from instability and towards increased stability. These changes result in the resolution of instability. Physiological homeostasis clearly involves a form of innate intelligence, because it orchestrates changes that are beneficial and lead to balance, stability and health. The changes are purposeful and have direction and this is the natural intelligence of the body.

However, an essential requirement for this body intelligence to be effective is the state of freedom. The body must be free to change under the direction of this innate intelligence, without any interference. If something prevents this freedom to change, then the body is prevented from restoring equilibrium, and physical suffering and disease will follow.

In fact, freedom is a fundamental requirement for homeostasis in any system, whether physiological, psychological or physical. On Earth, water flows down hill under the influence of gravity on its journey to the ocean, but it must have the freedom to move if it is to reach this state of maximum stability. If the water is frozen into a block of ice, or trapped in a rock pool on top of the mountain, then the water will not be free to move, and the journey to the sea will be interrupted, and the state of instability will persist. However, the moment that freedom of movement is restored, the water will resume its journey. Infact, all changes in the physical world are governed by the Second Law of Thermodynamics, which simply states that all systems seek the state of maximum energetic (*thermo*) stability and will change (*dynamic*) if given the freedom to change.

The principle of dynamic homeostasis observed in the body and in the physical world, applies equally to the psyche, and this is called *psychological homeostasis*. There is a natural state of energetic stability for the psyche, in which there is freedom from conflict and suffering. This is the state of *dukkhanirodha*, the extinction (*nirodha*) of suffering (*dukkha*), where there is no dissonance and no instability created through the reactivity of grasping, aversion and delusion. This is the natural state of maximum energetic stability, harmony and equilibrium, just as *dukkha* represents the state of instability and dis-equilibrium. If given the freedom to change, the psyche will naturally move towards this optimum state of inner stability by making intelligent changes that resolve inner conflict and *dukkha*. This natural intelligence is innate to the psyche and is called *satipanna*: the wisdom-intelligence that accompanies mindfulness and that directs change towards the resolution of *dukkha*.

However, the defining word is *freedom* to change, and if the mind is limited by conditioned habitual reactivity and blind attachment, then it is not free to respond in the best possible way to resolve *dukkha* and restore stability. Habitual reactivity puts constraints on the psyche and inhibits freedom. This limits the expression of *satipanna* and prevents the psyche from changing in an intelligent way. Just as water that is frozen or trapped as ice is prevented from moving on its natural journey to the ocean, so the psyche is unable to resolve *dukkha*, if locked into patterns of reactivity, created by blind attachment.

This is where mindfulness becomes so important, because mindfulness frees the psyche and allows *satipanna* to arise and direct the transformational processes that lead to the resolution of *dukkha*. It is no wonder that *panna*, which means wisdom-intelligence, is coupled with the word *sati*. Mindfulness is the main factor that restores freedom and that allows intuitive intelligence to flourish, and The Path of Mindfulness is the process of moving towards a state of maximum stability, balance and harmony at the energetic level. Mindfulness is equivalent to blowing warm air onto that block of ice, causing it to melt and freeing the water so that it can resume its purposeful journey towards the ocean. Therefore, we should strive to create this state of inner freedom, which allows the mind to respond intelligently, both internally in the mind, as well as externally in our relationships with people, and with our physical world and environment.

One of the most interesting aspects of *dukkha* is that like any other mental state, it has an internal structure based on attachments to thoughts, feelings, perceptions and the five *khandhas* or experience. The unaware mind builds these internal structures of mental suffering, without even knowing it, and then identifies with the monsters of its own creation. However, the Good News is that anything that has been built can also be disassembled, releasing the very energy that was used to create it. In effect, the path to the resolution of *dukkha* lies within the very structure of *dukkha*, and all that is required is that we create the condition of freedom, provided by mindfulness and allow *dukkha* to unfold into consciousness and resolve itself. The Path of Mindfulness is the journey that we take to uncover this natural path for every manifestation of *dukkha*, and in following this path dilligently, we gain liberation from the whole madness of *avijja* and *samsara*.

Mindfulness is the mental factor that allows the fire of *dukkha* to be extinguished, by freeing the mind and allowing *satipanna* to arise. The solution is always to be found in the problem, and the path to the resolution of suffering is mapped out in the internal structure of suffering itself. All that is required is that we awaken to *dukkha* and let our innate intuitive intelligence do the rest. Given freedom to operate, the psyche will always move towards less suffering and greater energetic stability. The Path of Mindfulness is not about trying to solve the problem of suffering through analytical thinking or psychological insight, but about how to free our conscious awareness so that *dukkha* can resolve itself, under the influence of *satipanna* and psychological homeostasis. *Satipanna* is the wisdom-intelligence that arises in the present moment when the mind is free to change in a way that leads to the resolution of *dukkha* and the underlying conflicts that sustain *dukkha*.

Energetically, *satipanna* directs internal changes that lead to greater stability in the psyche. Mental conflict, anxiety and anger and other states of dis-equilibrium are highly unstable and consume a great deal of energy. Under the guidance of *satipanna*, the psyche will naturally move from a state of energetic instability and disorder to a state of energetic stability and order. This movement from conflict to harmony; from cognitive dissonance to consonance; from instability to stability, is the process that leads to *dukkhanirodha*, the resolution of *dukkha*. However, for natural resolution to occur, there must be complete freedom in the mind, which means freedom from clinging to all forms of subjective reactivity. Conditioned habitual reactivity simply perpetuates ignorance (*avijja*) and inhibits beneficial change and this prevents the realization of *dukkhanirodha*.

The unpleasant feelings (*dukkhavedana*) that accompany suffering, as painful as they may be, have a positive function, which is to direct our attention to any underlying dissonance and conflict in the mind. If we develop a positive relationship with our suffering through mindfulness, then we will uncover the natural path that leads to the resolution of *dukkha*. All that we need to do is mindfully follow the change in feelings from *dukkhavedana* to *sukhavedana* and eventually to complete equilibrium and stability, which has the felt-sense of *upekkhavedana*. When there is *upekkhavedana*, then psychological homeostasis has been fulfilled and we feel this as a very profound form of happiness, called *upekkhasukha* that exceeds any form of conventional happiness. This change in feeling-energy is our guide on The Path of Mindfulness.

9 THE THREE DIMENSIONS OF MINDFULNESS

Mindfulness is not one thing, but describes a muli-dimensional form of conscious awareness, and it is essential to understand the full meaning of the term "mindfulness." Without a full understanding, mindfulness practice loses its power to transform, and becomes little more than another technique for promoting relaxation or concentration. Mindfulness includes three principle dimensions or factors to be cultivated. These are Vigilance, Relationship, and the Transformational dimension of mindfulness. Mindfulness meditation, called *vipassana bhavana* or insight meditation, is not one single technique, but a progression through all three dimensions, from vigilance, to relationship and finally to the transformational intelligence that liberates the mind from *dukkha* and the realm of habitual reactivity called *samsara*.

When we sit down to meditate, we should imagine that we are undertaking a journey that moves from the gross level of learning to stop our habitual reactivity, to the level of being in a dynamic and alive relationship with our experience. This journey is the journey of liberation through insight into the truth of experience, not as a set of concepts, but as a living process of unfolding in the present.

VIGILANCE

The first dimension of mindfulness is vigilance and conscious attention to whatever arises in each moment of experience, whether arising internally or externally. This is the most basic aspect of mindfulness practice, and the most common understanding of the term *sati*, which literally means to recall or remember to be present, and aware of what is happening while it is happening. Another closely related term is *appamada*, or heedfulness: making the effort to be attentive and awake. In Pali, the word for mindfulness is *sati*, a word derived from the Sanskrit *smrti*, which means to recall, or to keep in mind. This gives us an insight into the fundamental meaning of *sati*, which is to remember what you are doing, while you are doing it. Mindfulness means being fully present and fully engaged with your experience in the present, which is the complete opposite of reactivity and unawareness, collectively called *avijja*. It is the process of staying alert, and remembering to return your attention to the present when you become distracted by reactivity.

Sati is, first and foremost, a form of acute vigilance that keeps us firmly rooted in the present, because it is only when we are fully present for our experience that we can be said to be are truly alive. The two major hindrances to being fully present with our experience are *distraction* and *reactivity*. The mind naturally reacts to what is perceived through the senses, and naturally becomes distracted away from being fully present, and it is *sati* that serves the function of bringing our attention back to the present, over and over again. Without mindfulness, we readily become lost in daydreaming, inattention, unawareness and patterns of conditioned habitual reactivity. *Sati* is the antidote to this habitual sleepwalking or living death that destroys our aliveness, vitality and authenticity. For this reason *satipatthana*, The Path of Mindfulness is frequently referred to as the gate to the deathless (*amatapada*).

In practice, *sati* is the faculty of recognizing when you are *not* mindful and in that very moment of recognition, the state of mindfulness automatically returns. The exact nature of *sati* may be difficult to comprehend, but this is not important if you look at mindfulness as primarily the effort to recognize when the mind is reactive, to see when the mind is contracted and agitated. In that very moment of recognition, a space opens up, and in that space *sati* arises and the possibility for clear seeing and transformational insight is restored. Mindfulness is not a state that you create, but a state of conscious awareness that arises spontaneously in the very moment when you become aware of non-mindfulness. Therefore, it is often very helpful to think of mindfulness as simply the awareness of non-mindfulness, or as Krishnamurti described it,

Attention is the awareness of inattention.

This switch from reactivity to non-reactivity is like switching on the light in a dark room. The effect is instantaneous and all is illuminated, without any effort to *become* enlightened. The awakening happens spontaneously as a consequence of switching on the light and not because of what you do. This is the nature of experiential awakening, and it is in that microsecond of awakening that Buddha mind, or *bodhicitta* arises. It happens in each moment when you recognize inattention and respond to that inattention with mindfulness. The simple action of switching on the light is amazingly powerful, because it allows you to interact with everything in the room: to see danger, to see opportunity, to cook your dinner, in fact everything required for living. Mindfulness, *sati*, is simply remembering to switch on the light.

However, the switch works in both directions and we can just as easily become non-mindful and return to darkness, ignorance and reactivity. Therefore, to cultivate *sati* requires sustained effort to keep switching the light back on. The skill of mindfulness practice is to recognize as quickly as possible when we have slipped back into reactivity. For this reason, the practice of *sati* also involves the cultivation of another factor called *samadhi*, which means concentration and focused presence of mind, so that we can develop continuity of mindfulness. Throughout the Buddhist texts, you will find *sati* and *samadhi* mentioned together: the two inseparable twins of the Buddhist path of mental development. In fact the spiritual path for the purification of the mind involves five spiritual factors. These are faith and confidence (*saddha*), energy (*viriya*), *sati*, *samadhi* and wisdom-intelligence (*panna*). All five factors develop during the practice of mindfulness and mindfulness meditation (*vipassana*). Given the direct connection between *sati* and the liberation of mind and spirit, it is not surprising that the cultivation of *sati* lies at the very heart of Buddhist practice and meditation, and is the workhorse for psychological and spiritual transformation.

RELATIONSHIP

The vigilance factor of mindfulness, or *sati* is like switching the light on in a dark room: it brings you into conscious contact with the objects or phenomena of your experience. The relational factor describes the kind of relationship you make with the contents of the room have after you have made contact. This can be thought of as sustaining mindfulness after initial contact.

This relationship that we make with the objects of our experience has a very special quality. When the dust of our habitual reactivity settles, the air clears and we begin to see things as they really are. This pure objective knowing, without the reactions of the observer, is called *satisampajanna*, literally pure knowing through mindfulness. The quality of *pure knowing* is described, very succinctly, in the *Samutta Nikaya Sutta*:

> In what is seen, there should be just the seen;
> In what is heard, there should be just the heard;
> In what is sensed, there should be just the sensed;
> In what is thought, there should be just the thought.

Can you look at a beautiful object, without becoming infatuated and overwhelmed with desire? Can you touch excrement, without feeling revulsion? Can you look at your child or parent or employee and not label them according to your perceptions and prejudices? Can you listen to an angry or irritating person, without reacting with aversion? Can you listen to praise, without becoming conceited? Can you listen to a teacher, without blindly attaching to his views? Can you experience the disagreeable aspects of yourself, without becoming angry or disgusted? Can you see your pain and not react?

The qualities of a mindfulness-based relationship are many, but all arise out of the fundamental factors of *presence* and *engagement*. As the Vietnemese Zen master Thich Nhat Hanh said,

> The most precious gift we can offer others is our presence. When mindfulness embraces those we love, they will bloom like flowers.

Presence means that there is no self, no ego, no interpretor, no analyzer and no thinker reacting to the object of awareness. When you think about what you perceive, you are no longer perceiving, but reacting, and what you experience is not the original object, but your thoughts *about* the original object. This is not being fully present for the original object, but a distraction into your own projections and reactions.

Experience shows us the immense value of being fully present, as with a friend who wants to talk about something that is troubling them. More often than not, what they need most is for us to listen with complete attention, and simply be there for them. This quality of presence produces more healing than all our words of advice. Presence is the fertile ground from which insights and skillful actions arise, but we must start by listening, which is the primary skill of mindfulness. When our relationship with whatever we are experiencing is grounded in this open presence, then whatever eventually emerges as thoughts and acions will be very much more in tune with the needs of the present. Mindfulness has this quality of genuine and undistracted listening, like a mother waiting for her newborn to take its very first breath. The quality of presence is totally focused, yet soft and perfused with positivity and happiness. There is no thinking about the experience, just the experiencing itself in its purest form. *Sati* is often described as the "purification of awareness" in the sense that it strips away all extraneous reactivity and allows us to be fully aware of our experience as it is. The mind frequently wanders off into reacting, either in the form of thinking about what is being experienced, or simply becoming distracted by other thoughts. When you begin meditating, you will soon see how difficult it is to stay focused and how easily your attention becomes consumed by thinking, planning and analyzing. The most basic function of *sati* is simply to bring the attention back from these distractions to the original focus of meditation and to do this over and over again.

Along with presence, the factor of *engagement* is also a very important part of mindfulness. Mindfulness is more than just the passive recognition of sense objects, but includes an active element of investigation. This is called *dhammavicaya*, the investigation of mental phenomena, or *dhammas*. Mindfulness brings us into direct contact with sense objects, whether physical sensations or mental thoughts, feelings and perceptions, but then we must respond to this initial contact with the factor of *dhammavicaya*. This is why investigation is the second of the Seven Factors of Awakening described by the Buddha, after mindfulness, which is the first factor and foundation.

The Path of Mindfulness and the journey towards freedom and the resolution of *dukkha*, originates from this combination of *sati* and *dhammavicaya*. The Path of Mindfulness is above all else, a path of discovery, in which we move from the superficial to the deeper inner structure of our experience; from the gross to the subtle; from illusion to truth. The journey towards truth has no end, and requires that we cultivate an extraordinary openness of mind that relies on nothing other than the direct experiential knowing of the present moment. As expressed by Rene Daumal in his book, Mount Analogue,

> In the whole show there's nothing but mystery and error. Where one ends the other begins.

Life is a mystery and cannot be reduced to the level of beliefs and theories or any representation produced by thought. The "mystery" refers to the total and absolute reality that we call truth (*sacca*). The ego, in its attempt to control life, creates error and unskillful actions, because it is limited by conditioning. Any creation of the thinking mind (*sankhara*) is worldly, conventional truth (*sammutti sacca*) and limited by the distorted perceptions of the observer and his past. Knowledge about reality can never substitute for the actual or ultimate truth (*paramattha sacca*) and can never be more than a superficial snapshot of that ultimate truth. Such truth is not an abstract theory or ideology, but simply the direct experience of existence as it is in every detail.

Living with life as a mystery means opening to the whole drama of life with the freedom of mind that can fully engage with each moment, without reacting out of habitual conditioning. Full engagement leads to authentic living, in which we are open to receive life as it is, rather than imposing our superficial beliefs onto reality. In order to engage fully with life, the mind must first be empty to receive truth. Zen master Suzuki Roshi described this quality of openness as "Beginner's Mind," also called "Not sure Mind" by the Thai Buddhist meditation master, Ajahn Chah. Therefore, our spiritual path must involve cultivating a way of engaging with phenomena that is non-reactive and not conditioned by the past. This full presence and engagement is the fundamental nature of mindfulness: the process of bringing us back into the direct knowing of our experience, without the distortions of subjective and habitual mental reactivity.

Sati, the skill of being fully present and engaged, is a natural quality that we all have, and that we seek to develop and perfect through training. The successful hunter pays great attention to every detail of the landscape, noticing a broken twig here, a movement there, a sound or smell. His mind is completely open to everything in his field of awareness and equisitely interested in the smallest details. *Sati* has this quality of actively looking below the surface appearance of things, seeking out every detail of our present experience. Mindfulness is not just a passive process of observing things, but an active process of investigation into the deeper structure of things. This is how we should approach our mind when we practice mindful-awareness throughout the day, and during mindfulness meditation.

Mindfulness represents a very refined response to our experience that is truly wonderful and spiritual. To quote John C. Lilly,

> The miracle is that the universe created a part of itself to study the rest of it, and that this part in studying itself finds the rest of the universe in its own natural inner realities.

Above all, mindfulness is the Art of Relationship; a relationship based on conscious awareness and attention to reality. *Sati* allows us to experience the reality of things, without any perceptual filtering and without adding anything to the experience in the form of thinking, judging, analyzing or any other form of mental reactivity. The essence of mindfulness is awakening to experience, without the reactions of the conditioned mind, and without becoming infatuated with liking or disliking. Mindfulness is experiencing sensory phenomena just as they are, with complete objectivity. When we see things objectively, instead of reacting to them out of habit, we are opening to the truth of phenomena in all their rich detail.

You don't need to go searching for the truth, you simply need to open your eyes and see the truth right in front of you.

TRANSFORMATION

Mindfulness produces a fundamental shift in the psyche from the process of habitual reactivity to the process of direct experiencing. In the words of Dhiravamsa, a much respected *vipassana* teacher,

> You are the observing and you observe the reactions of the observer.

In each moment of mindfulness the mind temporarily ceases to react and there is simply the pure and direct knowing of whatever is being experienced. The *known* is as it is, the objective and independent reality of what is being observed whereas the *knower* describes the experiences created through *reacting* to what is observed. When there is no reactivity, the *knower* simply ceases to be and you become the *knowing* itself. You become *the observing*, rather than the *observer*; the *experiencing*, rather than the *experience*; the *knowing*, rather than the *knower*. This pure knowing consciousness is called *satisampajanna*, in which there is no division between the observer and the object observed, because there is no person reacting to the object, with likes and dislikes or other distortions of perception.

During mindfulness practice, we cultivate this natural relationship with phenomena by bringing our attention back, over and over again, from being the *knower* to being the *knowing*. This applies equally towards the contents of our mind, or externally towards our experience of the external world. With practice, even the "reactions of the observer" can be seen as mental objects to be recognized with mindfulness and known with *satisampajanna*. As we cultivate mindfulness, we learn to relate to both the *known* and the reactions of the *knower* and in so doing, we become free from both. This is the essence of the path to liberation described by the Buddha.

As we distentangle from our attachment and identification with the contents of our mind, we open up a spaciousness quality of

120

consciousness that is not limited by our habitual reactivity. When we relate to emotional suffering and *dukkha* with this spacious dimension of mindfulness, we create a highly creative and therapeutic space in which *dukkha* is free to transform and resolve. When *sati* is strong, *satisampajanna* is strong, and when *satisampajanna* is strong, then the wisom faculty arises and begins to orchestrate changes that lead to the resolution of suffering and liberation from the *dukkha*-producing realm of *samsara*. This factor is called *satipanna*, the innate wisdom-intelligence that accompanies *sati*.

10 MINDFULNESS AND VIGILANCE

Mindfulness (*sati*) is multi-dimensional, with active, passive and transformational dimensions that arise when we form an open and non-reactive relationship with our experience.

The active dimension consists of vigilance, watchfulness, alertness and heedfulness, called *appamada* in Pali. Such watchfulness is needed to maintain continuity of mindfulness and to recognize when the mind has slipped back into reacting. This is the most basic meaning of *sati*, literally remembering to stay awake and consciously aware of what is happening while it is happening. The passive dimension of *sati* is the response of opening to experience and forming a mindfulness-based relationship with our experience, so we can investigate experience and uncover its inner structure. This is the quality of *satisampajanna*, the relationship of pure knowing through mindfulness. The third quality of *sati* is the transformational dimension. This involves awakening to our innate intuitive intelligence of *satipanna* that leads to the transformation and resolution of *dukkha* and the liberation of the mind and spirit from habitual reactivity.

Thus, whenever we practice mindfulness, or *satipatthana*, we progress through each dimension, beginning with *appamada*, which allows *satisampajanna* to arise, which in turn creates the freedom and therapeutic space in which *satipanna* can arise, leading to intelligent change and transformation. Ultimately it is *satipanna* that acts as our inner guide and directs the process of transformation. It is this movement from reactivity to non-reactivity, from clinging to non-clinging, from ignorance to awakening that ultimately leads to the resolution of emotional conflict and all manifestations of *dukkha*.

Mindfulness brings about a fundamental change in how we relate to the contents of our mind, how we relate to other people and how we relate to the world in general. It begins with learning to recognize and stop the habitual reactivity and the blind identification with the reactions of the mind. It then proceeds to the next stage in which we cultivate and sustain a mindfulness-based relationship with our emotions or beliefs. When we stop reacting, we see more and in this greater clarity of insight, our inner wisdom-intelligence will arise, leading to transformation. However, the path begins with the most fundamental active dimension of mindfulness, which is learning to recognize reactivity when it arises. Through this simple awakening, we create the opportunity to stop the propagation of reactivity and to stop feeding the flames of blind attachment that feed *dukkha* and the endless round of habitual reactivity that is *samsara*.

VIGILANCE

Above all, the first function of mindfulness practice is to overcome ignorance (*avijja*) and the unawareness of what is happening in the present moment. The natural state for the mind is one of continual activity, moving like a humming bird from flower to flower, or like a monkey swinging through the trees in search of fruit. Whilst this is perfectly normal, it does reduce our conscious awareness to something more like daydreaming or sleepwalking in which we perform actions mechanically. This can be perfectly adequate for mundane activities, but it does lead to a degree of sensory impoverishment and inflexibility that leaves us vulnerable, because it reduces our ability to adapt intelligently to change. When we react to experience, what we see is our reaction and not the richness of what is before us. Our perception becomes mechanical, dull and impoverished. It is what we don't see that is most damaging, and incomplete awareness leaves us vulnerable.

In order to restore flexibility, adaptability and to revitalize the quality of our sensory experience, we need to develop an advanced degree of presence through mindfulness and vigilance. In effect, the most basic and primary activity of mindfulness practice is simply recognizing when mindfulness is absent and when we are not present and then responding by re-establishing presence in the here and now. This response to the recognition of non-presence is the heart of mindfulness practice that we will repeat over and over again during meditation and throughout the day. It is only through the clear awareness of reactivity, that reactivity can be stopped in its tracks.

The root meaning of the word "vigilance" means to "stay awake" and for mindfulness practice this means watching closely for the reactions of mind, speech and body. This active dimension of mindfulness is called *appamada*, in Pali, which means "heedfulness" and is the starting point for all mindfulness practice and meditation. *Sati* is often defined as a form of recollection or remembering to bring the attention back to the present so that one knows what is happening while it is happening. It takes considerable effort and patience to develop *appamada*, but it is absolutely essential if we are to overcome the entrenched habits of the reactive mind. In the Dhammapada we find the passage,

> Heedfulness is the Deathless path, heedlessness the path to death.
> Those who are heedful do not die, heedless are as if already dead.

Mindfulness is often referred to as the path to the Deathless (*amatapada*) that leads to the unconditioned (*asankhata*) state of consciousness in which there is perfect freedom from the conditioned (*sankhata*) contents of our mind. The state of consciousness that is conditioned by blind attachment to *sankharas* created by reactivity is the essence of death, because all *sankharas* are impermanent and subject to decay and eventual extinction. Those who are in the grip of conditioned mental reactivity are controlled by the *sankharas* that arise and pass away in their minds; they are condemned to a life of slavery and bondage, which is the death of the psyche. In contrast, the truly authentic and awakened human being has the inner freedom to fully engage and respond to life with intelligence and wisdom. To be truly alive, one must be free from the constraints of blind conditioning and the habitual reactivity of *samsara*.

We must be free to be happy and *appamada* is the beginning of the path to both freedom and happiness. In conventional understanding, freedom usually implies freedom *to do* what we like. From the Buddha's view, freedom means freedom *from* conditioned reactivity. The last words said by the Buddha on his deathbed are reputed to be as follows:

Vaya-dhamma sankhara, appamadena sampadetha.
Transient are all creations of the mind. Work out your
deliverance with heedfulness.

The cultivation of mindfulness is a skill that has to be learned, and
like any other skill, benefits from sustained practice. Your task is
to develop heedfulness and catch the reactions of *cittasankhara* as
soon as possible after they emerge so that you do not become
blindly attached to them and compelled to become the *sankharas*.
You do not have to do anything with the thoughts and feelings that
arise; it is sufficient to just know that they have arisen and then respond to them with mindfulness. In this way, we no longer perpetuate *avijja* and we do not allow *sankharas* to proliferate into all
manner of secondary reactivity. This is a difficult practice and requires great patience, but the benefits of developing the skill of *appamada* are immeasurable. Each moment of mindfulness is a step
on the path to the Deathless, and spiritual and psychological freedom that benefits all.

STOP, LOOK AND LISTEN

Whether mindfulness is practiced as vigilant awareness from moment-to-moment throughout the activities of the day or in focused
meditation sessions, the basic approach of mindfulness practice is
the same, and involves the three basic trainings in mindfulness that
we all learned as children to recite before crossing the road: STOP,
LOOK and LISTEN.

STOP: Notice when you are reacting and respond by letting go of
the content or story line of the reaction. This is *appamada*, which
is the beginning point of *sati*.
LOOK: Apply mindfulness and investigate the detailed structure of
your experience. This is *satisampajanna*.
LISTEN: Be attentive to the intuitive direction of change at the
feeling level and allow that change to take place. This is *satipanna*.

126

The Path of Mindfulness is a practice of learning to STOP being blindly seduced by thought reactions and emotional reactions, and STOP the secondary proliferation of further thinking and emotional reactivity (*papanca*). However, before we can stop reactivity from proliferating we must learn to recognize a reaction when it arises. With practice we can refine this skill even further, and recognize the impulse to react before the reaction takes form.

All mental reactions have an impulsive emotional quality, the force known as *tanha*, and we can refine our ability to detect reactions by looking for disturbances in the energy field of our consciousness. Reactions create agitation and tension related to wanting, aversion or delusion. All reactions create a degree of conflict and tension between our subjective *sankharas,* and reality as it is, and this tension is experienced as *dukkha*. When we train ourselves to recognize this mental agitation caused by reactivity, we are training ourselves to recognize *dukkha* as it arises, not as an abstract concept, but as a concrete reality. This is the primary mission for followers of The Path of Mindfulness: to awaken to *dukkha* in all its forms and to respond to it by forming a relationship with *dukkha*, based on mindfulness and compassion.

During the activities of the day, we should cultivate a keen attention to any agitations that arise in the mind, any manifestation of *dukkha* that may arise in our relationships; when we are speaking to a friend; driving a car, doing our work; or when we are thinking about the past or contemplating the future. Wherever tension arises, that is where we respond with mindfulness, and the objective of our practice is to develop vigilance to such a degree that no reactions escape our attention. During mindfulness meditation (*vipassana*), we take an even closer look at our mind and actively search for any manifestation of *dukkha* and respond to each of them with mindfulness.

In the very moment of recognition, there will be a temporary release from the impulse to react; a space opens up, and this brief moment has immense significance. If we respond with mindfulness, then the reaction is prevented from taking on form and proliferating. The response of mindfulness effectively interrupts the reaction and creates a space or interval in which there is choice. As

Victor Frankl, the respected Psychiatrist and Holocaust survivor, once said,

> Between a stimulus and response there is a space. In that space is our power to choose our response. In our response lies our growth and our freedom.

This in itself can make a tremendous impact in breaking the habit of reactivity and the more experience you gain in STOPPING, the more you will develop the power to resist reactivity. This is an art, but like any other skill it can be learned and improved with practice. Eventually, the response of mindfulness becomes a habit in itself, a skillful habit that leads towards balance and freedom from reactivity, rather than perpetuating further reactivity and suffering. This skill of vigilance and careful attention is the foundation for The Path of Mindfulness and all spiritual development.

STOPPING also requires that you take responsibilty for your own *dukkha* and recognize that, ultimately, it is your choice whether you react out of ignorance or respond out of wisdom. You recognize that you alone are responsible for your happiness or suffering, rather than blaming external conditions for causing your agitation and unhappiness. Living generates pain, but suffering, or *dukkha* is generated by your mind in reaction to the pain through blind attachment to habitual reactivity. The awakening insight that you will learn through mindfulness practice is that you do not have to be a victim of your emotional reactivity and that you do have choice, as difficult as those may be to implement.

The Path of Mindfulness is based on the clear understanding that you do not have to remain a slave to your habitual reactivity. If a reaction of anger, anxiety or fear arises, you do not have to become angry, worried or afraid. The only reason you react with these emotions is because you have become conditioned to react in that particular way and you are blind to this conditioning. Reactivity causes you to become ignorant of the cause of your suffering and this ignorance and conditioning is what you overcome through the practice of mindfulness. Literally, you are learning to say "NO!" to the compulsive drive to become angry, upset, worried, frustrated, depressed, or any of the multitude of reactions that as-

sail you during the day and during meditation. This is the courageous proclamation of the spiritual warrior who chooses to live on
his or her terms, rather than as a slave to habitual existence. In the
words of Dylan Thomas,

> Do not go gentle into that good night - rage, rage
> against the dying of the light.

Do not allow yourself to be seduced into becoming upset, disappointed, angry, worried or compelled by any other creation (*sankhara*) of the conditioned mind. It requires considerable effort and
courage to resist the force of habit, to rage against ignorance and
"the dying of the light," but the rewards of making the effort and
practicing mindfulness are immeasurable and will bring you many
rewards.

It is important to have the right attitude when you practice
STOPPING. After saying "NO!" to a reaction, you should then respond with *metta* and *upekkha*, positive openness and equanimity,
which is the essence of mindfulness. Mindfulness does not stop after the recognition of a reaction, but should always be followed by
a response of opening and investigation.   Mindfulness is turning
towards experience, and this includes all the manifestations of *dukkha*. Thought reactions and emotional reactions are not, in themselves the enemy; the problem is only in the way you relate to
them. If you blindly identify with them through ignorance, then
you will become attached to the reactions and they will become
habitual. If you react against them with aversion or wanting something different, then you simply reinforce the original primary reactions. Any form of reactivity has the undesirable effect of
repressing the original primary emotions, and building a reactive
superstructure that keep them imprisoned and repressed. Repression strengthens ignorance (*avijja*) and this prevents the resolution
of *dukkha*. The reactions of aversion, like greed and delusion simply feed reactivity and solidify the inner emotional conflict, making the mind less malleable and less able to transform and resolve
dukkha.

What is needed is an alternative response, a more healthy response, in which you greet each thought, emotion or other reactive

sankhara, with non-reactive mindfulness. This is meeting fire with water. In this stillness and spaciousness, you create a safe space in which reactions have a chance to soften, unfold and change. What is needed is an attitude of firmness to prevent the proliferation of further reactivity, coupled with kindness and sensitivity that creates the best conditions for bringing about change, and healing the pain of *dukkha* with the cooling water of wisdom and compassion.

After STOPPING comes the response of LOOKING. Mindfulness is the art of relationship based on careful observation, with an open mind that is not tarnished by the preconceptions of the ego, and is not tangled up in ego-reactivity. Looking in this way means the pure *knowing* of what is being observed as it is, without reaction, and this is called *satisampajanna*.

Looking begins with awakening to what arises in consciousness as thoughts, feelings and sensations, but mindfulness does not stop there. Mindfulness is a much more dynamic and active process of investigation in which we engage with the contents of our experience with a mind eager to learn. This is the factor of *dhammavicaya*, the investigation of phenomena, which is the second of the Seven Factors of Enlightenment described by the Buddha that lead to liberation from suffering. The first factor is mindfulness, and the factors that follow this solid foundation of mindfulness coupled with investigation are energy, rapture, tranquility, *samadhi* and equanimity.

Mindfulness, the first factor, is the process of establishing the right relationship with our experience, based on complete openness and non-reactivity, but this must be followed by a thorough exploration of what is inside our experience, what surrounds our experience; in fact exploring every detail of the inner structure of our experience. When we establish mindfulness of a thought or a feeling or an external object, we embark on an intriguing voyage of discovery. This is not a voyage of analysis and thinking about the experience, but a voyage of *awakening* and fully *knowing* our present experience in all its dynamic richness. Mindful-investigation does not involve a subjective observer, evaluating experience, because that would simply be another manifestation of mental reactivity, conditioned by the past. Instead, *dhammavicaya* is the process of allowing experience to unfold into conscious awareness, without the interference of an observer. This is why *dhammavicaya* has to be grounded in *sati*; it cannot arise in the absence of mindfulness. When mindfulness is established and sustained, then any experience, emotion, thought or other mind object will differentiate and unfold by itself. Being fully present to witness and know this unfolding truth is the primary vehicle to liberation and the resolution of *dukkha*.

Needless to say, in order for mindfulness to be effective, there must be active LISTENING so that we can receive the unfolding content of experience that arises from LOOKING. The particular type of listening that we use in mindfulness, is attention to the intuitive and experiential level of our experience. This means letting go of the words, thinking, concepts and the content level, and opening to the feeling level of our experience. This kind of listening is Noble Silence, because it is beyond the conditioned world of thoughts and opinions and mental content. This is the space into which experience can unfold and differentiate, unimpeded by the ego.

It is the awareness and knowing of this unfolding content that is the essence of freedom and in this freedom, the innate wisdom-intelligence factor of *satipanna* comes into existence. This is what directs the transformation that leads to the resolution of *dukkha*. The detailed awareness of the inner structure provides the concrete material which *satipanna* can work on to resolve *dukkha*. The healing is always a product of what is seen, just as *dukkha* and suffering are always a product of what is not seen. This is the healing space of the Buddha mind that is a natural feature of the human psyche, and that is revealed when there is freedom from conditioning; a freedom that comes from the relationship of mindfulness.

In the practice of STOP, LOOK and LISTEN, we cultivate mindfulness throughout the day at each and every encounter with our mental reactions. In meditation sessions, we develop this to a fine art and strengthen the factor of mindfulness and equanimity in the mind. Mindfulness begins with STOPPING, proceeds to LOOKING and is followed by active LISTENING and this cultivates freedom and choice and the ability to engage and respond in a balanced way guided by intuitive intelligence. This awakened state of living is quite different to the usual habit of blind conditioned reactivity.

NON-ATTACHMENT

As Ajahn Chah so eloquently expressed it,

> Do everything with a mind that lets go. Do not expect any praise or reward. If you let go a little, you will have a little peace. If you let go a lot, you will have a lot of peace. If you let go completely, you will know complete peace and freedom. Your struggles with the world will have come to an end.

The Path of Mindfulness is the path of non-attachment. In Pali, this is called *anupadana*, non-attachment to mental reactivity. This includes freedom from attachment to sensual desire (*kamupadana*), freedom from attachment to inner beliefs (*ditthupadana*), freedom from conventions (*silabbatupadana*) and most importantly of all, freedom from attachment to the subjective habitual reactions of the ego (*attavadupadana*). If you relate to the experiences of life, to the irritations and frustrations, disappointments and pain, as well as the joys and moments of happiness with this relaxed attention of non-attachment, then you will be free to fully experience life and free to respond wisely to the changing conditions of life.

Now it should be made clear that non-attachment is not the same as detachment, which implies a degree of aversion, avoidance and indifference. Non-attachment is actually a process of getting closer and more engaged with experience, including *dukkha*, but from a position of non-reactivity and equanimity (*upekkha*). The whole purpose of cultivating non-attachment is so that we can engage more fully and be more present for our internal mental experiences; to be more present with others in our personal relationships; and to be more present for our environment and our world. Non-attachment and full engagement go hand in hand, because it is only when the mind is free of attachment that it can receive and know what is happening in the present and this is essential for skillful engagement.

Mindfulness brings about non-attachment quite spontaneously, because attachment (*upadana*) depends on *avijja*, the unawareness of present experience, whereas mindfulness is the direct awareness of experience. The two are mutually exclusive and when ignorance is removed, attachment simultaneously falls away. This is taking the path of non-attachment to a far higher level than trying to deliberately let go, which is little more than the ego trying to control the mind. Allowing the ego to solve the problems of the mind is like asking the fox to guard the farmer's chickens. We should understand that the mind that is controlled by reactivity is not able to effectively rid itself of its own attachments and ignorance. All that it can do is replace one set of attachments with another set of attachments.

Mindfulness is a different kind of conscious relationship, in which there is no fragmentation of the mind into the controller and the controlled. When we follow The Path of Mindfulness we do not try to get rid of our attachments, but simply envelop them in the spaciousness of pure awareness. Without reacting further, without creating the superstructure of habitual secondary reactivity, reactions simply lose their power to dominate us. That power depends on ignorance, and if we replace ignorance with the pure knowing that comes with mindfulness, then reactivity is effectively neutralized. This is the mind letting go of itself, which is quite different than one part of the mind trying to control another part through coercion. Blind attachment sustains *dukkha* while non-attachment nourishes the transformation and resolution of *dukkha*. Mindfulness facilitates the shift from *dukkha* to the resolution of *dukkha*.

11 THE RELATIONSHIP OF MINDFULNESS

The active side of mindfulness is very important, because it helps us recognize when we are reacting. Without this basic recognition of what is happening as it is happening, nothing can change. Therefore, awakening to what is arising in our mind is the most fundamental step in the battle against *avijja*, and overcoming the domination of the mind by habitual reactivity.

In the very moment of mindful-recognition of an impulse to react a space opens up in which there is a brief moment of choice. In that moment of freedom, we have the choice to let go of the reaction, and avoid becoming compelled to react. In that brief moment of mindfulness, we discover freedom from *bhavatanha*, the compulsion to become and can now respond to the reaction, the *sankhara* and its associated emotional energy with sustained mindfulness. We form a mindfulness-basd relationship with the mental object that has arisen in consciousness. However, this relationship is based on non-reactivity, non-compulsive becoming and non-attachment. This is the relationship of *satisampajanna*, pure knowing of experience as it is, without any reactivity and without any movement of greed, hatred or delusion to what is being experienced.

However, this is just the beginning of the relationship of mindfulness. We need to follow through by opening the mind and heart to investigate the subtle inner structure of experience. The vigilant dimension of *sati* allows us to make contact with experience and stop the proliferation of habitual reactivity, and we are able to move between the different mind objects freely. This is the horizontal dimension of mindfulness, in which we move freely from one object to another, without becoming ensnared or seduced by our thoughts and emotions.

Besides the horizontal dimension, mindfulness also has a vertical dimension, in which we uncover the inner structure of our experience. When mindfulness is established, we naturally begin to see more of what is there. Mindfulness illuminates, and directs us away from the superficial appearance of things to experience the truth within. There is a natural movement from the gross surface structure to the subtle deep structure of experience; from ignorance to truth. This is the natural response of investigation into the reality of whatever we perceive with mindfulness, and is called *dhammavicaya*. Whether you are watching a waterfall, listening to a friend or focusing on the contents of your mind, the response of mindfulness means that we take a keen interest in whatever is perceived through the six sense doors of seeing, hearing, smelling, tasting, touching and thinking. Rather than our usual reaction of carelessly dismissing objects according to our past conditioning and attachment to beliefs, we choose to respond to all phenomena with a freshness of mind and an apetite to investigate and learn.

INNER STILLNESS

Mindfulness is deliberately making the effort to be fully present with whatever is experienced, internally or externally, with a mind that is silent and open. This is the art of listening, and requires inner stillness and deep sensitivity so that we fully experience the present moment. Zen master Gensha described this presence of mindfulness as,

> a stillness, which abides in the present.

The mind has a very strong tendency to react to what it sees, hears, smells, tastes, touches and thinks. It becomes caught up in activity and looses this inner stillness, and the function of mindfulness is to repeatedly return our attention to that place of inner stillness and tranquility.

However, stillness and tranquility by itself is not the point of The Path of Mindfulness. What is far more important is to develop this stillness *in relationship* to the objects of our experience, whether external sense objects or the inner mental objects of thoughts, memories and emotions. If agitation arises in the mind, mindfulness allows us to *relate* to the agitation, without becoming overwhelmed by the agitation, which is our usual respone. If anger arises, mindfulness allows us to be still and observe the anger. If fear or anxiety arises, mindfulness allows us to sit with these emotions, listening with complete stillness and complete presence.

Mindfulness is the response of stillness to the pain and happiness, gain and loss, success and failure, praise and blame and all the chaos of changing conditions that visit us in daily life or in our meditation sessions. This unique stillness in relationship to the world is called *samadhi*, from *sam*, which means totality, *a-*, towards and *-dha*, to hold. *Samadhi* is the state of mental stability and harmony that comes from having the right relationship of mindfulness with the objects of our experience.

Whatever the object perceived, we seek to develop this stillness from one moment to the next, such that every aspect of our life is touched by this stillness. The stillness of being fully present is extraordinarily powerful and transformative. With this noble stillness, we can perceive the full richness of experience, and transcend the conventional world of illusion and superficiality. In the words of Mahatma Gandhi,

> In the attitude of silence the soul finds the path in a clearer light, and what is elusive and deceptive resolves itself into crystal clearness. Our life is a long and arduous quest after Truth.

The more we see of the truth, the more freedom we will know. Stillness is freedom, and freedom from the constraints of our habitual reactivity creates a fertile therapeutic space in which transformation can take place, and from which skillful and comopasionate actions arise. In this stillness, the wisdom-intelligence of *satipanna* flourishes and purifies our actions and, "what is elusive and deceptive resolves itself into crystal clearness." We struggle so hard to find the answers, when all that is really needed is that we cultivate an inner stillness and attentiveness and allow the psyche to heal itself, and present solutions based on our innate and intuitive intelligence.

Complete openness and stillness of the thinking mind allows new insights to arise, which facilitates creativity and problem solving and supports the resolution of core emotional complexes. As J. Krishnamurti said,

When the mind is still, tranquil, not seeking any answers or any solution, neither resisting nor avoiding - it is only then that there can be a regeneration, because then the mind is capable of perceiving what is true; and it is truth that liberates, not your effort to be free.

Krishnamurti was keenly aware of the supreme importance of the still mind; the Noble Stillness that does is not perturbed by the subjective reactions of the ego. The ego can solve things at the superficial level, but not at the deeper level of our core emotions. The effort to control emotions by the ego, or the force of discursive thinking, invariably creates division and fragmentation in the mind, and such inner conflict creates more suffering.

When Noble Stillness and *satisampajanna* arise, then in that very moment, the reactive ego dies and allows us to experience the wider and deeper intuitive level of experiencing. When there is no interruption from the ego, our experience responds by unfolding from the inside out; a totally different mode of change than that imposed by the ego. The Path of Mindfulness is one of awakening to this natural intuitive unfolding, and relating to our experience as a dynamic changing process. It is in the stillness of pure knowing that the mind is purified and becomes liberated from the mechanical constraints of *samsara*.

SAFE HAVEN

The best way to work with emotional reactivity, or any form of *dukkha*, is to create a space around the emotion. In that space, the emotion can exist in safety, without being threatened by the judgmental and controlling ego. Often, just this simple attitude of respect and acceptance is enough to bring about transformation and healing. Many emotional conflicts will resolve themselves if we simply provide a safe space for them, and attend to them by being fully present and non-reactive. This phenomenon is called Contact Resolution, and is one of the main mechanisms through which mindfulness heals suffering. If your friend is in pain, the best action is often to simply hold him or her in your arms and comfort them. This quality of being present and creating a safe space for their suffering is often more important than any advice that you might give.

The Path of Mindfulness teaches us to relate to our inner *dukkha* in the same way, being fully present and non-threatening; caressing the pain with great attention and love. This is the perfection of mindfulness as a spiritual power, called *sammasati*, or "right mindfulness." Mindfulness is much more than just the bare recognition of mental phenomena; it is a *response* to experience, filled with compassion and friendliness, the spiritual expression of *metta*. Whenever we are practicing mindfulness, we should remember this and never lose sight of the spiritual dimension of mindfulness. Mindfulness is not just about "showing up," but what you do when you are there for your experience.

Spaciousness, which is synonymous with freedom, is always beneficial to a mind in pain, because freedom allows things to change. There is a popular Zen proverb that the best way to control a wild bull is to place it in a very large field. When there is plenty of space surrounding the bull then there is much less risk of being hurt by the bull, no matter how fierce it is. By the same token there is much less chance that the bull will hurt itself. This quality of creating a safe therapeutic space in which painful emotions can exist is central to mindfulness practice. Besides creating a safe haven, the spacious dimension of an open mind allows things to move, change and unfold at the experiential level. Openness creates the right environment for transformation and resolution of inner conflict by allowing things to untangle and unfold in conscious awareness. Consciousness is in fact another name for this therapeutic space, but this variety of consciousness is unconditioned and not constrained by the contents of the thinking mind. Conscious awareness that is free from attachment to content is free to be fully present for all mental phenomena, including suffering.

BARE ATTENTION

Bare attention is a term used by many *Dhamma* teachers to describe mindfulness and gives us an idea about the simplicity and uncomplicated nature of *sati*. It is bare, in the sense that nothing is added to the direct experience of an object. There is no "dressing up" of experience by adding layers of interpretation based on be- liefs and preconceptions. Mindfulness is the witnessing and know- ing of any experience in its pure, original state, which is closer to objective reality and to absolute truth. Mindfulness is always about bringing the mind back from the world of illusion to the truth of things as they are. To quote Robert Frost,

Anything more than the truth would be too much.

All the subtle, and not so subtle reactions of the thinking mind are definitely more than the truth; they are created through our reac- tions to truth, which is never the same as original truth. Mindful- ness is a response that simplifies experience into the direct knowing of experience as it is happening in the present moment. When you practice mindfulness, you will soon begin to notice a profound change in your perceptions and you will discover a richer dimension of experience. As Marcel Proust said,

The real voyage of discovery consists not in seeking new lands but seeing with new eyes.

The mind is always more than ready to form opinions and react to sensory experience by labeling and categorizing, which is seeing through the "old eyes" of past conditioning. However, truth can never be reduced to labels and concepts, and these superficial rep- resentations are one of the many faces of *avijja*. We tend to project our ego onto experience, which obscures the truth and keeps us confined within a superficial world of illusion. Knowing with bare attention means putting aside prejudices from the past and dwell- ing in the pure knowing (*satisampajanna*) of things in the present. Without the distortions of the past, we are more likely to respond with intelligence and wisdom (*satipanna*) to the present, because we are at last able to see reality as it is, without distortion. With bare attention the truth illuminates the soul and we see with new eyes, the eyes of wisdom and freedom.

We are so habituated to react to sense experiences that we never actually see what is in front of us. All we see are our reac- tions: cognitive reactions of thinking about what we are experiencing; perceptual reactions and memories; and emotional reactions of wanting and aversion. Every type of reaction is actually a diversion from the direct awareness of things as they are and this takes us away from the pure knowing of things in their primary state. When we are not able to see things as they really are, we become less able to respond wisely to the present moment, because we cannot see the subtlety of what is needed.

In other words, the obstruction of knowing, or *avijja*, prevents the arising of intuitive intelligence (*satipanna*). This is particularly relevant when working with emotional complexes, where the process that leads to transformation can be very subtle and not obvious to the thinking mind. If we are unable to see this experiential subtlety, the emotion will not be able to change. The movement of bare attention allows us to move from the superficial to the depth of our experience, from the gross to the subtle, and this is the most important movement that happens during mindfulness meditation, or *vipassana*.

CHOICELESS AWARENESS

Choiceless awareness was a favorite term used by the influencial Indian philosopher J. Krishnamurti, who emphasized the importance of direct experience, without the interference of all the prejudices and expectations of the subjective mind. As Krishnamurti said,

> Freedom is not a reaction: freedom is not choice. It is man's pretence that because he has choice he is free. Freedom is pure observation without direction, without fear of punishment and reward. Freedom is without motive; freedom is not at the end of the evolution of man but lies in the first step of his existence. In observation one begins to discover the lack of freedom. Freedom is found in the choiceless awareness of our daily existence and activity.

Freedom means many things, but the essence of psychological freedom means that we can fully engage with the present, without

141

the baggage of the reactive conditioning from our past. There is little freedom when the past conditions the present, because the possible responses to the present will be limited. This lack of flexibility and intelligent responsiveness to the present is the characteristic of slavery and spiritual ignorance, and the root of suffering.

Krishnamurti taught us that the time for applying choiceless awareness is in every aspect of our daily life and not just in meditation, and this is what makes the practice of mindfulness a spiritual path, rather than just another technique for the ego to use to control the psyche. It is through the very practice of awakening to everyday experience, moment to moment, that we discover true freedom. With this understanding, life and meditation become one and the same.

Choiceless awareness means that we allow experience to unfold naturally, without interference, but this does not mean that we cannot take the initiative and choose a subject to contemplate with mindfulness. The underlying purpose of mindfulness practice is to facilitate the resolution of *dukkha* and the conditions that give rise to suffering and conflict. If you are affected by a painful memory or you have a specific worry about the future, then the skillful response is to bring such memories or worries into the present as subjects for mindfulness meditation.

However, the practice of mindfulness of past recollections or future worries is not the same as indulging in thinking and worrying. In the practice of mindfulness, the primary focus is to establish an objective relationship with the *present* experience of the selected painful memory or anxiety-thoughts. Present awareness is like a screen onto which you can project mental phenomena for investigation. It is a space into which you can place thoughts, feelings and reactions for observation. After you have selected a subject for meditation, you then exercise choiceless awareness and allow the emotion to unfold in its own way, without interference. This is very important, because how things unfold is not a rational or linear process, but a highly complex process that involves many factors that you cannot know ahead of time. This is the nature of experiential unfolding, which is directed by the psyche and not by the ego.

Contemplation with mindfulness provides one of the best tools available to prepare for the future, by allowing us to cultivate balance and non-reactivity, as we contemplate our anxiety and fears. Mindfulness of the past creates the best environment for resolving the emotional reactivity of any past traumas that have become repressed and solidified in the mind. Suffering is suffering, whether it arises from the past, present or anticipation of the future. However, the resolution of suffering can only happen in the present, therefore all manifestations of *dukkha* should be brought into the present and cared for with mindfulness. In the therapeutic space of mindfulness, all manifestations of *dukkha* have the freedom to transform and resolve themselves under the direction of *satipanna*, our intuitive intelligence. However, this healing can only occur when there is complete freedom from any movement of the thinking mind and this is to be found in the choiceless awareness of *dukkha*.

12 TRANSFORMATION THROUGH MINDFULNESS

Perhaps the most significant insight gained by the Buddha on his enlightenment is that when you touch *dukkha* with mindfulness, it changes, and when you develop a relationship based on mindfulness, then in this relationship *dukkha* transforms and resolves itself.

After we encounter a sensory experience, either internally in the form of a thought or emotion, or externally through the sense organs, we are faced with a critical decision point. We can either react according to habitual conditioning or we can respond with non-reactive mindfulness. Reactivity simply intensifies mental stress and *dukkha*, like pouring oil onto a fire. Reactivity also perpetuates *samsara* by reinforcing the subjective reactive habits of the self so that they repeat over and over again. But perhaps the most unfortunate aspect of reactivity is that it effectively prevents resolution (*dukkhanirodha*) by distracting our attention away from suffering into secondary reactivity. Reactive Displacement has the effect of repressing primary reactions; and hidden from consciousness, repressed emotions are unable to change and resolve themselves.

The other possibility available to us is that we respond to *dukkha* with mindfulness, which is the response of pure knowing, without becoming entangled in the contents. With this pure knowing, we are able to see what is most skillful and wholesome and respond accordingly. We allow action to arise out of the totality of the situation, rather than blindly reacting out of habit.   Mindfulness supports therapeutic change in many different ways and is avery effective tool for stress reduction and for promoting general psychological health as described in the Mindfulness-based Stress Reduction (MBSR) program developed by Jon Kabat-Zinn of the University of Massachusetts Medical School. This program teaches mindfulness to help individuals develop present, body-centered awareness as a way of counteracting the proliferation of negative thinking and rumination that sustains emotional stress. This approach is also very effective for the treatment of depression and anxiety disorders in Mindfulness-based Cognitive Therapy (MBCT).

Besides using mindfulness to cultivate general present-centered awareness, there is another approach in which mindfulness is applied directly to painful emotions to facilitate beneficial changes. This is called Mindfulness Meditation Therapy (MMT). Meditation refers to the focused application of mindfulness on an object, such as the breath or physical sensations, to develop present-centered awareness. In MMT, the meditator makes the emotion the primary object for meditation. In this form of psychotherapy the therapist guides the client to develop a mindfulness-based relationship with his or her present experience of an emotion. With practice, the individual learns to maintain a stable relationship with his or her emotional trauma, anxiety or pain, without becoming reactive, and this opens the way for inner transformation and resolution. Mindfulness Meditation Therapy is the direct application of mindfulness to facilitate the resolution of emotional suffering, or *dukkha*.

Mindfulness Meditation Therapy proceeds through three primary phases: RECOGNITION, RELATIONSHIP and RESOLUTION.

The first benefit that comes from cultivating a mindfulness-based relationship with *dukkha* is that it breaks the prolifertion of habitual reactivity. Reactivity keeps us in bondage and ignorance, and keeps the emotional complex repressed. Nothing can change until we are able to establish a mindfulness-based relationship with our inner emotions.

Through careful and systematic attention, we learn to recognize our reactions and then we learn to recognize the *impulse* to react, before it manifests. We learn to see anger before it takes on the form of unskillful words and actions. We learn to notice reactions of frustration, irritability, impatience and disappointment, before they take hold. We learn to recognize the impulse that preceeds emotional reactions of fear and anxiety. Individual transformation, or transformation of conflict within relationships and families, depends on being able to recognize our habitual reactivity. As long as we remain blind to our reactivity and remain in the grip of *avijja*, nothing can change and *dukkha* will continue indefinitely.

Mindful recognition is an immensely important skill, especially if we also tune in to our habitual tendence to proliferate secondary emotional reactivity. If we cultivate an attentive relationship with reactions and refrain from reacting further with self-criticism and aversion or blind identification, then we open up a space in which real change becomes possible.

The second phase in MMT is to develop this non-reactive relationship and establish a *therapeutic space* around the emotional complex. This is called the RELATIONSHIP phase, where we build and sustain a relationship based on openness, compassion and stability of mind. In the mindfulness-based relationship, we cultivate complete presence with the felt-sense of the emotion.

The term "presence" is a particularly good description of the mindfulness-based relationship and indicates the sense of turning towards experience, including *dukkha*, rather than turning away from experience, which is exactly what happens when we react. When we are with a friend in need, or a child in pain, it is more often the quality of our presence that is sought, rather than our advice. In this same way, we can learn to be fully present for our inner pain, with complete attention, openness and friendliness, which is called *metta*. Through mindfulness we establish a safe zone in which the emotional complex can exist, unmolested by the ego and its patterns of secondary reactivity, and in which we as the observer can exist free from the compulsion to react. The direct experience of this quality of presence has a profound effect and is central to the therapeutic process. When both the observer and the observed are at peace with each other, transformation becomes a reality.

The third phase in MMT occurs spontaneously in the therapeutic space established through mindfulness, and involves the experiential unfolding and differentiation of feelings. This process leads to the transformation and eventual resolution of emotional reactivity and is called the RESOLUTION phase of Mindfulness Meditation Therapy.

All emotions including anger, depression, anxiety and fear or phobias have an internal structure, and there is a direct relationship between internal structure and the intensity of the emotion. A change in feeling produces a corresponding change in the internal structure and a change in the structure of an emotion changes the intensity of feeling. This is known as the Structural Theory of Emotions, which is central for understanding the process of psychological transformation.

In our usual state of reactivity and ignorance, we become blind to this inner structure and only see the superficial outer appearance of the emotional complex. However, with focused mindfulness, we discover that what first appeares in our consciousness as a solid emotion, like anger or fear, is actually a composite of many parts in the form of specific feelings, specific memories, specific bodily sensations and specific experiential imagery. This process of *differentiation* is extremely important in the therapeutic process and is greatly facilitated by mindfulness practice. Anger differentiates into fear, which further differentiates into sadness, which may give rise to internal imagery. This imagery differentiates further and we become aware of the sub-modalities of the imagery in the form of size, color, position and movement. Each of these subtle details encodes feeling energy, which accumulates and comes together to produce the emotional reaction.

Mindfulness is a movement in conscious awareness from the gross to the subtle; from the superficial to the actual; from the abstract to the concrete. Like the layers of an onion, mindfulness uncovers each layer of the inner structure of our core emotions to reveal finer and finer details. It is the very process of uncovering this detailed structure of experience and especially at the concrete level of the sub-modalities of inner imagery that leads to transformation and resolution of emotional complexes.

Emotional complexes are formed through the accumulation of patterns of secondary reactivity formed around a core primary emotional reaction, such as a traumatic memory. Through time, we become ignorant of the detailed structure of our emotions and all that remains is a superficial and abstract surface representation, which is very hard to change. It is only when we begin to consciously experience the specific objective content of the emotion that change becomes possible. This is an example of Sensory Enrichment, which is a natural consequence of mindfulness practice; we simply see more. It is a general rule that the more aware we become of the details of our experience, the greater the chance for beneficial change. It is the lack of conscious awareness, or *avijja*, that sustains and perpetuates habitual emotional reactivity, and it is what you don't see that does most harm. A primary function of mindfulness practice is to illuminate what was previously unknown and replace ignorance with clear knowing in the present.

Experiential Transformation occurs as the result of two fundamental psychological processes. These are described as Contact Resolution and Experiential Resolution. The process of Contact Resolution describes the direct healing effect that comes directly from forming a mindfulness-based relationship with emotional suffering. Experiential Resolution describes the healing that results from the unfolding of the internal structure of an emotion into specific contents.

CONTACT RESOLUTION

Perhaps one of the most remarkable effects of mindfulness (*sati*) is that the very act of making mindful contact with the feeling level of our inner emotional suffering is, by itself, transformational. When we focus mindfulness repeatedly on a painful feeling, it is quite usual to experience a softening in the intensity of the feeling. This is called Contact Resolution: the spontaneous healing that arises simply through responding to mental pain with mindfulness. This is not thinking about our pain, but being present with our pain and making contact with it through mindfulness.

From everyday experience, we know how important it is to listen with a completely open mind; to be fully present for our friends and loved ones when they are in pain. As is so often the case, it is not what we do or say that is as important as the quality of being with that person. Being attentive and compassionate, without any trace of reactivity, is what facilitates healing. A person needs to know that it is safe to open up, and the attitude of silent listening, the Noble Silence of mindfulness, creates this safe space. In this very same way, mindfulness creates a safe space in which repressed emotions can unfold and heal themselves. It is often sufficient to just touch the feeling level of the emotion with mindfulness, and simply be there for the emotion, with compassion, friendliness and patience. Repeat this over and over again and in time, you will develop a totally different way of relating and engaging with your inner *dukkha*. The quality of engaged-presence is one of the most transforming aspects of mindfulness. Put simply, when we touch *dukkha* with mindfulness, it responds by healing itself. As we let go of our suffering, which is what happens when we are mindful, it responds by letting go of us.

Being present means suspending the activities of the thinking mind and simply resting in complete open awareness to whatever we are contemplating. In the words of Eckhart Tolle,

> When you surrender to what is and become so fully present, the past ceases to have any power. The realm of Being, which had been obscured by the mind, then opens up. Suddenly, a great stillness arises within you, an unfathomable sense of peace. And within that peace there is great joy. And within that joy there is love. And at the innermost core there is the sacred, the immeasurable, That which cannot be named.

Healing the broken heart and spirit is brought about by engaged-presence, in which we learn to dance with the inner emotional suffering that is *dukkha*. This innate healing dance is beyond the world of concepts and ideas, but lies in the wisdom that arises when we let go of trying to fix things, and relax into the expansiveness of the pure knowing of things as they are.

EXPERIENTIAL RESOLUTION

Many of us experience patterns of habitual emotional reactivity that are persistent, that undermine our happiness, and that create havoc in our personal relationships. Working with this core emotional reactivity is one of the prime activities for *vipassana* meditation, because such complexes are a very potent source of *dukkha* and the prime mission for *vipassana* meditation, and *Dhamma* practice as taught by the Buddha, is to bring about the resolution of *dukkha*. Therefore, it is essential to search inwardly to find these inner demons and work directly on them with the tools of mindfulness meditation. The only way that we can transform them and become free of our emotional reactivity is by facing them, and this means embracing them with mindfulness.

Emotions are simply the outward expression of inner knots of "frozen" feeling energy that has become aggregated into a core emotional complex. In Mindfulness Meditation Therapy the central approach is to facilitate, through the application of mindfulness, the unfolding of this frozen inner feeling energy. Repeated mindfulness contact allows the frozen inner complex to unfold and it is the conscious awareness of this unfolding content that brings about transformation.

The Structural Theory of Emotions informs us that inner transformation happens when there is a change in the inner structure of the emotion. Through focusing mindfulness on the present felt-sense of an emotion, intangible and abstract emotions differentiate into tangible mental objects in the form of specific feelings, images and symbolic representations, which form the internal structure of the emotion. One of the most direct effects of mindfulness is that what first appears solid begins to differentiates into parts. An emotion seems solid on first appearance, but when you look more closely with mindfulness, you see the emotion as a complex system of moving parts. It is in the direct conscious awareness of this detailed inner structure of the emotion that brings about transformation and resolution of core emotional complexes.

Experiential unfolding begins with mindfulness (*sati*), which leads to *satisampajanna*, the intuitive awareness in which mental contents are seen with clarity and full consciousness in the present. Through *satisampajanna* the psyche gains access to all the data available from the depths of the mind, rather than being restricted to the incomplete and superficial products of reactivity. In this totality of experience arises the intuitive intelligence of *satipanna*, which directs the process of transformation, and that eventually leads to the resolution of *dukkha*. However, the process of transformation begins when we make conscious the inner structure of our experience. As Carl Jung said,

One does not become enlightened by imagining figures
of light, but by making the darkness conscious.

Consciousness awareness is the working space in which the psyche transforms and resolves inner emotional conflict, to create greater stability. To achieve this, the psyche must have access to the concrete experiential details of the inner structure of our emotions. The essence of Mindfulness Meditation Therapy and *vipassana* meditation is to make conscious the experiential details of our inner experience, not in the form of thoughts about experience, but in the direct present experience of body sensations, feelings and experiential imagery.

An emotion, like anger or anxiety, can seem very solid and impossible to change, but this is an illusion created by ignorance (*avijja*) of the deep structure of the emotion. This state of *avijja* is created and maintained by habitual reactivity in which we react with avoidance or resistance to the emotion of anger or depression. When *avijja* is dominant, these powerful emotions become our inner demons that control us and proliferate suffering and *dukkha*. They take on an illusory form in the same way that the shadow of a mouse projected onto a bedroom wall takes on the form of a monster. But, the fear that we experience is generated by the illusion, not reality. It is generated by the reaction to the aggregate of the emotional complex, rather than to the specific feelings and thoughts that make up an emotion like anxiety, depression, anger or grief.

Therefore, what is needed is to dissect the illusory emotional complex into its component parts: the intuitive feelings, memories, beliefs, and the inner symbolic imagery that always lies at the core of strong emotions. It is very difficult to change an abstract and superficial emotional construct, such as anger, anxiety or depression, because there is nothing tangible to grab hold of. However, once we reduce the emotion into its subtle experiential content, then we have something much more tangible to work with. Mindfulness provides the right inner therapeutic space in which an emotional complex will differentiate and unfold. When we meditate with mindfulness on an emotion, it will naturally and spontaneously differentiate into a variety of feelings that have aggregated together to form the complex structure of the emotion. Mindfulness practice can be thought of as the "reverse engineering" of the emotional complex, allowing us to rediscover the reality beneath the outward, illusory appearance of things.

If the mind becomes stuck at the level of blind superficial reactivity, then it is prevented from changing and the emotional complexes become frozen like a block of ice. This is the nature of emotional suffering, where emotional energy becomes frozen into *sankharas*, and this leads to reactivity and *dukkha*. When we bring mindfulness to these hard, frozen places, they respond by melting and becoming fluid again. Illumination with mindfulness brings warmth to each emotional knot and this promotes transformation and healing. The deeper we penetrate into the actual reality of experience with the warmth of mindfulness, the more we are able to change, or more accurately, the more our mind is able to change itself.

Emotions are complex aggregates of feeling energy, and mindfulness allows us to see these different qualities of feeling. An emotion like anger may seem very solid, but after *vipassana* meditation on the anger, it usually differentiates into all maner of more subtle feelings. We may notice a feeling of betrayal, which differentiates into sadness, followed by fear, which further differentiates into a feeling of emptiness. In other words, the structure of the emotion of anger contains many feelings that have been combined to form the emotion. Transformation happens when the emotional complex unfolds into conscious awareness and we clearly see each these feelings. In experiential transformation, you allow the experience to change by itself through this process of differentiation, and not from analytical thinking about the experience or what it means. You allow feelings to change in their own way, guided by your intuitive intelligence, rather than by your ideas about what is supposed to happen.

As is so often the case, the solution to our suffering lies within the suffering itself. What prevents suffering from naturally resolving is our inability to be fully present. We become seduced into secondary reactivity, in the form of avoidance, seeking more pleasurable thoughts and activities. Or we react with aversion and actively suppress the emotion through willpower. These secondary reactions of wanting and aversion take us away from the source of the *dukkha*, and this inhibits transformation. The other main form of reactivity that prevents transformation and the natural resolution of *dukkha* is delusion, where we blindly identify with the reactions that arise. This causes us to be overwhelmed by our reactivity, and nothing can change in a mind that is chained to becoming angry or depressed, sad or upset.

The Path of Mindfulness gives us the opportunity to break free of our usual habitual reactivity of wanting, aversion and delusion so that we can, perhaps for the first time, be fully present with our anger, grief, sadness, disappointment and frustration. Mindfulness helps us awaken to *dukkha* as it is, and it is through awakening to *dukkha* that *dukkha* will transform and resolve itself. This is the First Noble Truth: the truth of suffering as taught by the Buddha. In order to resolve suffering, we must first awaken to suffering, internally and externally.

13 THE SEVEN FACTORS OF AWAKENING

The process of experiential transformation that happens during mindfulness practice and *vipassana* meditation involves seven key mental factors, which, when developed, lead to the resolution of *dukkha*, and freedom from *samsara*. These are known as the Seven Factors of Awakening, called *bojjhanga* in Pali, which is derived from the root *budhi*, to "awaken." These seven factors are mindfulness (*sati*), investigation of the true nature of mental phenomena (*dhammavicaya*), energy (*viriya*), rapture (*piti*), tranquility (*passaddhi*), concentration and stability (*samadhi*), and equanimity (*upekkha*). These factors build on each other in a sequence, beginning with the all-important foundation of mindfulness.

Mindfulness

The seven factors of awakening and transformation proceed in a stepwise fashion, where each factor becomes the foundation for the next and not surprisingly, the first foundation for transformation is mindfulness, *sati*. Nothing can change until we break free of our habitual reactivity, and we are able to open our heart mind to fully contemplate *dukkha*. Our fundamental enemy is blind reactivity, and mindfulness is our primary weapon against the unawareness, or *avijja*, that sustains reativity.

After we have learned to recognize our patterns of reactivity, we must proceed to the second part of the response of mindfulness, which is to establish a relationship with our inner experience. When we have established a mindfulness-based relationship, we create a therapeutic space in which experience can unfold and differentiate. With *sati* as foundation, *satisampajanna* and *satipanna* arise, and all three interact to facilitate transformation and the eventual resolution of *dukkha*, if suffering exists. A solid foundation in mindfulness also protects us from falling victim to mental reactivity, which will always arise as a natural function of the mind. But, even more than this, mindfulness provides the foundation that allows us to fully experience life, to be fully present with all that we experience, both internally and externally. It leads to sensory enrichment and full authetic living in the world. With mindfulness well cultivated, life becomes a vibrant dance in which we live in perfect balance with all that we encounter.

Investigation

The second factor is *dhammavicaya*, the investigation of *dhammas*, which means that we choose to investigate the inner structure of our experience. If we are meditating on an emotional reaction, then we investigate the emotion and look beneath the surface and allow the emotional complex to differentiate.

Mindfulness is like a spotlight that serves to illuninate, but this is not sufficient by itself to resolve suffering. For mindfulness to become a transformational force, it must be combined with investigation, which means moving beneath the superficial appearance of things to see the totality of things as they are. It is not sufficient to just recognize *dukkha* and the mental afflictions; we must proceed to the second step, which is to investigate them in depth. Therefore, it is the combination of *sati* and *dhammavicaya* that lays the foundation that leads to the transformation of emotional suffering and for our eventual liberation from *samsara*.

When we establish *sati-dhammavicaya*, we simultaneously awaken to the universal characteristic of *anicca*, the impermanent and dynamic nature of all phenomena. No longer stuck at the superficial perception of things, we allow experience to become fluid and malleable and allow it to change in accordance with its innate nature. Living in harmony with *anicca* is a fundamental characteristic of the awakened mind and is a natural consequence of mindfulness, and facilitates the process of intelligent change that leads to the resoltion of *dukkha* and emotional suffering.

All forms of *dukkha* are states of psychological and spiritual instability in which emotional energy is trapped in the internal structure of the emotion. Nature does not tolerate instability and will always seek to resolve instability, if there is freedom in the mind. When we harmonize with *anicca* we simply allow things to change in the therapeutic space of inner freedom provided by mindfulness and conscious awareness.

When we have established *dhammavicaya*, we not only see more of the detailed structure of our experience, perceptions and our emotions, but we also gain direct insight into what needs to change such that *dukkha* resolves itself. This is opening to the inner truth of our suffering, and it is this truth that liberates, not the efforts of the ego. In essence, we provide the freedom of consciousness that allows the psyche to heal itself, which it is very capable of doing. However, it we have to create the right conditions that allow the natural and intuitive flow of intelligent change. Any resistance or attachment to form simply obstructs this innate and intelligent change. In fact, *dukkha* can be defined as the suffering that results from the resistance to change, the reactivity against *anicca* that inhibits the innate intelligence of *satipanna*.

Besides awakening to *anicca*, the practice of *satidhammavicaya* also helps us awaken to *anatta*, or not self, not mine. *Anatta* is simply a way of describing a relationship to experience that is free from attachment (*upadana*) to the habitual reactions of a self or ego. Clearly, nothing will change if you continue to blindly identify with your habitual patterns of emotional reactivity. There must be freedom to relate to all experience, internal or external. We must also have the freedom to relate to each emotional reaction that arises out of conditioning; to each manifestation of *dukkha*, and this requires a relationship based on mindfulness and not on further habitual reactivity of the ego (*atta*) conditioned by the past.

With the combination of mindfulness and investigation, we are in that very moment, letting go of our attachment to the superficial ego and allowing things to unfold in a natural way. We become the *knowing* of this process of unfolding and change, and this is the essence of our real self as a dynamic process, rather than as a static collection of habitual reactions. *Anatta* does not mean that we have no self, but rather that we are infinitely more complex than anything we can know. Awakening to *anatta* means that we awaken to ourself as a process that is not fixated on the contents of our conscious experience. We are the knowing of our emotional reations, our thoughts and beliefs, but none of this content constitutes our essential self.

Through these awakenings to *anicca* and *anatta*, *dhammavicaya* represents the flowering of wisdom, *panna*, and it is this wisdom-intelligence that heals, transforms and liberates us from the grip of *dukkha* and the causes of *dukkha* to reveal the purity and happiness of the original Buddha mind, which is our true nature.

Energy

The third *bojjhanga* is energy, *viriya*. This represents the courageous application of energy and effort required to sustain mindfulness and investigation so that awakening can occur.

When we are in a blind reactive mode of feeling angry, frustrated or worried, the mind follows a familiar and habitual path that simply perpetuates suffering. It requires effort to overcome these negative habits of contracted and conditioned thinking. We need to direct our efforts intelligently, which means that we are always keenly aware of what is skillful and wholesome and leads to the resolution of suffering.

The Buddha described four kinds of effort that should be developed. The first right effort is to root out the underlying patterns of reactivity that cause us to act unskilfully. The second right effort is to stop unwholesome reactions that have arisen, through the application of mindfulness. On the positive side, the third right effort is to develop dormant wholesome responses that lead to freedom, happiness and well-being, and the fourth right effort is to cultivate these qualities once they have arisen.

Right Effort, which is one of the factors of the Noble Eightfold Path, requires that we make the effort to identify *dukkha* and any form of emotional suffering and instability that exists in the mind, and investigate each with care and attention. The Path of Mindfulness is a courageous path of actively searching for *dukkha* and choosing to embrace our emotional suffering face-to-face. Meditation is not an escape from suffering, but the opportunity to work on our suffering with mindfulness, compassion and wisdom. With this understanding, we can choose to make our anger, depression, fear, grief or disappointment the very objects for our meditation. We become the hunter, rather than the victim, and we deliberately search for inner suffering, rather than waiting for it to find us. We might call this a "search-and-destroy mission," as we seek to uproot our mental afflictions, but actually it would be better to describe this noble path as a "search-and-heal" mission.

However, there is more to *viriya* than just the application of effort. *Viriya* refers to the spiritual energy of the psyche that supports life and brings vitality into our being. When we become locked into patterns of habitual reactivity, we loose this vitality and aliveness, and become slaves. The purpose of mindfulness meditation is to liberate this trapped energy so that we become more alive and more able to engage passionately with life. We wake up from our sleep and discover our true essence and authenticity as a living, dynamic being, imbued with the spiritual energy of *viriya*.

Rapture

As *dukkha* resolves in the therapeutic space of mindfulness, emotional energy is released back into the psyche. The release of trapped emotional energy is experienced as the energizing feeling of rapture (*piti*), which is the fourth factor of awakening. This is the rapture of empowerment that permeates the whole psyche. It is like the joy of a slave who finally sheds his chains and rejoices in his freedom. It takes a lot of energy to maintain habitual reactivity and *dukkha*, and elation naturally follows when we break free from the chains that keep us bound to our reactivity. The more we investigate the detailed inner structure of our emotions, the more likely it will be that they change, releaseing trapped energy in the process. This is the tase of freedom, which is the sweetest of all tastes and the greatest of all pleasures.

Besides the happiness that comes from the release from bondage and from *dukkha*, there is another quality of elation that is called Sensory Enrichment and that comes from waking up to the fullness and the inherent richness of life. Living in the grip of reactivity limits and distorts our perception of both internal and external sensory experience, and we see only the lifeless superficial appearance of things. This produces dullness in the mind and a sense of insufficiency and emptiness. Superficiality and ignorance lead to sensory deprivation at both the experiential and spiritual levels, and *dukkha* is intimately connected with attachment to the superficial appearance of things.

Contrast this with the alive and engaged investigation of experience that comes with mindfulness coupled with investigation. There is a natural and universal excitement that comes from learning new things and coming to know the intricacies and wonders of nature. The more we tune in to the experience of the truth of things, the more we feel connected. If all you see of a waterfall is your own distorted perceptions, then you are denying yourself the richness of experience that is naturally inherent in that phenomenon. If you can see and experience the same waterfall with a mind that is completely open, present and engaged, then your experience will be infinitely more rewarding.

The same principle applies to how you engage in a hobby or any other activity. The more engaged you are, the more you will enjoy the experience. This is the rapture of sensory enrichment and the natural joy that arises when there is *sati-dhammavicaya* and when we are fully engagement with all the different aspects of our life and relationships.

Tranquility

After the elation that follows from the release of trapped emotional energy, the psyche finds a new state of balance, stability and tranquility. This is the fifth factor of awakening, called *passaddhi*. The release of psychological and spiritual energy brings peacefulness, not only to the mind (*citta passaddhi*), but also to the body (*kaya passaddhi*). The mind and body relax into the experience of freedom, and this quality of being settled and at rest provides the foundation for all spiritual growth.

As the mind settles, it is like the sky clearing after a thunderstorm, or a lake returning to a mirror-like stillness after a storm. Just as the natural resting state for water is complete stillness, so the psyche will return to its natural state of tranquility, if given the freedom to change. This is a profound inner calm that is produced by the healing action of our innate wisdom-intelligence, or *satipanna*. The mind returns to its natural pure state of calm and stillness, no longer agitated by the winds of attachment and ignorance.

Samadhi

Following resolution and the re-integration of emotional energy into a more stable state, the mind becomes naturally very steady and collected. This state of stability is called *samadhi*, the sixth factor of enlightenment.

When the mind becomes more energetically stable and unified, we are better able to interact with phenomena, and are less likely to become reactive and agitated. The mind becomes steady in the face of the experiential complexity of our world, able to "multi-task" without losing balance. *Samadhi* is not so much a state of concentration, which is the usual translation of the word, as a state of stability and inner strength in relation to the contents of our experience. Certainly, when this mental stability is well developed, it becomes easier to establish concentration and focused attention, but that is more to do with the application of *samadhi*; the application of a steady mind.

The word *samadhi* is derived from *sam-*, meaning "complete, all together, integrated," *a-* meaning "towards" and *-dha* meaning, "to hold or contain." *Samadhi* refers to a state of stability and composure in the relationship that we have with the contents of our mind. It is that quality of mind that can hold and contain any sensory experience, pleasant or painful, without becoming reactive and corrupted by the forces of attraction, aversion and blind identification.

Samadhi and *sati* are frequently mentioned together throughout the Buddha's discourses, and along with energy (*viriya*), faith (*saddha*) and wisdom (*panna*), forms the five spiritual factors that facilitate transformation and liberation from *samsara*. *Sati* and *samadhi* are the inseparable twins that work together to generate *panna*. Mindfulness counteracts reactivity and allows the mind to settle down and tune in to experience. In turn, *samadhi* supports mindfulness, because a settled mind is better able to observe the mind. In fact, *samadhi* should always arise out of a foundation of mindfulness, rather than through forced concentration. Conventional concentration is analogous to looking through a microscope and focusing on a very narrow field to the exclusion of other things that might be happening. *Samadhi*, on the other hand has a much broader focus that allows us to embrace whatever arises in the mind. In actuality, *samadhi* covers the whole spectrum, from highly focused attention on a single object at one end, to the open awareness of changing phenomena at the other end. However, the theme that unites all forms of *samadhi* is stability and non-reactivity in relationship to phenomena.

In *vipassana* meditation, we develop the form of *samadhi* that is able to greet all the unfolding content of our experience: all the thoughts, memories, perceptions, feelings and physical sensations, and yet remain free from attachement and reactivity. We even learn to become non-reactive to conditioned reactions themselves, when they arise. This great nimbleness of mind is one of the characteristics of *samadhi* that we develop during *vipassana* meditation, and is called *khanika-samadhi*. Usually translated as momentary concentration, or moving *samadhi*, this mental factor allows us to maintain clarity and freedom, no matter what arises, internally or externally. We are able to be fully present and fully engaged with anything that arises in the mind or in our world and remain free to respond out of wisdom, rather than react out of habit. This can be described as the "dance of *samadhi*," because just like a dance, one has to be free to respond to the subtle changes of your partner, and yet remain stable and not pulled off balance by your partener's movements. As in a dance, stability comes from intelligent responsiveness and cannot be forced. The state of *samadhi* is not a forced state of concentration as is sometimes prortayed, but a very skillful enagagement with all the ups and downs of life, as we experience them from moment to moment.

In practice, the factor of *samadhi* means that we develop stability in our relationship to whatever arises in our experience, including the emotional reactions of the habitual ego. Anxiety, anger, grief or suffering may arise, but when *samadhi* is present, we are no longer seduced into further secondary reactivity. *Samadhi* simply describes the state of freedom from the compulsion to react. With *samadhi* well established, we can be fully present for our pain, without reacting with worry, aversion or the proliferation of further emotional reactivity and suffering. *Samadhi* also helps us be fully present for the pain and suffering of others, and the stability of *samadhi* is the beginning of true compassion and true unconditioned love, known as *metta*. In general terms, we can say that *samadhi* protects us from the excesses of greed, hatered and delusion so that we can be more present, not only for our own needs, but the needs of others as well.

Traditionally, *samadhi* describes the state in which the mind has overcome the Five Hindrances (*nivarana*) of sensual desire, ill will, apathy and mental fatigue, agitation and worry, and spiritual doubt. We are no longer seduced into habitual patterns of blind wanting or aversion, or endless thinking and worrying. We no longer allow ourselves to be overwhelmed by life or by our subjective emotional reactions when things don't go to plan.

If wanting arises, we see it as just the objective phenomenon of wanting. We don't identify with it, become it, or react to it; we simply see it as it is, an as a phenomenon to be known, fully. If hatred arises, we simply see it as a hate-thought. We don't let ourselves become entangled in hatred, but observe the hatred with mindfulness. If apathy or rigidity arises, we observe this state of mind as it is, without reacting or becoming apathetic. If anxiety or agitation arises, we relate to these thought-emotions with mindfulness, rather than proliferating speculative thinking and worry. If uncertainty or doubt, or feelings of low self-confidence arise, we don't blindly accept them and become these emotions, but observe them with mindfulness. This is how we can keep the dance of *samadhi* alive and moving. We settle on nothing and attach to nothing, but engage mindfully with everything.

Equanimity

With the mind stabilized, unified and free from the force of reactivity, we now find ourselves able to live and respond fully to life. We can respond to the desirable or the unpleasant sensual experiences of life, without becoming seduced into patterns of blind attachment and reactivity. This freedom to respond with equanimity is the seventh factor of spiritual awakening, called *upekkha*. Liberated from the compulsive grip of the habitual reactivity of the ego, we are free to respond to life with complete presence of mind. This quality of non-reactive pesence allows us to respond with balance, clarity, compassion and wisdom. When *uppekha* is well established, then we can begin to experience the true nature of compassion and love.

Just as *sati* helps us perfect the art of relationship and presence with whatever we experience, internally or externally, *uppekha* helps us develop the art of responding to whatever we experience, internally or externally, with real freedom, choice and balance.

To transform our lives, we must take the challenge and face every manifestation of *dukkha*, from the petty irritations and disappointments of the day, through to the intense pain of trauma, loss and grief. If we choose to work with *dukkha* in all its forms, then *dukkha* will be changed from being our enemy, to being our teacher, and we will grow and become stronger. It is only through awakening to *dukkha* with mindfulness and investigation that we can unleash the natural process that leads to inner transformation and freedom. Only then can we develop the noble qualities of compassion, kindness, genuine virtue and wisdom in our relationship to other people and to our world.

14 THE APPLICATIONS OF MINDFULNESS

Mindfulness meditation, or *vipassana* sessions, are for the purpose of applying mindfulness in depth to heal inner conflicts, dissolve underlying attachments and liberate the mind from patterns of habitual reactivity. However, meditation sessions should be regarded as an integral part of a much bigger picture, which is the development of mindfulness throughout the day in our moment-to-moment living. As the Buddha said in the *Satipatthana Sutta*,

> Mindfulness, O disciples, I declare is essential in all things everywhere. It is as salt is to the curry.

Ultimately, The Path of Mindfulness practice is for developing mindfulness in all aspects of life, as outlined in the Noble Eightfold Path, so that mindfulness becomes the foundation for all the activities of body, speech and mind. Right mindfulness practice (*sammasati*) should begin the moment you open your eyes in the morning and continue through the day until the very last moment before falling asleep. Every moment of mindfulness is of great value, whether in meditation or daily activities, because each moment of mindfulness helps counteract the force of reactivity and ignorance, and helps cultivate equanimity and freedom so that we can discover what is skillful and wholesome action.

The Path of Mindfulness, or *satipatthana* in Pali, includes three levels of mindfulness practice: AWARENESS, CONTEMPLATION and MEDITATION. We can think of mindfulness practice as a continuum between the vigilance of moment-to-moment mindfulness throughout the day at one end, and concentrated *vipassana* meditation sessions at the other end. In between these two extremes, we can also apply mindfulness in short periods of contemplation and reflection on emotional reactions as and when they arise during the day.

Whenever we practice mindfulness, the objective is the same, which is to become more present and more aware of every part of our internal and external experience. Similarly, the purpose of our practice is the same, which is to purify the mind and purify our ac-

tions so that every action and thought is directed towards the resolution of *dukkha* and the causes of suffering, internally and externally.

MINDFUL-AWARENESS

Mindfulness practice, in any context, begins by cultivating awareness and waking up to what you are doing, both mentally and
physically, in the present moment. It also means becoming more
aware of your sensory experience of the world, seeing things in
more detail and in "full color," rather than seeing only the black-
and-white perceptions of the limited reactive mind. You learn to be
more awake and more present with everything that you encounter:
whether externally as sense impressions through the five sense
doors, or internally as thoughts, emotions and other mind objects.
The foundation for all mindfulness meditation is just this: learning
to be *present* for anything that you encounter through your sesnses.

Sensory Awareness

You can strengthen Sensory Awareness by deliberately choosing to
cultivate mindfulness during any activity such as walking, breathing, or washing the dishes. As you gain experience through deliberate practice with one task, you then expand this mindfulness to
take in more and more physical activities until mindfulness becomes a continuous response to life. The goal is to develop unin-
terrupted mindfulness throughout the day and to be aware of
whatever you are doing while you are doing it.

Mindfulness of breathing, called *anapanasati* is a technique
greatly favored by the Buddha for developing the faculty of mindfulness. He taught this simple practice as the foundation from
which we can cultivate the four *satipatthanas* of body, feelings,
thought reactions, and truth. Practicing mindfulness of in and out
breathing helps us develop the acuity of awareness needed for
working with the much more challenging habitual reactions and
powerful feelings that tend to dominate the mind. We breathe
every minute, and indeed our life depends on this activity, yet how
often are we actually aware of our breathing?

166

The practice of *anapanasati*, like all mindfulness practice, helps us awaken to the detailed structure of experience. When we investigate breathing, we see that it involves a flow of many subtle physical sensations. In reality, there is no such thing as an in-breath or an out-breath. These are just labels. The reality is in the changing sensations, and nothing else. This provides our first glimps of *anicca*, impermanence, and *anatta*, not self. There is no separate entity called breath that can be dissected away from this continual process of changing sensations. This is the essential insight that we carry to all other areas of our experience, including the emotions and beliefs that form our personality. These too will be subjected to this same investigation with mindfulness, and we will also learn to let go of the superficial initial perception of mental objects to reveal the subtle details of the experience in depth. This movement from superficiality to reality is the essence of all mindfulness practice, and it is in this process that we discover freedom from *dukkha*.

The practice of *anapanasati* begins with simply being aware of taking an in-breath and an out-breath. The awareness proceeds to noticing whether the breath is long or short, fast or slow, shallow or deep. Some breaths may be very smooth, while others are eratic. Soon, we begin to realize that even a simple and unquestioned activity like breathing is actually a complex movement of changing sensations. Being aware of sensations is the first function of mindfulness; the enrichment of sensory awareness that comes from paying close attention is the second function of mindfulness. The third function of mindfulness that we develop through this simple practice is to develop the still center of pure knowing, which is *samadhi*, or steadiness and stability of awareness.

Each physical sensation arises as a sense object in this field of awareness; it exists for a brief moment, and then passes away. We observe this happening over and over again, without interference or any sense of trying to make things happen. We are learning to be the center of our conscious awareness, which is the pure knowing of sensations, as they arise, do their dance, and pass away. We become the *knowing* itself, and this represents a major shift away from unknowing, or *avijja*, and reacting based on attachment. Sensory phenomena move around this center while we remain still.

167

This *pure knowing* is called *satisampajanna*, and represents a fundamental shift from being reactive, to being responsive. This shift in perception allows us to relate to phenemena with freedom and in this state of freedom, innate intelligence can transform, heal and purify. Therefore *anapanasati* is useful as a preparation for mindfulness of the mind and its reactive contents, and a prelude to *vipassana* meditation, or the in-depth investigation of mental contents through mindfulness.

Mindful-Awareness of Habitual Reactivity

Through the practice of general sensory awareness, we lay the foundations for the next, and more challenging task, which is to cultivate mindfulness of our patterns of habitual reactivity as they arise during the day. The sooner we learn to recognize the many impulses to react, the easier it will be to prevent unskillful reactions of body, speech and mind from manifesting. Throughout the day, we can train ourself to recognize reactive impulses as soon as they arise and respond to them with mindfulness. This is something that we repeat over and over again until no impulses to react go unchecked. This is a fundamental part of deconditioning the mind from years of accumulated habitual reactivity.

Most people can recognize anger or other intense forms of emotional reactivity, but remain oblivious to the more subtle forms of agitation, such as disappointment, frustration and irritation. Suppose you want to go for a walk, but it starts raining. Habit causes you to react with a feeling of disappointed. Be vigilant and notice the impulse to react before it takes hold, and respond to the impulse with mindfulness. The more you practice responding with mindfulness instead of reacting, the more you will develop the power of mindfulness as an alternative to habitual reactivity. Reactivity is simply a learned habit based on ignorance and unawareness. These can be directly overcome through mindfulness training and simply learning to recognize each and every habitual reaction as it arises and stopping right there.

Driving a car is a wonderful opportunity for practicing Mindful-Awareness. You find yourself in heavy traffic and start to react with impatience. STOP. Catch yourself and respond with mindfulness. If you react out of habit, then you will simply make yourself miserable and create more *dukkha*. This is how *dukkha* arises and perpetuates itself. Every time you react out of blind attachment, you strengthen *dukkha*; every time you STOP and respond with *sati*, you weaken the force of habit and the cause of *dukkha*. This is the beginning of the path to freedom and it is really very simple, but the art is to recognize reactions as soon as they arise and to respond with mindfulness. There is nothing that you need to do, other than recognize the impulse to react and respond with mindfulness.

A driver cuts in front of you. Your habit is to react with anger. STOP and say "No! Thank you. I choose not to react that way." Don't be seduced by the impulse to react, and become the anger. It is nothing more than a habit, and like any habit it thrives on ignorance, but all habits can be changed by cultivating mindful-awareness. It is also worth reminding yourself that there is no law that compels you to react with anger. Any reaction is simply a conditioned response that has been acquired unconsciously. In the end, it is your choice whether you perpetuate *dukkha* through reacting, or cultivate choice through the practice of mindfulness.

Each and every impulse to react is either going to create more *dukkha* through blind reactivity, or that same reaction can be used as an opportunity to undo the habit of reactivity and gain greater mental stability and freedom. In this way you actually use your habitual reactivity as a vehicle for developing greater freedom, choice and happiness, instead of simply feeding the habit of *samsara*. The more you develop awareness of your reactivity throughout the day, the more chance you will have to break the habit and begin a process of change for the better.

Throughout the day you will be bombarded by impulses to react with anger, frustration, disappointment, sadness and worry, as well as temptations to indulge in obsessive sensory gratification, fantasy and other forms of escape. Many of these impulses to react are minor, like swarms of biting insects while others may be quite painful or emotionally intense, like the bites from wild dogs. Obviously, it is essential to train yourself to be mindful of intense reactions, such as anger or jealousy, as these can have far reaching negative effects on your state of mind and happiness. But, it is also just as important to train your awareness to detect the "biting in-

169

sects," of smaller irritations, because their negative effects are cumulative. The practice of Mindful-Awareness helps you recognize each and every impulse, no matter how big or small, so that you can cultivate freedom and choice, and prevent unskillful actions from taking form. This will be a great improvement over blind habitual reactivity, in which you have no choice and very limited freedom.

Of course, sometimes the impulse to react may be very strong and requires more attention than we can give it during the heat of the moment, and this leads to the next level of mindfulness practice, the practice of Mindful-Contemplation.

MINDFUL-CONTEMPLATION

A further development of Mindful-Awareness in active daily life is to find a few minutes to "sit" with any strong emotional reactions that may arise. Mindful-Contemplation is essentially a mini-meditation session, in which you devote more time to explore the feeling level of the emotion or impulse to react. This is a form of *cittanupassana*, the contemplation of mind states, which is intermediate between the practice of Mindful-Awareness and *vipassana* meditation.

When you notice anxiety, anger or any form of mental agitation, try to find a few minutes to simply be mindful of these states of mind and the underlying feelings. The primary task is to simply make contact with the emotion and give it space in which to exist and change. A few quality moments spent being mindful with our inner emotions can have profound effects over time. You do not need to try and resolve the emotion or analyze it during these periods of Mindful-Contemplation; it is sufficient to simply be present with each of them. In many ways, these mini-meditation sessions are more important than long, formal meditation sessions, because they allow you to access emotional reactions soon after they arise and when they are still fresh in your mind. Often, anger, worry or fear will not arise outside of real life situations with all the associated stimulatory triggers, and of course, this is precisely where you most need to cultivate mindfulness.

170

The practice of *cittanupassana* in meditation or in reflective contemplation is simply learning to be present with your emotions with patience and non-reactivity. There is no need to do anything other than give them your full attention, and trust in your intuitive intelligence (*satipanna*). You will be surprised how many problems will resolve themselves quite effortlessly if you stop feeding them with worry or other secondary reactivity. This may seem like a path of non-action, but what you are actually doing is opening your mind to the totality of your experience, both internally and externally, which you cannot see when you are locked into worrying or reactive thinking. The spontaneous healing that can arise as a consequence of being fully present with our pain is called Contact Resolution and mindful-contemplation provides the opportunity to have many of these quality encounters throughout the day. Mindful-Contemplation is like a runner taking a few minutes to massage his muscles and relax the inner tension. This simple practice can prevent muscles from cramping and causing injury and pain. The practice of Mindful-Contemplation can also stop the mind from cramping and becoming contracted and creating further *dukkha*.

MINDFULNESS MEDITATION

Meditation is simply the focused application of mindfulness and vigilant awareness to explore things in depth. Mindfulness Meditation includes the mental factors of mindfulness (*sati*), concentration (*samadhi*) and investigation (*dhammavicaya*) that allow us to explore the inner structure of our experience. There are, of course, many different types of meditation, but the meditation described throughout this book is called *vipassana* meditation, or "insight meditation." This kind of meditation cultivates insight into the detailed inner structure of experience, combined with insight into process of transformation that leads to freedom from suffering. *Vipassana* meditation is an in-depth exploration of the inner world of our experience, and through this direct knowing, we discover liberation from the attachments and reactivity that create and sustain emotional suffering.

171

The term *vipassana* has the root *vi* meaning "behind" or "within," *pas*, which means "seeing," and *na*, which means "knowing." A common translation of *vipassana* is "insight," although *vipassana* insight operates at a much deeper experiential level and refers to the *process* of seeing and knowing, rather than any insight-knowledge produced. *Vipassana* insights are not ideas, concepts or knowledge that we acquire and then use to change our behavior, as might occur in conventional psychotherapy, but the process of transformation that results from what is seen. In *vipassana* meditation it is the direct knowing itself that leads to the awakening of intuitive and transformational wisdom-intelligence. *Vipassana* is awakening to the truth in each moment of our ongoing experience, and it is the dircect perception of this truth that leads to freedom. Krishnamurti expresses this beautifully in the following passage:

> When the mind is still, tranquil, not seeking any answer or any solution, neither resisting nor avoiding – it is only then that there can be a regeneration, because then the mind is capable of perceiving what is true; and it is truth that liberates, not your effort to be free.

As with all mindfulness practice, *vipassana* meditation is the process of establishing a special kind of relationship with our inner experience, with our core emotions, thoughts, memories and beliefs. This special relationship is a movement in stillness, openness, listening with complete attention and full presence with whatever we choose to investigate with mindfulness. Through this quality of complete presence, which is *satisampajanna*, we create a therapeutic space that allows access to the deeper and more intuitive level of our experience. Meditation provides a more intimate and complete level of relationship than is possible in the chaos of daily life and Mindfulness Meditation is the perfect complement to the practice of Mindful-Awareness and Mindful-Contemplation.

In *vipassana* meditation the focus is on developing pure undeluded knowing (*satisampajanna*) of mental phenomena (*dhammas*) as they arise in present moment-to-moment experience, but with the added factors of investigation (*dhammavicaya*) and concentration (*samadhi*). *Vipassana* meditation is an exploration of the depth of experience, which is essential for the resolution of emotional suffering, and for developing experiential insight and wisdom. It may not be possible during the practice of general mindful awareness throughout the day to explore our experience in depth, so it is useful to set aside a period of time for the focused application of mindfulness on the emotional content of the mind. However, whether we are engaged in general mindfulness practice or *vipassana* meditation, the direction is the same, which is to know phenomena directly in a way that leads to liberation from the grip of habitual reactivity.

Mindful-Investigation

Mindfulness begins with the wakeful vigilance of *sati* that brings us into mindful-contact with our present experience, whether arising internally or externally. Establishing this non-reactive awareness and compete presence is the second step of mindfulness practice called *satisampajanna*, and the beginning of the process of transfromation. However, it is only the beginning and we must take a third step after making contact, which is to investigate our experience in depth. This will reveal the vertical dimension, the deeper structure of our experience, which is not obvious and not apparent, but becomes apparent through investigation. To quote Ray Mears, the popular teacher of outdoor survival skills,

> The secret of survival is to learn to look into the wilderness rather than just at it.

Investigation into the structure of our experience is called *dhammavicaya*. The term *dhamma* refers to the objective reality or truth of any mental phenomenon. Therefore, *dhammavicaya* means investigation into the actual objective truth of experience, which can only be revealed when we stop reacting, because the reactivity of the subjective ego simply diverts our attention away from what is actually present.   Mindfulness is not simply being aware of sense objects and mental objects as they arise, but a dynamic response to what arises. This is the response of investigation, *dhammavicaya*, and this is why *dhammavicaya* is listed as the second of the Seven

Factors of Enlightenment, after the first foundation, which is *sati*. Mindfulness naturally leads to investigation and the combination of *sati-dhammavicaya* paves the way for transformation.

Each mind moment (*citta*) consists of a dynamic collage of mental factors: the five *khandhas* of thought reactions (*sankhara*), perceptions (*sanna*), associated feeling tones (*vedana*), consciousness (*vinnana*) and the physical aspect of experience (*rupa*). This collage of inner experience becomes condensed into a thought or emotion that takes shape and arises in consciousness as a *sankhara*. However, a *sankhara* is nothing more than a superficial representation of experience. Just as a word is not the thing it represents, so the initial conscious form of a thought, belief, emotion or other *sankhara* does not equate to the totality of our experience. Unfortunately, the mind has a strong tendency to become identified with these abstract labels, and becomes dissociated from the reality of the underlying deep structure of our experience. This is the nature of *avijja*, which has the effect of inhibiting transformation, and keeping alive our dysfunctional and habitual patterns of reactivity.

Nowhere is this more apparent than in the realm of our inner emotional suffering. For example if anxiety arises, we typically identify with the surface appearance of the emotion, the *sankhara*, and loose sight of the specific perceptions, feelings, memories and thoughts that form the inner structure of the emotion. In effect, we become attached to the supeficial illusion and shadows cast by our anxiety-*sankhara*, and in this state of ignorance and delusion, nothing can change and the anxiety cannot transform and resolve itself. This blind attachment to the *sankharas* that arise in the mind is the fundamental cause of all our suffering, and it is this blind attachment that we seek to dissolve through the practice of mindfulness.

The mind always benefits from investigation into the truth of mental phenomena, of *dhammas*, and as we uncover the inner structure of our emotions and beliefs, we will begin to see the rich and dynamic reality of what lies below the surface, and it is the conscious illumination of this inner reality that leads to transformation. This is what Krishnamurti means by the statement, "It is the truth that liberates, not our efforts to be free."

When we follow The Path of Mindfulness, the direction of our practice is always to move from the superficial to the actual inner structure of our experience; from the abstract to the concrete; from the gross to the subtle; from illusion to truth. With Mindful-Investigation, we see experience as a process that is continually changing, unfolding, and rich in detail. When we relate to experience, including our experience of *dukkha* in this way, we begin to harmonize with the truth of experience as a dynamic process of change and we create the freedom in which intelligent change can occur.

If all we see is the surface structure of our experience, then only partial change is possible. If we open to the totality of experience through Mindful-Investigation, then complete transformation becomes a reality. In order to heal *dukkha*, we must first awaken to suffering, and then investigate suffering through focused mindfulness to uncover the truth beneath the surface. As truth becomes conscious, our innate wisdom-intelligence will have the material needed to bring about complete transformation.

15 THE CULTIVATION OF MINDFULNESS

In the *Satipatthana Sutta*, the Buddha describes in great detail the importance of mindfulness (*sati*) and how *sati* is to be applied, cultivated and established. The suffix *–patthana* means "foundation, to establish, to keep steadfast," so *satipatthana* means to develop, cultivate and establish mindfulness. *Satipatthana* is the Pali term for The Path of Mindfulness; the path of awakening to each moment of our life and being fully present and fully engaged with each experience as it arises and unfolds. *Satipatthana* is at the very heart of Buddhist meditative practice, and developing the skill of mindfulness is essential for spiritual development and for the purification of the mind.

It is understood that the purification of our mind through the elimination of negative habitual reactivity also leads to the purification of our actions. Through freeing our mind and heart, we enhance our ability to be truly present for others so that we may bring peace and happiness into their lives, as well. Therefore, *satipatthana* is the primary vehicle for the purification of *Sila*, or morality and right behavior. *Satipatthana* is also the primary means for developing *Panna*, the wisdom-intelligence that leads to the resolution of suffering. *Satipatthana* is also essential for the development of *Samadhi*, the cultivation of mental stability and non-reactivity in relation to internal and external phenomena. These three roots of *Sila*, *Panna* and *Samadhi* are the embodiment of the Noble Eightfold Path, which can best be understood as the cultivation of mindfulness in all aspects of our life.

The *Satipatthana Sutta* begins with the unambiguous statement:

> Monks, this is the direct path for the purification of beings, for the overcoming of sorrow and distress, for the disappearance of *dukkha* and discontent, for the gaining of the right path, for the realization of *Nibbana*, namely the four *satipatthanas*.

The Path of Mindfulness is described as the direct path, because it works with the moment-to-moment experience of life, rather than trying to transform the mind indirectly through the beliefs. One of the immediate consequences of a direct path is that we can experience the fruits of liberation from *dukkha* from moment to moment. Liberation is not a goal that we reach after years of study, or the application of methods that we are told will transform our suffering. Liberation is to be experienced now, in the midst of our world of chaos and *dukkha*.

Besides developing the skill of being fully present and engaged with whatever arises in our experience, *satipatthana* has another mission that should not be forgotten. This is the contemplation of experience in order to uncover *dukkha* in all its manifestations. The primary mission of the Buddha was to teach us how to resolve suffering and the underlying causes of suffering, and this requires an active investigation of our experience to seek our *dukkha*. We might describe *satipatthana* as a "search and heal" mission to search out *dukkha* in the body and mind and then bring the healing energy of mindfulness to that place of blind attachment and suffering. It should be added that this is a "search and heal" mission and not a "search and destroy" mission, because suffering can never be removed by violence, but rather by transcending the whole field of conflict with the Eye of Wisdom and the Heart of Compassion, which is the fundamental nature of *satipatthana*.

There are four primary domains to our living experience where we should endeavor to cultivate mindfulness. These are mindfulness of the body and physical activities (*kayanupassana*), mindfulness of the feeling quality of experience (*vedanupassa*), mindfulness of mental contents and habitual mental reactivity (*cittanupassana*) and mindfulness of the natural laws pertaining to mental phenomena (*dhammanupassana*). The Buddha described the four *satipatthanas* as follows:

> Here, a monk abides contemplating the body in the body; he abides contemplating the feelings in the feelings; he abides contemplating the mind in the mind; and he abides contemplating dhammas in the dhammas, diligent, clearly aware and mindful, having put aside worldly greed and grief.

Contemplating mind in mind means that we penetrate beneath the superficial appearance of mental objects to reveal the inner structure of experience. As we let go of the gross structure, the subtle inner structure is revealed and we become aware of the deeper structure of our thoughts. What seemed like a solid emotion differentiates into a complex assembly of feelings, memories and peceptions. The same formula applies to the investigation of the body, investigation of feelings and the *dhammas* of the mind. *Satipatthana* is the investigation of experience with an open and receptive mind, and the natural consequence of this kind of awareness is that we begin to see existence as a dynamic, unfolding process of changing phenomena. This natural movement from the static perception of self to seeing self as a dynamic process is the essence of *anatta*, no self. We directly see that nothing has a permanent existence that can be defined and everything that we experience is continually changing and evolving, arising and passing away.

As we watch the unfolding of experience in the body, feelings, mind and *dhammas*, the *Sutta* tells us to "put aside worldly greed and grief." This statement urges us not to allow ourselves to become entangled in the contents of our thoughts, worries and fears, but to simply be mindful of our worries and fears. It does not mean that we should turn away from our pain, but, on the contrary, we should turn towards our suffering and form a relationship with it based on mindfulness. Mindfulness means being fully present, which is not possible if the mind is scattered and preoccupied with plans and daydreaming, or full of regret about the past. If worry and fear exist, the point is to be mindful and observe the phenomena of worry and fear objectively and with an open and receptive mind. What we want to avoid is reacting to the worry and fear with further worry and fear or further reactions of wanting, aversion and delusion.

There is an important refrain that occurs rthroughout the *Sutta* that describes the full extent of what should be attended to with mindfulness:

In this way, in regard to the mind (body, feelings, *dhammas*) he abides contemplating the mind internally, or he abides contemplating the mind externally, or he

179

abides contemplating the mind internally and externally. Or, he abides contemplating the nature of arising in the mind, or he abides contemplating the nature of passing away in the mind, or he abides contemplating the nature of both arising and passing away in regard to the mind. Mindful that 'there is a mind' is established in him to the extent necessary for bare knowledge and continuous mindfulness. And he abides independent, not clinging to anything in the world.

We encounter physical sensations through the physical senses of seeing, hearing, smelling, tasting or touching. These physical sensations may arise internally in our own body or they may arise externally as we come into contact with the world. We also encounter mental objects in the form of perceptions, memories, thoughts and feelings that arise from within, or we encounter perceptions, memories, thoughts and emotions externally in response to external stimuli.

The other essential part of The Path of Mindfulness, as explained in this passage, is the contemplation of the arising of experience and the passing away of experience in both body and mind. This is an extremely important part of mindfulness practice and is central to the entire process of awakening and liberation. Mindfulness means seeing the whole show and not just the highlights. Awakening to phenomena arising means that we have developed a high acuity of awareness, such that nothing escapes our attention. However, seeing things as they arise is just the beginning: we must sustain our mindfulness and allow the experience to unfold into full conscious awareness. It is the experience of the whole dance, from beginning to the end that leads to awakening and transformation. This is the essence of awakening to *anicca* in action and to allow experience to flow unimpeded by attachment and clinging.

Mindfulness is not a passive process, but an active process that creates the right conditions in which beneficial change can occur. Without mindfulness, change becomes chaotic and does not move in harmony with the innate intelligence of what needs to happen and what needs to change. When we are meditating in this way, with direct insight into *anicca*, the mind and psyche are free to move and change, without interference from the ego and its attachments. This allows wisdom-intelligence (*satipanna*) to ditect change in a beneficial direction that will ultimately lead to the resolution of *dukkha*. Being mindful of the whole cycle of arising and passing away is simply another way of saying that we are open and not resisting the natural process of transformation and resolution of *dukkha*. However, conscious awareness, which is the opposite of *avijja*, is essential to allow *satipanna* to operate effectively.

Anicca simply informs us that everything, including emotional suffering, is a dynamic and ever changing process. In our "normal" state of consciousness, which is dominated by habitual reactivity and ignorance, we blindly cling to our habitual reactions and this inhibits intelligence and the possibility of intelligent transformation. Therefore, the essence of *satipatthana* is to avoid clinging to anything that arises in the mind or body, but to "abide independent, not clinging to anything in the world."   This does not mean that we are indifference to internal or external phenomena, but that we maintain balance (*samadhi*) and equanimity (*upekkha*) in relation to whatever is experienced. This is the response of mindfulness, and the response of freedom. Hence *satipatthana* is not simply a practice to purify the mind; it is the realization of awakening and to liberate the mind from *samsara* in each and every encounter with the sense world.

It is also emphasized in this refrain, that the approach of *satipatthana* is to establish a mindfulness-based relationship with whatever we perceive. We practice to the extent necessary to establish "bare knowledge and continuous mindfulness." Bare knowledge or bare attention is a primary characteristic of *sati* as described previously and this is the nature of *satisampajanna*, or pure knowing, without the corruption of reactivity in the form of judgement, analysis or interpretation. The prime activity of mindfulness is simply to establish an open and receptive relationship with sense experience, including thoughts, memories, perceptions and emotions, and then remain in this relationship with sustained mindfulness.

Sustained mindfulness requires *samadhi*, mental stability and non-reactivity, and this is essential to allow the completion of the process of transformation as described above. In this way, we create a transformational and therapeutic space around whatever we experience, and this is the nature of freedom and non-clinging. Nothing can change if we don't have this inner freedom, but when we do live in this way, then we are living in harmony with *anicca*, and this is living in a way that will lead to freedom from *dukkha*. This is simply allowing the psyche to heal itself in its own way, which can only happen when the mind is free from reactivity and thinking about what it is experiencing. The psyche has extraordinary powers to heal suffering and trauma if only we can let it do its job. The Path of Mindfulness is a path of getting out of the way of the psyche and letting it do its work, through the alignment with *anicca* and *satipanna*, to resolve suffering and discover our true inner happiness and well-being.

The Pali term *anupassana* means seeing, observing and investigating our experience. It is derived from the prefix *anu-*, which means "on" and the suffix *-passana*, which means "insight knowledge," as in the word *vipassana*. It is most usually translated as "contemplation," but we need to be careful, because contemplation is often taken to mean an activity of thinking about an object, whereas mindfulness is the direct experiential knowing of whatever is being contemplated, without the overlay of thinking. The word "contemplate" comes from the Latin *contemplari*, to "gaze attentively, "to observe" and "to mark out space for observation," and this is actually much closer to the true meaning of *anupassana*. The notion of creating a space around the object of experience is very much a quality that we associate with *sati*, and mindfulness is always accompanied by a sense of spaciousness and openness.

Another translation of *anupassana* is "experiential knowing." The term "experiential" is a very important term in Buddhism and psychotherapy and refers to the direct conscious awareness of experience in the present, rather than trying to interpret experience through a system of beliefs. Experiential knowing means seeing what is actually happening, while it is happening in the present. This direct knowing is the unique quality of mindful-awareness that has the power to bring about transformation and liberation of the mind and spirit.

Satipatthana is the art of developing an acute awareness of whatever enters our field of consciousness and to awaken to experience in the present moment. Every experience is a drama between three charaters: the *knower*, the *known* and the *knowing*, or the *observer*, the *observed* and the *observing*. The *knower* and the *observer* are manifestations of the self, the ego that reacts to what is experienced according to past conditioning. The *known* and that which is *observed* constitutes the actual reality and truth of the sense object. Besides self and object there is another ground, the ground of pure knowing, or *satisampajanna*, which is not self and not object, but the ongoing fluid process of direct experiencing and which is not the reactivity of the self. This awakened *knowing* contains both the object and the subjective reactions to the object, both the *known* and the *knower*. *Satipatthana* is the art of learning to be the *knowing* of both the sense objects and the subjective habitual reactions to those objects. Mindfulness practice is the process of becoming established in the *knowing* aspect of conscious in all the myriad encounters with the sense world of mental and physical phenomena.

KAYANUPASSANA

The first area for the cultivation of mindfulness is called *kayanupassana*, in which we direct mindfulness onto the physical sensations of the body and all physical activities involving the body. We are continually bombarded with physical sensations that may arise internally or from our contact with the world, and the purpose of *kayanupasana* is to develop our mindfulness of all these sensations as they arise throughout the day. Through mindfulness and the cultivation of clear knowing (*satisampajanna*), non-clinging (*upekkha*) and non-reactivity (*samadhi*), we develop a great inner stability in our living relationship with the physical world. This is body-centered *samadhi*, or *kaya-samadhi* that provides a foundation and refuge for our practice of *satipatthana*. The body is the foundation for the mind and spirit and we need to make this foundation as strong as possible to support the development of both mind and spirit. Therefore we begin mindfulness practice by cultivating full presence of mind at the physical level of sensations.

Mindfulness of Physical Sensations

The first level of *kayanupassana* involves developing awareness of the physical sensations of seeing, hearing, smelling, tasting and touching. At the beginning of a session of meditation it is beneficial to focus awareness on the external sensations associated with sitting, such as sensations in the legs, back and neck. Some of these may be painful, others pleasant, but all provide an opportunity to develop mindfulness, grounded in the present.

Body sensations are good objects for meditation, because they are relatively simple, and most are free from the complications of associated emotional reactivity. It is relatively easy to be mindful of common physical sensations, without becoming caught up in thinking or becoming lost in painful memories or anxiety about the future. By focusing mindfulness on these neutral sensations, we strengthen the skill of mindfulness, which will be very beneficial when we progress to the greater challenge of focusing mindfulness on the contents of the mind. We can use mindfulness of physical sensations to develop *samadhi*, the very strong sense of stability in the midst of the chaos of changing phenomena. We become the center of our experience, rather than seduced by the peripheral world of changing phenomena. As we sit in the middle of the storm of physical sensations, we develop the faculty of pure knowing, or *satisampajanna*, as an alternative to conditioned reactivity. *Samadhi* begins in the body and from there we can develop stability in our relationship to feelings and mental contents, but to have *vedana-samadhi* and *citta-samadhi*, we must first develop *kaya-samadhi*.

Although the foundation of mindfulness of the body is simply learning to recognize and be present for physical sensations and physical movements, *kayanupassana* also includes a series of contemplation on specific aspects of the body as a way of further developing mindfulness. One of the most popular mindfulness trainings is mindfulness of breathing (*anapanasati*). In this form of meditation, we observe the subtle physical sensations of in-and-out breathing.

As we sustain mindfulness, we observe that breathing is a complex flow of bodily sensations, of movement, heat and cold and pressure. Through practicing mindfulness of breathing, awareness naturally moves from the gross and superficial level to the finer details of experience. This is an example of sensory enrichment, which is one of the most important functions of mindfulness practice, and which will be invaluable when we begin meditating on the more challenging contents of the mind, such as the emotions. Our usual experience of an emotion is very abstract and superficial and it is only when we uncover the subtle and more concrete structure of an emotion that we will be able to bring about beneficial changes. Mindfulness is the pre-eminate skill for doing just this, of translating the abstract into the concrete, of enriching our experience through the differentiation of the superficial appearance of experience into detailed experiential structure. Mindfulness of the subtle inner structure of breathing is a way of cultivating this movement in depth of experience, away from the superficial and illusory outward appearance of things.

During *anapanasati*, you will also see first hand how the mind readily becomes distracted, and you will see just how agitated and reactive the mind really is. This provides you with an excellent opportunity to develop the primary skill of mindfulness, which is vigilance (*appamada*). In *vipassana* meditation the object is not to try and make distractions go away, but to simply respond to them with mindfulness. This means that we learn to know a distraction as a distraction, just like any other sense object that enters our field of awareness; we learn to receive it as it is, without any further reactions of wanting, aversion or blind acceptance. In the pure knowing of a distraction, it will go through the usual cycle of arising, existing and pasing away, without any need for us to try and make it go away. Allowing things to change naturally in this way, rather than grasping at them or reacting with resistance is one of the most important skills of mindfulness practice, and is central when working with emotional complexes and *dukkha*.

Mindfulness of Activities

The second aspect of *kayanupassana* involves cultivating mindfulness of physical activities such as walking, eating, driving a car, washing the dishes, or working at the computer. We wish to develop mindfulness of any activity that involves the body, including speech, as we interact with people and friends and family, as well as with the physical and material world. The purpose of activity-based mindfulness practice is to become acutely aware of what we are doing while we are doing it. This is intended to counteract the usual lack of awareness that accompanies so many of our activities. This does not mean being self-conscious, nor does it mean restricting spontaneity, but rather that we have an open mind that is alive and vibrantly engaged in everything that we do.

Through cultivating mindfulness of activities, we develop a certain nimbleness of awareness, able to respond to a rapidly changing world. This is a very important part of the cultivation of the still inner center of *samadhi*. It is easy to be calm during meditation when we are doing very little, but much harder to maintain *samadhi* when we are absorbed in the busyness of life. The Path of Mindfulness means that we cultivate mindfulness of all activities of body, speech and mind. We train to be like a Samurai warrior who is completely present and attentive to every movement of his enemy. As the enemy lunges towards him, the Samurai responds with a perfect countermove that redirects his energy. Such attention to the detailed movements of self, others and the world becomes a skillful dance with the unfolding phenomena of our on-going experience. Although the Samurai is armed with a sword capable of cutting through a tree, it is the quality of his attention that is his strongest weapon. The Path of Mindfulness is an art form in which we learn to dance with life and respond with great sensitivity to each unfolding experience. There is no place for the ego in the dance of mindfulness; it simply gets in the way and makes us clumsy. In the dance there is neither the knower nor the known, but the being of pure knowing that embraces both.

Whether at work or play, the more mindful we are, the more we will enjoy what we are doing, because one of the most noticeable effects of mindfulness is that it enriches experience. The Path of Mindfulness enriches all aspects of our life, and the more present we are with what we are doing, the more we will enjoy what we are doing. Like the kiss that awakened Cinderella from her perpetual sleep, everything touched by mindfulness springs to life. Mindfulness is the kiss of life, just as ignorance is the kiss of death. In the practice of The Path of Mindfulness, we choose to embrace all aspects of conscious experience with *sati* and live fully in each moment. Even mundane activities such as walking or washing the dishes can provide a tremendously rich ground for training in mindfulness. Drinking a cup of tea can become a dance of great beauty and great hapiness, as in this quote from the teachings of Thich Nhat Hanh,

> Drink your tea slowly and reverently, as if it is the axis on which the earth revolves - slowly, evenly, without rushing toward the future. Live the actual moment. Only this moment is life.

By practicing mindfulness of the simple activities of life, we develop *samadhi* in relation to those activities, and this is the same composure and steadfastness of mind that creates the perfect conditions for healing *dukkha*. Through cultivating mindfulness of body sensations and activities, we develop a solid foundation, a base to which we can return, and from this secure place we can venture out and heal *dukkha* both internally and externally wherever it occurs. But, besides the healing effect and equanimity that mindfulness brings to our lives, it should also be remembered that mindfulness also simply makes life more satisfying and enjoyable. Nothing is missed, and every experience becomes a magnificent reward in itself. All we have to do is open our eyes, and drink from the rich experience of the river of life.

Old age, sickness and death

Besides using *kayanupassana* as a skillful means of developing *sati* and *samadhi*, we must remember the original purpose of *satipatthana*, which is to seek out *dukkha* and heal it. The body is a process: it grows and develops, and then after reaching its peak, the body ages, becomes sick and eventually dies. As the Buddha said,

> And this, monks, is the Noble Truth of dukkha: birth is dukkha, and old age is dukkha, and disease is dukkha, and dying is dukkha.

This does not mean that birth, aging, sickness and death are suffering in the absolute sense, but that they are fields of experience in which suffering can arise and will arise if the mind is dominated by *avijja*. It is important to reflect and contemplate birth, old age, sickness and death and investigate how we relate to the experience of these events in our lives. How do we react to aging? Does getting old generate worry, anxiety and regret? If there is sickness, do we react with fear? How do we relate to the prospect of dying? We need to contemplate these realities and search out the suffering that we generate through our conditioned subjective reactivity.

We can choose to continue reacting and continue to suffer, or we can choose to respond to our *dukkha* with mindfulness, and bring the healing power of *satisampajanna* to the experience of living and dying. The choice is ours: to react, or to respond. Reactivity leads to more suffering; responsiveness, which is mindfulness in action, is to live in freedom from suffering.

There is no law that requires us to live in fear of aging, sickness and dying. We create this fear and anxiety through our blind attachment to our conditioned reactivity. The purpose of reflection on aging, sickness and dying is not to burden the mind with more anxiety, but to liberate the mind and spirit from *avijja* and the psychological clinging that keeps us bound to our subjective habitual reactivity. This is an example of the active "search and heal" dimension of *satipatthana* practice. We don't wait for *dukkha* to come and ambush us; we take the initiative and meet it directly on the field of mindfulness, with careful attention and compassion. We learn how to comfort our suffering by holding *dukkha* in our heart with the healing spaciousness of mindfulness. Fear feeds on ignorance, the deliberate or unconscious avoidance of suffering, but fear is simply energy that has been trapped in the *sankhara* of fear. It is mindfulness and *satisampajanna* that allows this negative energy to transform into positive energy that can nourish our being.

The second major field for cultivating mindfulness is *vedanupassana*, mindfulness of feelings. When we practice *vedanupassana*, we pay very close attention to the three qualities of feeling energy that arise along with senses experience. These energetic qualities are *dukkhavedana*, *sukhavedana* and *upekkhavedana*: painful feelings, pleasant feelings and neutral feelings.

Feeling energy is extremely important, because it gives meaning and power to our thoughts and beliefs. Without this energy to sustain them, thoughts, beliefs and other *sankharas* would simply dissolve like bubbles in a waterfall. It is feeling energy that drives the actions and reactions of body, speech and mind. It is, therefore, essential that we cultivate a conscious relationship with the feeling energy associated with our reactions, in order to avoid becoming a victim to reactivity, and so that we can begin to explore ways of releasing this trapped energy.

A negative emotional reaction such as anger or anxiety contains the negative feeling energy of *dukkhavedana* that has become crystallized into a particular negative reaction, a *cittasankhara*. A positive emotion such as happiness or joy contains *sukhavedana* that has been channelled into a positive *cittasankhara*. The neutral feeling of *upekkhavedana* is the quality of neutral feeling energy that gives power and meaning to those beliefs and perceptions that we blindly accept as true.

Clearly, the really important subjects for *vedanupassana* meditation are the feelings that fuel the emotional reactions of greed (*lobha*), hatred (*dosa*) and delusion (*moha*). The emotional reactions of greed (*lobha*) include longing, lust, envy and jealousy and any reaction that contatins the compulsive drive to acquire. The emotional reactions of aversion (*dosa*) include anger, hatred and ill will and the compulsive drive to destroy. The emotional reactivity of delusion (*moha*) includes fixation on beliefs, conceit, arrogance and self-righteousness as well as the delusion of blind identification and attachment to our patterns of reactivity that creates most of our suffering.

All emotional reactions depend on the strength of the underlying feeling energy of *vedana* and when that energy is very strong it becomes the obsessive-compulsive force of *tanha*, or craving. The stronger the *tanha*, the stronger the resulting emotional reaction will be. By focusing mindfulness on the feeling energy or feeling tone that underlies an emotional reaction, we can access the very powerhouse that fuels our reactivity and if we can produce a change at the level of feeling, then we can disarm the compulsive force of *tanha*.

As with *kayanupassana*, through cultivating mindfulness of the feeling energy of our experiences as an object to be investigated will strengthen the quality of our relationship with our emotions. Mindfulness helps us move away from reactivity, towards a relationship based on full presence and engagement. We can observe objectively and surround the experience of our feelings with the spacious quality of mindfulness. In this way we develop *vedana-samadhi*, or inner stability in our relationship with our emotions. This provides the therapeutic space and inner freedom in which negative emotions can differentiate and unfold, leading to their transformation and resolution.

CITTANUPASSANA

The third area for establishing mindfulness is in our relationship to the contents of the mind, called *citta* in Pali. Thoughts, memories, emotions, beliefs and other mental objects arise in a continuous stream as we come into contact with sense objects. Cultivating awareness of the contents of the mind is called *cittanupassana*, or "mind watching" and this is the most important foundation for counteracting the habitual reactivity of the mind. All spiritual work begins by awakening to the reality of the mind and removing the cloak of ignorance (*avijja*) that prevents change and sustains habitual reactivity. You cannot change what you cannot see, and one of the key activities of mindfulness practice and *vipassana* meditation is to illuminate the unseen manifestations of reactivity. In this practice we learn to recognize thoughts as they arise and learn to respond to thought reactions with mindfulness, rather than simply being seduced into further reactivity. We learn to observe emotions as they arise, rather than falling under their spell. We learn to respond to our beliefs, views, opinions and perceptions with mindfulness, rather than blindly accepting them as true. Nothing is blindly accepted as truth, and instead we choose to observe all *cittasankhara* with mindfulness and equanimity, and with a mind that "abides independent, not clinging to anything in the world."

When we follow The Path of Mindfulness, we understand that we are responsible for our sorrow as well as for our happiness, and this means taking responsibility for our habitual patterns of thinking. Instead of blindly accepting negative thoughts and states of mind, we choose to relate to them with mindfulness. We learn how to see thoughts and memories, or any other mental phenomena, as objects that we can observe objectively in the same way that we might observe a tree or a table or any other external sense object. If the thought arises, "I am depressed," or "I am upset," we do not simply give in and become depressed or upset, but respond to the thought with the bare recognition that, "a thought has arisen in me," and then establish a relationship of mindfulness with that thought.

We begin to experience in depth that we are not our thoughts; we are not our emotions; we are not our beliefs. Thoughts, emotional reactions, memories and beliefs are seen as visitors to our home: we greet them with respect and friendliness, but we do not have to agree with them or follow their bidding. In this way we develop *citta-samadhi*, or stability in our relationship to mental contents. We learn to sit perfectly still and respond with full presence to each of the thoughts and memories, perceptions and emotions that come to visit us. When we do this, we are cultivating inner freedom and this freedom leads to great integrity and authenticity. We discover that our truest identity is as the home in which our visitors arrive.

cittanupassana requires mental dicipline, and this means learning to control the reactive thinking mind. As the Buddha said,

> To enjoy good health, to bring true happiness to one's family, to bring peace to all, one must first discipline and control one's own mind. If a man can control his mind he can find the way to Enlightenment, and all wisdom and virtue will naturally come to him.

However, it should be understood that to "control one's own mind," cannot be done effectively by the activities of the conscious thinking mind, the ego, because the mind that is fragmented by reactivity cannot heal itself. As Albert Einstein said,

> No problem can be solved from the same level of consciousness that created it.

When the Buddha talks about control, he means creating a totally different relationship with the mind that is based on mindfulness and the intuitive wisdom-intelligence (*satipanna*) that transcends the reactive content of the thinking ego-mind. This kind of discipline and control arises when we let go of thinking and the activities of the ego, and open to the total experience of the present. The path to "Enlightenment" is to be found through the practice of mindfulness, which is opening to reality, rather than thinking about reality or imposing our beliefs and ideas onto reality. Therefore, our primary activity in *cittanupassana* is to learn to recognize when a thought or emotion has arisen and to respond with mindfulness and establish a relationship with the mind object, based on mindfulness. This provides the right conditions in which transformative *satipanna* will arise.

DHAMMANUPASSANA

Through cultivating mindfulness of the body, mindfulness of feelings and mindfulness of thoughts and emotions, we start to develop a completely different relationship with the contents of our experience that is not based on reactivity, but on direct knowing of things as they are. We begin to see how phenomena arise, do their dance and then pass away, and that this process of change obeys natural laws that exist independent of the ego or beliefs. We see how *dukkha* arises whenever there is clinging to mental phenomena and resistance to the dynaminc flow of change. We begin to awaken to the natural laws of *anicca*, *dukkha* and *anatta*, or impermanence, suffering and not-self, respectively, and we see how these laws apply the phenomenon of conscious experience. The term *Dhamma* includes these and other natural and unchangeable laws, and the insight into these laws as they operate in the mind is called *dhammanupassana*.

At a very practial level, *dhammanupassana* means relating to our ongoing experience in terms of the Four Noble Truths: awakening to suffering; awakening to the underlying attachments that create and feed suffering; awakening to a different way of being that is not based on reactivity and suffering; and awakening to the The Path of Mindfulness as the primary means that leads to the resolution of reactivity and suffering. The contemplation of *Dhamma* means that we learn to recognize and know directly and clearly what is happening in the mind and know whether it is wholesome (*kusala*) and contributes to the ending of suffering, or whether it is unwholesome (*akusala*) and perpetuates suffering. As we develop *dhammanupassana*, we develop the innate wisdom of *satipanna* that allows us to see the difference between *kusala dhammas* and *akusala dhammas*.

Through practice we develop *dhamma-samadhi*, or stability and harmony in our relationship to the natural processes of the mind, so that the *Dhamma* becomes our refuge and guides us in everything we do. As with all the *satipatthanas*, what we are trying to cultivate is a living, moment-to-moment harmony with *dhammas*, *cittas*, *vedana* and *kaya*. It is awakening to "real-time" existence as it is, without interference from our habitual patterns of reactivity and without interference from the ego, or *atta*. It means that we see the body as body, feelings as feelings, thoughts as thoughts. We experience first hand how all of these phenomena exist as an unfolding process that is fundamentally not I, not me, and not mine. We see how clinging to that which is impermanent and unstable produces suffering, and how non-clinging provides the right conditions for genuine happiness.

Wherever we start in our *satipatthana* practice, we will arrive at *dhammanupassana*, because mindfulness puts us in touch with the true nature of mental phenomena. Mindfulness is the absence of reactivity, which means the absence of clinging and *avijja*. The Path of Mindfulness is the path of non-attachment and non-clinging that leaves the mind open to perceive truth and *Dhamma* in every moment. When there is no reactivity and no clinging, then we are able to awaken to *annica*, *dukkha* and *anatta* as living insights that operate automatically and without effort in every moment of our life. This is the perfection of *satipanna*, the innate wisdom-intelligence that we all possess. The relationship of pure knowing through mindfulness means that we awaken to *anicca* and live in harmony with the dynamic and impermanent nature of phenomena. We relate to thoughts, emotions and beliefs not as static truths, but as temporal manifestations of an ever-changing process. As we look closely at each emotional reaction that arises in daily life, we see that it does not exist as a solid "thing," but as a constellation of more subtle feelings and inner thoughts and perceptions. As we become mindful of the subtle experiential structure of our emotions, the entire field changes and purification through insight begins. As we awaken to *dukkha* through mindfulness, we create a healing space around the suffering and this provides the freedom in which change can occur at the experiential and intuitive level. Reactivity is the ignorance of *dukkha*, the force that keeps us chained to the past. Mindfulness is the antidote to *avijja* that brings healing intelligence back into the midst of the inner disorder and instability of the mind.

As we awaken to *anicca* and *dukkha*, we also awaken to *anatta*. This does not mean that we cling to theories about not-self, but that we live in an ongoing relationship with phenomena in which there is no interference from the *knower*, the conditioned ego-mind, or *atta* that reacts to whatever it perceives. To awaken to *anatta* means that our essential identity becomes the *knowing*, the pure conscious experience of the *known* that is free from both the *known* and the reactivity of the *knower*. This is the essence of *anatta*, and *dhammanupassana* means that we live in an ongoing relationship with whatever we experience, painful or pleasant, based on this awakening to *anicca*, *dukkha* and *anatta*.

16 Meditation On The Mind

The natural state for the mind is Buddha mind, the state of pure wakefulness. This innate awakened mind is free from attachment to habitual reactivity and the products of habitual reactivity. Unfortunately, the mind has a strong tendency to attach to the mental objects that arise through conditioning, and this causes agitation and emotional suffering. Thoughts arise and the mind is seduced into following the thoughts; emotions arise and we are seduced into identifying with the emotions. This attachment to the activities of self or ego takes away our basic freedom and choice. What results are unskillful and harmful actions of body, speech and mind, lacking in compassion and wisdom. We become the victims of our thoughts, beliefs and emotions and suffer accordingly.

Therefore, the path of spiritual awakening must involve a valiant and unceasing effort to overcome our entrenched patterns of habitual subjective reactivity. If we can achieve this, then we will uncover the innate wisdom and purity of mind that is our original nature. This will provide the foundation for developing true compassion and skillful acion in our relationships with self, with other people, and with the physical world. All spiritual practice must begin with a fundamental resolve to purify and free the mind from the tyranny of habitual reactivity, as expressed in the opening lines of the *Dhammapada*:

> Mind precedes all mental states. Mind is their chief; mind is their maker.
> If with an impure mind a person speaks or acts suffering follows him like the wheel that follows the foot of the ox.

> Mind precedes all mental states. Mind is their chief; mind is their maker.
> If with a pure mind a person speaks or acts happiness follows him like his never-departing shadow.

The mind, called *citta* in Pali, when dominated by ignorance and habitual reactivity, becomes the "impure mind." The mind that is free of conditioning and that is responsiveness, rather than reactive, modulated by *panna*, rather than *avijja* is the "pure mind." Consequently, the purification of mind is central to The Path of Mindfulness and *vipassana* meditation. We must actively search for all traces of blind attachment and habitual reactivity that create agitation and instability in the mind. We do not wait for *dukkha* to take control, but choose to actively search for all traces of emotional dissonance and suffering and attend to each with mindfulness. This ardent application of mindfulness to investigate the mind is called *cittanupassana*, which literally means, "mind watching."

These opening verses of the *Dhammapada* are particularly interesting and give much insight into many aspects of the path of *Dhamma*. The ox refers to the ego, the rather dull and limited part of the mind that is dominated by fixed patterns of habitual reactivity, in the same way that the ox is chained to the cart. When our mind and psyche are governed by the ego, we become dull and inflexible and unable to respond or engage intelligently and compassionately with life. Suffering results and does not go away. Consequently, the heavy burden of suffering follows us as we repeat our habitual paterns of emotional and behvioral reactivity, or *samsara*. The ox represents the unawakened mind, dominated by *avijja*, that is mechanical and lacking vitality and authenticity.

Contrast this with the effortless nature of the awakened mind that is not chained to habitual reactivity. A shadow has no weight and creates no *dukkha*, no emotional instability and dissonance. The never departing shadow refers to the Buddha nature of Original Mind that is always present. Not being chained to reactive thoughts, beliefs and emotions, the Original Mind, or *bodhicitta*, is free to engage fully with life, without creating suffering. The pure mind is the mind that is free from blind habitual conditioning, where *sati*, *satisampajanna* and *satipanna* are dominant and work together in harmony.

Awakening through mindfulness allows the wisdom-intelligence of *satipanna* to arise, and this leads to skillful and wholesome actions that are not conditioned by the past. This is why the purification and liberation of the mind is so central to the path of Buddha *Dhamma* and why such great attention is given to searching out *dukkha*, the sign of the ox mind. The purification of the mind requires liberation from the forces of reactivity and ignorance. Only when the mind is completely free from these forces can it fully engage with life and respond wisely and compassionately. We must free the mind and spirit, collectively called the psyche, from the reactive patterns of the ego, the compulsive reactivity of thinking based on blind attachment to inner beliefs. There is an ancient Chinese saying,

Watch your thoughts, for they become words.
Choose your words, for they become actions.
Understand your actions, for they become habits.
Study your habits, for they will become your character.
Develop your character, for it becomes your destiny.

Everything begins with the mind, and the spiritual path for the purification of the mind and heart must place the mind at the very center of mindfulness practice and meditation. The Buddha emphasized that the only way to effectively liberate the mind and heart from *samsara* is to work directly with the mind, with the beliefs, emotional reactions and other *cittasankharas* that arise out of habit and ignorance. Hence *cittanupassana*, the contemplation of mind, should become the foundation for our mindfulness practice and *vipassana* meditation.

Ajahn Chah was renowned for his emphasis on the importance of mindfulness of the mind, as in the following passage:

The untrained heart races around following its own habits. It jumps about excitedly, randomly, because it has never been trained. Train your heart! Buddhist meditation is about the heart; It's about developing the heart or mind, about developing your own heart. This is very, very important. Buddhism is the religion of the heart. Only this. One who practices to develop the heart is one who practices Buddhism.

197

Cittanupassana meditation or "mind watching" involves observing with mindfulness, each state of mind as it arises in the present. If there is anxiety, then we respond to the anxiety with mindful-investigation, rather than becoming entangled in the barbwire of worrying. If there is agitation, then we respond to the mental object of agitation with mindful-investigation, rather than becoming agitated. If there is anger, then we respond to the anger with mindful-investigation, rather than becoming angry. If depression arises, then we observe the depression, without becoming entangled in negative thinking. If there is sadness, then we observe the sadness, without becoming sad. If there is fear, then we observe the fear, without becoming afraid. If a thought arises, we observe the thought, without becoming lost in thinking. We train ourselves to see each thought, belief and emotion that arises as an object, which we choose to observe and investigate with mindfulness. This relationship of mindfulness and investigation does not involve thinking about our experience, but simply acknowledging what arises and staying with the pure direct knowing of the mind objects. We look at them as visitors that have come into our space. We greet each and sit down with each in the relationship of pure mindfulness.

The reactions of the mind are very seductive, and when there is unawareness and *avijja*, we tend to blindly identify with the reactions that arise and *become* the thought, belief or emotion. When something doesn't happen according to expectation or desire, the mind blindly reacts and we *become* disappointed or angry. When we remember a painful event, the mind reacts out of habit and we *become* upset. A minute later we remember something pleasant and we *become* happy. Reactivity creates successive states of mind, or *cittasankharas*, and ignorance causes us to become the thought or emotion as dictated by past conditioning and attachment and the compulsive force of *bhavatanha*.

We must develop the active side of mindfulness to restrain this tendency to be seduced by every thought and emotion, every *sankhara* that arises in the mind. Consequently, the very first skill that we need to develop in *cittanupassana* meditation is vigilance (*appamada*). We need to wake up from our usual state of daydreaming and mindlessness, and resist the pull of reacting so that we can fully engage with each thought, each emotion and each reaction as they arise, without attachment and further reactivity. We learn to take care of our guests.

Once we have recognized that we are reacting, we can stop right there, and begin the most important part of *cittanupassana*, which is to open the eye of direct conscious awareness, or *satisampajanna*. Through *satisampajanna*, we establish an objective relationship with the thought or emotion as a mental object to be investigated. No longer distracted by reacting or thinking about what we are experiencing, we are able to be fully present, and experience beigins to unfold, revealing details of the inner structure of the experience. In other words, we see and experience more as we tune in to whatever we are observing with mindfulness. This paves the way for *vedanupassana* meditation, the mindful-contemplation of the feeling energy associated with mind states. It is in this creative interface with intuitive feelings that transformation takes place, because all mind states depend on feeling energy (*vedana*) to give them power. Thus, mindfulness of mental states naturally progresses to mindfulness of the underlying feeling tone of the thought, memory or emotion.

BECOMING THE OBSERVER

The core skill in mindfulness meditation and *cittanupassana* is to become an observer of the phenomena of experience as they arise. Specifically, this means learning to observe all the reactions of the mind arising internally, or externally through contact with the outside world. If a thought or emotion arises internally then we observe it. If a thought or emotion arises in reaction to an external object, a person, place or event, then we observe those reactions. Nothing should fall outside the watchful eye of *cittanupassana*. The goal is to be there for our experience and to be fully present and fully conscious. In perhaps one of his most famous descriptions of *vipassana* meditation, Ajahn Chah describes The Path of Mindfulness as follows:

> Try to be mindful and let things take their natural course. Then your mind will become still in any surroundings, like a clear forest pool. All kinds of won-

derful, rare animals will come to drink at the pool and you will clearly see the nature of all things. You will see many strange and wonderful things come and go, but you will be still. This is the happiness of the Buddha.

Letting things "take their natural course," means that we are receptive to the innate intuitive intelligence of each situation. When we awaken to our experience through mindfulness, we are in that very same moment awakening to *anicca*, the natural flow of change. This freedom allows things to take their natural course and change, without the corrupting influence of the reactive ego. Above all, things take their natural course when we stop attaching and identifying with the *sankhras* as they arise. When guided by a sensitive and alive awareness, change will always lead towards maximum stability and the resolution of *dukkha*, as directed by *satipanna*. With *satisampajanna* we relate to things without reaction, which means that we don't grasp on to the *sankharas* of our experience. Instead, we allow experience to change under the guidance of intelligence (*satipanna*) and this is the in-the-moment realization of *anicca*.

With sustained mindfulness, "your mind will become still in any surroundings, like a clear forest pool." This stillness and composure is the state of *samadhi* that develops naturally when there is mindfulness. From this still center, the mind can relate to everything with equanimity (*upekkha*), friendship (*metta*) and non-attachment (*anupadana*). Developing the mind that is still in any surroundings allows us to awaken to our Original Mind, or *bodhicitta*, that is not conditioned and not reactive, and as we develop The Path of Mindfulness, this becomes our refuge as the "clear forest pool." Like the pool, *bodhicitta* welcomes all the animals of the forest, from the fierce tiger to the poisonous snake; from the elephant to the smallest insect, and this openness of heart is the expression of *metta*.

The "rare animals" that come to drink at the pool are the shy voices of our intuitive intelligence that we do not normally see when the mind is reactive, but that arise during *cittanupassana-vipassana* meditation. When we awaken to the subtle realm of our "rare animals" the world opens up before us, and our experience is enriched and nourished by the details of what we see. We become dynamic and intelligent living beings that respond to life, instead of cold and mindless robots that can only react out of habit. As we develop and cultivate mindfulness, all experience becomes enriched and every object of experience becomes a "rare animal" that we can appreciate and come to love.

Mindfulness is the expression of freedom, and when we are grounded in freedom, we can engage with all phenomena, pleasant or painful with a sense of wonder and interest, instead of reacting out of fear and aversion, or the compulsion to acquire and control. When we relate to the "strange and wonderful things" of our thoughts and emotions with pure, objective mindfulness, then they become our teachers. Fear and anxiety become our teachers; anger and hatred become our teachers. Happiness and tranquility become our teachers; beauty, order and stability become our teachers.

All becomes possible when we open to the truth of experience as it is, with an open mind and heart and a willingness to learn. This is the relationship of freedom that leads to true and lasting happiness. The equanimity and stillness of *bodhicitta* allows us to fully engage with life, without compulsion and without reactivity, but with a natural compassion that is unbounded. This state of inner and outer harmony is indeed the true "happiness of the Buddha," and it is our birthright, to be realized in each moment of life. The path of Buddha *Dhamma* is about awakening to this happiness right now, in every moment. It is not some distant esoteric state of consciousness to be achieved in the future after years of study and practice, but something to awaken to right now through The Path of Mindfulness and *vipassana* meditation.

THE ART OF SITTING

A session of *vipassana* meditation is often simply called *sitting meditation*. The term *sitting* is very appropriate, because it conveys the qualities of patience, attentiveness and non-reactive awareness that you have when sitting with a friend. You know from experience, that the most important attitude is to listen with an open mind and an open heart. This attitude of warm and receptive presence is the expression of *metta*, or loving-kindness, which is the essence of mindfulness as we apply it during *vipassana* meditation.

Meditation sessions can be anything from fifteen to forty-five minutes long, but you should not force yourself to practice longer than feels comfortable. It might be more appropriate to do three fifteen-minute sessions with breaks, rather than one long session. Meditation should not be an exercise in endurance; it is the quality of meditation that is most important and how well you are able to sustain mindfulness. Five minutes of high quality sitting is preferable to forty-five minutes of forcing yourself beyond your comfort level. The quality of your meditation will improve with practice, especially when you approach it in this relaxed way. As always, you start with where you are and find what works best for you, rather than trying to follow some prescribed method. There is no simple technique that will substitute for what evolves organically through your practice of sitting and observing the mind.

Make a special place in your home for meditation that is quiet and comfortable. It is helpful to establishing a routine and it is useful to set aside a certain time each day for practice. Regular practice is important, as it is with any skill that you are trying to develop. With practice your mind will become progressively more tuned in to the process of being present and you will find it easier to settle into meditation. Whether you sit on the floor or in a chair is not important; you need to experiment to find what works best for you. It is often very beneficial, but not essential to meditate with a group, because there is something very powerful in the energy transmitted within a group that aids the development of *samadhi*. Humans are social animals and when they meditate together there is a connection at the non-verbal level that is mutually supportive.

Meditation is not about following conventions and you do not need to become a Buddhist to meditate. You will become a Buddhist by default if you practice The Path of Mindfulness, and are genuinely interested in cultivating awareness and compassion in a way that leads to happiness, well-being and the resolution of *dukkha*. What interested the Buddha was helping people awaken to *Dhamma*, or the truth of experience, rather than adopting the conventions, beliefs and rituals of a religion. In fact, he strongly advised against attaching to any conventions and rituals. Your temple for worship is your heart and mind and the path of awakening to the truth of experience in each moment of living.

It is usually helpful to begin with a few minutes of *kayanupassana* meditation to settle the mind, and there are many techniques to choose from. You might begin with simple body scanning, to notice the various sensations throughout the body. You may notice a tingling sensation in the stomach or a pain in the back. Notice the physical sensations of contact with the chair you are sitting on or the sensations of heat or cold in the room. From this focus on body sensations, you can also develop awareness of external sensations, such as sounds from other people in the room, or from outside. In this way you begin to cultivate mindful-awareness, in which you are the observer at the center of your sensory experience. You remain still, watching and experiencing phenomena arising and passing away, without grasping onto anything or pushing anything away. This is exactly the same attitude that you will take when you turn awareness towards the thoughts and emotional reactions of the mind and this simple practice provides an excellent prelude to *cittanupassana*.

The practice of mindfulness of breathing, called *anapanasati* is one of the most popular preliminaries to *vipassana* meditation. This involves simply noticing the in-and-out breathing in a relaxed and natural way. You do not try to modify your breathing, as in some yoga practices, but simply observe with mindfulness what is happening at the level of physical sensations. This will naturally focus your attention and strengthen your *samadhi* and mindfulness, as well as refining the level of your awareness. When you begin to notice the mind becoming more settled, then you can let go of *anapanasati* and turn your attention to the contemplation of the mind, or *cittanupassana*.

MEDITATION AND THE STILL CENTER

The mind ressembles a pool of water, in which the surface is continually stirred up by reactive thoughts and emotions such as worrying about the future, regretting something said or done. *Vipssana* meditation begins when we deliberately cultivate mindfulness of all these activities of mind that create agitation. As we recognize each thought reaction as it arises, we create a moment of choice, and in that moment we can decide to let go of the thought or to investigate it in greater depth. In that very moment of recognition and letting go we open up a space in the mind that is non-reactive and not agitated. This is a natural state of tranquility that arises as a direct consequence of mindfulness. We cannot create this still center, but simply return to it over and over again through our mindfulness of mental agitation. It is the recognition of non-mindfulness that takes you back to the still center.

This state of inner stillness and silence is called *samadhi* and during meditation, we use mindfulness to bring us back to this still place, over and over again. This is your reference point from which you can engage and relate to the contents of your mind. Such stillness allows you to penetrate beneath the agitated surface to see the true structure of your experience, and this inner knowing is essential for transformation. Through mindfulness practice and meditation, you will become progressively more tuned in to the still center at the heart of your psyche, and it will become a tremendous source of freedom, strength and stability that will help you in all aspects of life. As Chuang-tzu said about the power of *samadhi*,

To a mind that is still, the whole universe surrenders.

The still mind of *samadhi* arises when there is *sati* and when we allow thoughts, beliefs, emotions, impulses and perceptions to arise and pass away, without any taint of further reactivity against them or entanglement in their content. This inner stillness is not static, but a movement in equanimity, in which we greet each sensory experience and mind object, with openness and without becoming reactive. There is nothing to do except be silent and mindful, observing the stream of thoughts and feelings that arise, without clinging to any of them. In this way you establish "mindful presence," which is the opposite of reactivity, where you are distracted and agitated by what arises.

The mind will often wander and become distracted by extraneous thoughts and worries. This continual movement in thinking is a perfectly natural activity for the mind and you should not fight against it, because resistance will simply create more tension and more agitation. The appropriate response to the wandering mind is simply to develop vigilance and notice when the mind has wandered and then gently, but firmly bring the attention back to the primary object, which in this case is the still center of non-thinking.

The faculty of *sati* and *samadhi* will strengthen over time and you will develop a natural resistance to the hyper-reactivity of the mind. The only time that you would *not* let go of a distracting thought is if it carries an emotional charge, in which case you should temporarily switch your attention to this mental object and investigate it with mindfulness. You must be careful about what you discard as unimportant, because that is a judgement made by the reactive ego, and you may end up missing a very important part of the healing process. Sometimes, the irrelevant details turn out to be very important, and at other times what seems like a profound psychological insight, turns out to be ineffective. Therefore, it is advisable to approach *all* thoughts that arise in the mind with equanimity and openness, and a willingness to investigate them fully with mindfulness, before returning back to the still center.

This form of meditation, in which you cultivate inner stillness and tranquility through mindfulness of agitation and reactivity in the mind, is an important part of *vipassana* meditation. It teaches us to to be aware and tuned in to the continual arising and passing away of phenomena, without becoming attached to the contents. This form of general mindfulness meditation practice provides the foundation for more focused *vipassana* in which we deliberately seek out *dukkha* for mindful-contemplation and investigation.

SEARCH FOR DUKKHA

After you have established mindfulness and *samadhi* in relation to the contents of your mind, it is helpful to begin actively scanning the mind for any hint of *dukkha*, any vestige of attachment and subjective emotional reactivity that constricts the heart and mind and causes dissonance. When you look inside, does it feel relaxed and balanced, or agitated by conflict and anxiety? We should actively search through the major areas of our life, of our relationship to Self, Other and World. We can do this by posing a series of questions such as:

How do I feel in relation to myself, right now?
How do I feel in relation to my family, right now?
How do I feel in relation to my work, right now?
How do I feel in relation to my world, right now?

You then repeat this self-examination by focusing on past memories and future concerns as you contemplate your relationship with yourself, others and the world. You may find that the mind is already very peaceful and free from agitation, worry or other manifestations of *dukkha*. If this is the case, then meditate on this state, and fully experience and appreciate the inner joy that you have. It is just as important to fully experience inner stability and well-being as it is to focus on instability and *dukkha*. It is through our experience of what is skillful and wholesome and free from suffering that the psyche learns new ways of being.

If you detect emotional suffering or some form of dis-ease, then your response should be to simply "sit" with the present experience of this discomfort, being mindful and creating lots of space around the painful emotion. As always, the response of mindfulness is to develop complete presence through which you can investigate the deeper structure of the emotion and cultivate equanimity and compassion towards each manifestation of *dukkha*. This is the response of turning towards your suffering and choosing to be fully there for it with mindfulness.

After you have accessed a particular emotional state, pleasant or unpleasant, it is often useful to find a word that best fits the emotional complex. The word acts as an anchor that allows you to access the particular emotional state throughout your meditation. It helps you monitor the resolution process and determine if the emotion has become more or less intense. The other great benefit of a word anchor is that it helps the process of objectification, so that you can relate to painful emotions, without becoming overwhelmed by them. The word label helps you see the emotion as an object that has arisen in you, but is not you.

After you have successfully established a mindful-relationship with the present state of consciousness (*citta*) arising from contemplation of the present, past, or future, then you are ready to proceed to the next step of *vipassana* meditation, which is to investigate the underlying feeling energy that empowers each of these mind states. This is the next level of *vipassana* meditation, called *vedanupassana*.

17 MEDITATION ON FEELINGS

The purpose of *vipassana* meditation is not simply to investigate the deeper structure of experience, but to become exquisitely sensitive to what needs to change. In other words, *vipassana* meditation has a purpose, which is to allow intuitive wisdom-intelligence, or *satipanna*, to arise and direct inner transformation in a way that leads to the resolution of *dukkha*. When the mind is dominated by conditioned habitual reactivity and *avijja*, then change becomes chaotic and destructive, leading to conflict and further suffering. But, when mindfulness is present, then chaos is replaced by intelligence and the changes that ensue will lead to greater stability and harmony in the psyche. Nothing can halt the march of change, the truth of *anicca*, but we do have a choice on the direction of change. Either change leads to further suffering and disorder, or change leads to liberation and happiness. It all depends on the presence or absence of mindfulness.

It soon becomes evident to anyone practicing mindfulness meditation, that within every dissonant state of *dukkha* there is also an innate directionallity, a kind of positive pressure that naturally leads to the resolution of that suffering. In effect, the path to the resolution of instability is encoded in the inner structure of that state of *dukkha* when it was created.

We can see this most clearly in the natural world. For example, if a bottle of water is emptied ontop of a mountain, the water will naturally begin a journey downwards towards the ocean. The water moves towards greater energetic stability under the direction of its own innate intelligence. In this same way, *dukkha* will naturally resolve itself into a more stable energetic state within the psyche, if given the freedom to change. *Vipassana* is simply the insight, or awakening, that puts us on this natural path that leads to the resolution of *dukkha*, and mindfulness provides the freedom in which intelligent change can take place.

This process of Psychological Homeostasis, the movement towards energetic balance and equilibrium happens at the experiential and intuitive level, far beyond the control of the ego and the thinking mind. This is why investigation with mindfulness is so effective, because it penetrates beneath the superficial surface to reveal the deeper dynamic structure of experience. The innate wisdom-intelligence that guides this process of psychological homeostasis is called *satipanna*. This intuitive intelligence will arise whenever there is *sati* and *satisampajanna*, and *vipassana* meditation is the process of awakening to this innate intelligence.

Satipanna arises the moment we let go of our preconceptions and reactive thinking. We do not make change happen by applying psychological insights gained from meditation or elsewhere, but simply by bringing about a state of inner freedom in which change can occur spontaneously, under the direction of *satipanna*. Most of our work involves learning to stay out of the way, rather than trying to solve problems through the intervention of the thinking ego-mind. Just as the water will reach the ocean if given the freedom of movement, so the psyche will heal itself if given the freedom provided by mindful-awareness.

During *vipassana* meditation, we deliberately tune in to the intuitive and experiential feelings that are embedded in our experience, and use these intuitive feelings as a guide to facilitate the changes that lead to the resolution of suffering and the cultivation of well-being and happiness. Therefore, the investigation into the depth of our experience must include the mindful-investigation of the feelings (*vedana*) that accompany the mental states observed during *cittanupassana*. This means letting go of the contents of our thoughts and emotions, and searching for the feeling tone and feeling energy that powers these thoughts and emotional reactions. This important part of *vipassana* meditation is called *vedanupassana*, the investigation of feelings, and is the second of the Four Foundations of Mindfulness (*satipatthana*).

Vedana refers to the general felt-sense or feeling tone that accompanies an experience and which can be pleasant, painful or neutral. A pleasant or positive felt-sense is called *sukhavedana*, while a painful or negative felt-sense is called *dukkhavedana*. Alternatively, experience may have a neutral felt-sense, called *upekkhavedana*, which is neither pleasant nor painful, but nonetheless powerful in its effect. The associated *vedana* gives meaning and power to thoughts, beliefs, emotions, memories and perceptions. *Vedana* is the glue that holds experience together and without it, memories, negative thoughts and emotional reactions would not become lodged in the mind, but would simply evaporate like drops of water in the hot sun.

Mental pain is analogous to physical pain in that its primary purpose is to direct attention to the cause of our pain so that you can see what must be done to resolve it. If you perceive a burning sensation in your hand, you respond by looking at your hand, and you will intuitively take the appropriate action and move your hand away from the fire. The appropriate response to the pain is dictated by awareness of the cause, and your innate and intuitive intelligence (*satipanna*) automatically directs the appropriate action that leads to the resolution of the pain. You do not have to think about what to do and in fact, thinking would be a distraction that may prolong the suffering.

Mental pain (*dukkhavedana*) has a similar function and is intended to direct your attention to the source of your mental suffering (*dukkha*). If you respond with mindfulness to the sensation of *dukkhavedana*, then you create the right conditions in which *satipanna* will arise, and this intuitive intelligence will guide internal transformation and resolve the underlying *dukkha*. However, there must be the freedom in which *satipanna* can arise and operate, and this requires mindfulness and *satisampajanna*, the clear and direct perception of things as they are.

In *vedanupassana* meditation, we do not focus on the meaning of our thoughts or emotions, but on the feeling energy, which is often called the *felt-sense* or *feeling tone* that accompanies each thought or emotion. Mindfulness and investigation are applied to unveil the *vedana* that permeates our mind states, beliefs and emotional complexes and gives them power. This is the heart of *vedanupassana* meditation: a journey into the subtle awareness of intuitive feelings as a guide to facilitate transformation and liberation.

Tuning in to our intuitive feelings of *dukkhavedana* and *sukhavedana* also has great value in our personal relationships. The more sensitive and open we can be to our intuitive feeling level, the more in touch we will be with the needs of others and with the unique needs of each new situation. Compassion requires an extraordinary sensitivity to the subtle feeling level of experience as it unfolds in the present, so that we can intuitively feel what is wholesome and appropriate.

INTUITIVE FEELINGS AS OUR GUIDE

The heart of meditation at the feeling level is to use the changes in felt-sense as our guide for transformation and compassionate action. This means tuning in to the subtle shifts in the intensity of *dukkhavedana*, *sukhavedana* and *upekkhavedana*.

The principle of Psychological Homeostasis informs us that given the freedom to change, the psyche will always move in the direction that leads towards the resolution of *dukkha*. Mindfulness and *satisampajanna* provides this freedom, or therapeutic space, in which *satipanna* can arise and transformation can happen, just as habitual reactivity sustains *dukkha* by inhibiting *satipanna* and the freedom to change. When suffering resolves in this way, it is naturally accompanied by a shift in feeling tone from *dukkhavedana* to *sukhavedana* and finally to *upekkhavedana* and we can monitor these changes during *vedanupassana* meditation.

When *dukkha* resolves, it is accompanied by a release of trapped feeling energy (*vedana*) from the highly constrained state of attachment, to a state of non-attachment and freedom. This release of energy is experienced as *sukhavedana*. In experiential psychology, this change is called a *felt shift* and provides an indication that something beneficial has happened internally.

During experiential transformation, there is a further progression from *sukhavedana* to *upekkhavedana*. This represents the completion of the reintegration of feeling energy back into the psyche and a return to a state of stability and equilibrium (*upekkha*). This resolution happens as we let go of inner attachment to reactivity; but it is not you who lets go, it is the mind letting go of itself.

This process happens all the time in everyday life. For example, you may be consumed by anxiety (*dukkhavedana*) about an upcoming job interview, but once you are actually in the interview, the tension subsides and you feel a surge of enthusiasm (*sukhavedana*) and after it has finished, everything returns to normal (*upekkhavedana*).

When we focus mindfulness on painful emotional state of *dukkha*, we may experience a powerful release of energy from *dukkhavedana* to *sukhavedana* as the emotional complex begins to unfold and transform, but eventually the euphoria subsides as this emotional energy reintegrates back into the psyche. This state of stability and balance produced by the resolution of suffering is accompanied by the felt-sense of *upekkhavedana*, which is a much higher state of happiness associated with peace and freedom.

TRANSFORMING NEGATIVE EMOTIONS WITH MINDFULNESS

Vedana should not to be confused with emotion, because an emotion has a very complex structure, whereas *vedana* simply describes the energetic state of an experience. *Vedana* is undifferentiated feeling energy, whereas emotions have a structure composed of thoughts, memories and physical reactions in the body. An emotion takes shape when the energy of *vedana* becomes crystallized around these thoughts, memories, beliefs and actions.

Emotions arise as products of habitual conditioned reactivity. Our past compels us to react in certain ways and when the conditions are right, emotional reactions arise in the mind. It is very easy to identify with these emotional reactions because they are so compelling. However, this is a form of delusion called *moha*, the seductive face of *avijja* that causes us to become identified with mental reactions (*sankharas*). Something goes wrong and we *become* upset, and act out the emotion in the form of conditioned paterns of negative thinking and behavior. *Moha* causes us to identify with the reaction and become upset. If anger arises as a primary reaction and we identify and attach to this reaction, then we *become* the anger, and it will dictate how we think, feel and act. *Moha* prevents change by limiting our freedom, so you must develop mindfulness as an antidote to *moha* and *avijja*. Through the practice of mindfulness, we learn to avoid identifying with emotional reactions and learn to see them simply as mental objects that arise in the mind. Emotions may seem very personal, but actually they are not. We did not invite them in to our mind; they force themselves in, uninvited due to blind conditioning.

213

The Path of Mindfulness and particularly *vipassana* meditation and Mindfulness Meditation Therapy is a very skillful way of working with emotions in which we essentially de-construct emotional complexes and illuminate their internal structure. All emotions have an internal structure composed of specific feelings, memories, perceptions, beliefs and imagery. This inner structure is like the workings of a Swiss watch. When you gain a thorough familiarity with the internal mechanism and individual parts, then you have something very tangible and concrete to work with. You cannot repair something as complex as a watch without this direct knowledge and the same applies to our emotions. We are seduced by the superficial and immediate appearance of our emotions; we identify with this and remain completely ignorant of the inner workings. This is the state of ignorance, or *avijja*, that is the central problem that sustains emotional reactivity and *dukkha*. The Path of Mindfulness is a deliberate path of dispelling *avijja* by the simple and persistent application of mindfulness and investigation (*sati-dhammavicaya*) to uncover the inner deep structure of our emotional complexes.

No one wants to experience sadness, fear, anger, anxiety or depression, but avoidance and aversion or resistance will not make them go away. Trying to replace negative thoughts with positive thinking may keep painful emotions at bay for a while, but this will not stop them reappearing in the future. Similarly, using meditation to try and empty the mind of thoughts in an attempt to create a state of tranquility is simply another form of resistance and avoidance. The emotional reactivity will return the moment we stop meditating.

Understanding that avoidance and repression are not skillful, the Buddha taught us that the only effective way to resolve *dukkha* is to face our suffering directly and compassionately with mindfulness. This is the First Noble Truth of suffering, which states that we must awaken to suffering, wherever it exists, internally or externally. We awaken by establishing a relationship of non-reactive mindfulness with the feeling level that lies at the heart of all emotional reactions. Mindfulness provides the right conditions for the transformation and resolution of *dukkha* just as unawareness, or *avijja*, inhibits transformation and resolution.

Mindfulness creates a therapeutic space of non-deluded, pure knowing, or *satisampajanna*. This creates the right conditions in which intuitive wisdom-intelligence (*satipanna*) can arise, and this guiding intelligence is what leads to transformation and liberation. *Vipassana* meditation, when focused on emotional suffering as the object of meditation, creates the right conditions in which *satisampajanna* and *satipanna* can arise and facilitate the transformation and resolution of emotional suffering. This form of *vipassana* meditation is the primary tool in Mindfulness Meditation Therapy. In this approach, we allow emotional complexes to heal from within, which is much more effective than anything we might try to do to them through thinking. We do not heal emotional suffering; it heals itself, and mindfulness combined with investigation provides the right conditions in which this natural healing can take place.

Reframe the emotions

When an emotion arises, it is usually in the form of a personal statement, such as, "I am anxious; I am angry; I am frustrated; I am disappointed; I am afraid; I am sad." The reference to "I" is a statement of subjective identification with the emotion and this is the root reaction of delusion (*moha*) that causes the emotion to dominate consciousness. If you remove the "I" then the emotion becomes reduced to an objective phenomenon that can be observed with mindfulness. Therefore, it is helpful to change "I am..." statements into "I notice..." statements, such as "I notice anxiety in my mind; I notice anger; I notice frustration; I notice disappointment; I notice fear." Then we become the one who notices, rather than the emotional content of the reactive mind.

This simple process of reframing emotional reactions creates a space between you as the knower or observer and the emotion as a mental object that you can observe. This helps prevent you from becoming overwhelmed by emotional reactions. It also allows you to cultivate a non-reactive relationship with the emotion, which is essential for intelligent change. Through this simple exercise in reframing the emotion, you effectively stop yourself from becoming entangled in the emotional reaction. Instead, you become the *container* of the emotion. Cultivate an objective relationship, based on mindfulness, with your anxiety, anger, disappointments, fear or any other of the numerous emotional reaction that torment us, and you create the ideal conditions for transformation and liberation.

Establish a Safe Zone

We must take special care when working with powerful core emotions such as depression, anger or the intense emotions associated with childhood trauma and abuse. There needs to be a safe working relationship, so that you do not become overwhelmed by your emotions. Without this therapeutic space you will become vulnerable to secondary reactivity and the proliferation of negative thinking and further suffering. Forming the right relationship with emotional suffering requires positive friendliness (*metta*) and patience (*khanti*), which are natural qualities that accompany mindfulness. It's all about learning how to greet the emotions as they appear. Greet them like guests; be courteous, be vigilant and know where they are at all times.

The emotional afflictions are not enemies to be uprooted and destroyed. That is the way of violence and contrary to The Path of Mindfulness. *Dukkha* is not our enemy, but our teacher whose function is to show us the way to non-suffering. Therefore, the best way to begin to establish a safe relationship with our suffering is not to react against it with resistance, but to learn to be present with it and know it as it is with an open mind and heart. Through repeated mindfulness contact we begin to replace the original reactions of aversion with a more stable state of presence. There is a cumulative effect from making frequent contact with any painful emotion and in time, mindfulness will become the natural response to the emotional reaction, instead of habitual secondary reactivity. This simple action of responding to suffering instead of reacting is the expression of true compassion, and it is this response of mindfulness heals all that it touches.

Through frequent mindful-contact, you will become more familiar with your emotional reactions and you will naturally become less reactive. The more we see of the details and inner structure of an emotion, the less overwhelming it will be. This may seem counter-intuitive, but fear depends on abstraction and ignorance, and mindfulness counteracts this. If we encounter a cobra in the wild, our first reaction will most likely be one of fear and panic. However, if we stop and focus mindfulness on the snake, we will naturally begin to learn more about the reality, or truth, of the snake. We see how it reacts to our movements, how quickly it moves its head and whether it feels threatened or not. All of this information allows us to respond to the cobra in a skillful way, and it is exactly the same when we relate to *dukkha* with mindfulness. Ignorance breeds *dukkha*; mindfulness dispels ignorance and heals *dukkha*.

If the emotion becomes too strong, then simply step back, open the eyes and take a break for a minute or two. There is no rush; practice with patience and compassion towards yourself. The relationship of mindfulness is like a dance in which you make continual adjustments to the needs of your partner and the needs of the dance. Every step you take in the "dance of mindfulness" is a small yet significant victory, so allow yourself plenty of time to become a skillful dancer when working with strong emotions.

Access the feeling level

If you are troubled by a traumatic memory, then carefully recall the memory and picture the event in your mind, just to the extent necessary to access the associated feelings, without becoming caught up in thinking about the event, which will simply perpetuate emotional reactivity.

Surround the emotion with lots of space and approach it in small steps so that you can maintain a mindful and comfortable relationship with the associated feelings. It is often very helpful to first practice approaching and withdrawing many times in quick succession, taking no more than a quick glimpse each time. The purpose is to make *mindful contact* with the present felt-sense of the emotion. This does not involve thinking about the emotion, but *sensing* the emotion. Do this as many times as you need until you can sit comfortably with the felt-sense of the memory, without becoming overwhelmed. Learning to develop this balanced way of relating to painful memories is an essential part of establishing the mindfulness-based relationship with the emotion. Learning not to react is a very beneficial skill in its own right, as well as also creating the right space in which core emotions can begin to unfold and change internally.

If you are worried about the future, then picture a possible future scenario. Again, adjust your position until you find a safe zone where you can sustain mindfulness of the feelings and avoid being overwhelmed by emotional reactivity and thinking. Make frequent mindfulness contact and learn to dance with the felt-sense of the anxiety about the future. Keep just the right distance, as you would with a dance partner: not too close and not too far away.

Memory images or imagined future images provide a reference point, an anchor, to which you can return at periodic intervals to monitor your progress during meditation. The purpose of such recollections is not to wallow in painful memories or worrying about the future, but to learn a different way of relating to these experiences that allows you to access the deeper inner structure of the associated emotion, without becoming reactive. It may take considerable practice, approaching and withdrawing over and over again, but in time you will be able to sustain contact for longer and longer periods of time with traumatic memories, or intense anxiety about the future, and maintain balance, or *samadhi*.

This repeated mindful-contact is a form of contact desensitization, and is an essential tool for the treatment of traumas and phobias. But most importantly, mindful-contact paves the way for working with the internal structure of the emotions in a way that will lead to transformation and resolution.

Another useful tool to help you access the feeling energy that surrounds an emotion is to find a word anchor that resonates with the feeling. Allow a word to emerge from the emotion and check it to see if it really fits with the internal felt-sense of the emotion. You may be focusing on anxiety and the word "heavy" emerges as a good fit. This technique of finding word anchors is used to great benefit in a psychotherapeutic technique called Focusing, developed by Dr Eugene Gendlin, one of the founders of the schools of Experiential Psychotherapy. As experiential unfolding takes place, you will find that the word anchors also change. "Heavy" may change to "sad" and later to "black" before resolution is complete.

After you access the feeling level of an emotional complex, simply allow yourself to rest there, being mindful of the feeling tone and bring your attention back to the feeling over and over again. If you become distracted by thoughts then gently acknowledge each thought, let go of thinking, and return to being mindful of the felt-sense. Often, these frequent transitions between distracting thoughts and mindfulness of the primary emotion can be very important. Distractions can be thought of as a safety mechanism that allows the psyche to process feeling energy in small bite-sized chunks. You should look at distractions as a natural part of the process of transformation, rather than something to be resisted.

It is not necessary to do anything or to try and understand anything about the feelings that you are experiencing. The whole focus is on simply being present with mindfulness and *satisampajanna*. This intuitive awareness is much more transformational than any insight knowledge or ideas that you may acquire. The conscious presence of mindfulness contact is often sufficient by itself to produce major changes in an emotional complex, even if nothing else happens at the level of psychological insight. This is the phenomenon called Contact Resolution, in which the simple act of making mindful-contact with inner suffering brings about healing. Mindful contact is healing: it brings warmth to what has become froxen; it softens and makes malleable that which is hard and impenetrable; it breathes life into that which is dead.

At other times there may be considerable movement as the inner experience of an emotion unfolds. This process is called Experiential Resolution and is more common with intense emotional complexes such as trauma or phobias. The emotion may give way to a tremendous volume of dynamic and changing phenomena: shifting feelings, memories, word labels and experiential imagery as well as changes at the physical level, such as crying. We all know the powerful healing effect of crying, and in the same way the direct experience of all the experiential details of the unfolding process brings about healing at a very deep level.

Take time to cultivate the mindfulness-based relationship with your feelings. This is one of the most valuable things that you can do, and it is worth doing with care and attention. In many ways, the practice of contacting inner emotions with mindfulness is like blowing warm air onto a block of ice. As the ice melts, the water is set free to continue its natural flow towards the ocean, where it finds complete peace and stability. Often, all that is needed is that you relate to your pain with love, compassion, gentleness and the equanimity of mindfulness. The power of this quality of mindful-presence for facilitating healing cannot be overemphasized. True mindfulness (*sammasati*) is the attitude of loving kindness (*metta*), openness, compassion and genuine interest, even towards the most unpleasant aspects of our experience. This change in relationship allows the contracted and rigid parts of the mind to soften and become malleable, which creates the ideal conditions for change.

Explore the inner structure of the emotion

Through mindfulness of the felt-sense of a core emotion, you can begin to explore and investigate the inner structure of the emotion. All emotions have an internal structure, and this inner structure is based around experiential imagery, because the psyche thinks in pictures, not words, and uses imagery to organize the emotions.

We may think that emotions arise out of strongly held beliefs, but actually beliefs and thinking originate from a much deeper level of organization in the psyche, which is provided by inner core imagery. Inner experiential imagery encodes feeling energy and holds this energy in place and in a form that gives rise to an emotion. When we focus mindfulness on the felt-sense of an emotion, like anger or anxiety, we start to uncover this inner imagery, and this provides a rich source of specific and concrete material that makes transformation possible. You can't change what you can't see, but the moment you become aware of experiential imagery you have something tangible to work with. In short, as the imagery changes, so too does the emotion.

Sit with the emotion. Walk around it. Hold it in your hands. Observe it with careful attention to detail.

What does it look like? Is it big or small, stationary or moving, in color or monochrome? Does it have a shape or is it amorphous? Is it organic or inorganic, alive or dead?

What does it feel like to the touch? Is it hard or soft, rough or smooth, brittle or malleable, hot or cold?

What does it sound like? Does it make any sound? Is it trying to say something?

What does it smell like? Does it have a pleasant perfumed scent or an unpleasant smell?

What does it taste like? Is it sweet or bitter?

By exploring these and other structural details of the emotion that you are contemplating, you will make it much easier for the emotion to differentiate and unfold through changes in the inner imagery, and this promotes transformation and resolution. In general, ignorance (*avijja*) promotes reactivity and inhibits change, whereas conscious awareness of the inner structure of experiential imagery promotes beneficial change and healing.

Allow experiential unfolding

When you have established a mindfulness-based relationship with the feeling level of an emotion, the feelings that have become aggregated into an emotional complex will begin to differentiate. It is important to follow these subtle changes in the quality of feeling and be fully mindful of each component feeling as it unfolds. It is the process of making these individual feelings conscious that leads to the transformation of the emotional complex.

What seemed like an impenetrable fortress of depression or anger will begin to differentiate into more subtle feelings that form the structure of the emotion. This is the process of objectification, in which the abstract nature of an emotion differentiates into tangible objects in the form of specific feelings. Touching each of these individual feelings with mindfulness and knowing them fully will begin the process of deconstruction of the fortress of the emotion, brick by brick. What seemed impenetrable is now penetrated, and this is the beginning of the process of experiential differentiation that will eventually lead to resolution.

What keeps emotional reactivity alive is ignorance of the individual feelings, memories and imagery that make up the internal structure of the emotion. It is our delusional attachment to the superficial and abstract appearance of our emotions that keeps them alive. As you expose each component into the light of conscious awareness, you are harmonizing with *anicca* and allowing the emotion to change according to *satipanna*. The whole complex becomes dynamic and malleable, as freedom is re-established

through mindfulness. This will, in time, inevitably lead to the resolution of your emotional suffering.

Revisit the feeling often

At frequent intervals during *vedanupassana* meditation you should
return your attention to the original thought-emotion that you
chose for contemplation. You may find it useful to use a word anchor, or visualization to help you conjure up the emotion. If it was
anger, then re-access the anger by remembering the specific situation that led to the anger. Determine for yourself whether there has
been any resolution in the intensity of the emotional reaction. By
doing this in an objective and scientific way, you learn what is
helpful and what is not. Repeat another session of *vedanupassana*
meditation on the same emotion and observe the associated *vedana*
to see if it is the same or if it has changed.

With this degree of attention through focused mindfulness
combined with investigation (*sati-dhammavicaya*) the emotional
reactivity is bound to change. Ignorance is the major factor that
sustains and fuels emotional suffering and if you systematically
counteract this *avijja* with applied mindfulness, then it is only a
question of time before the emotional complex will fall apart and
resolve itself. Mindfulness is one of the most effective ways to
promote healing, but it will take time to undo the years of habitual
reactivity, so you must be patient and persevere.

18 EXPERIENTIAL IMAGERY AND MINDFULNESS MEDITATION THERAPY

During mindfulness meditation or in a session of Mindfulness Meditation Therapy (MMT) it is very common for repressed emotional energy to represent itself in the form of dream like imagery called *experiential imagery*, and we can use this imagery very effectively to facilitate transformation. Experiential imagery refers to inner visual representations that arise out of the emotion itself. There is something about the experiential image that feels intuitively right and *resonates* with the felt-sense of the emotion. Experiential imagery is not the same as visualization, in which you deliberately create an image, but arise quite spontaneously and intuitively from our inner feelings. Not surprisingly, mindfulness provides the ideal quality of subtle awareness that allows such intuitive imagery to arise. We do not make the imagery, but allow it to arise out of the silent awareness of our inner experience.

Sometimes, experiential images are easy to interpret, but more often than not, they seem to have a life of their own that is beyond rational interpretation. Fortunately, we do not need to interpret or understand their meaning; what is much more important is to simply *experience* them. We can think of experiential imagery as the psyche expressing itself in the field of conscious awareness through the language of pictures. The psyche uses imagery to organize experience and emotions internally, and the imagery gives a framework around which experience, memories, feelings and beliefs are assembled. This is called the Structural Theory of Emotions, in which the inner structure is based on experiential imagery.

There is a particularly strong connection between feeling energy and the structure of experiential imagery, and if the emotion changes so will the imagery. By the same reasoning, a change in the structure of experiential imagery will produce a change in the intensity of the emotion. This is called Image-Feeling Reciprocity and has profound implications for our inner process of transformation. It is very difficult to directly change an emotion, like depression or anger, because it is so abstract. In contrast, it is very much easier to change the structure of an image, because it is concrete and has a specific form. Every subtle change in color, position, size, context and the other sub-modalities of the imagery will produce corresponding changes at the feeling level and in the intensity of the emotion. Discover the subtle internal structure of the imagery and you have a very powerful tool for healing emotional suffering. As always, the starting point for working with experiential imagery is to focus mindfulness on a chosen emotional complex. We make the emotion the object of our meditation and allow imagery to arise from the present felt-sense of the emotion.

Experiential imagery may first appear as a particular color, which later differentiates into a particular shape with a certain texture and position in our inner visual field. During Mindfulness Meditation Therapy, we allow the imagery to change in its own way, without any interference or attempt to analyze what we encounter. What is most important is the direct conscious experience of the imagery as it unfolds, and not the interpretation of what it means. If you allow the imagery to change freely, under the guidance of the intuitive wisdom-intelligence of *satipanna*, then what emerges will naturally lead towards the resolution of *dukkha*. When there is mindfulness, the psyche will use imagery to process feeling energy and bring about resolution of inner emotional conflict. As always, this process of transformation is governed by the principle of psychological homeostasis and will always lead to the state of maximum energetic stability. We are, quite simply, allowing the psyche to heal itself through the natural language of imagery. The psyche thinks in pictures, not words and imagery acts as a catalyst for transformation and healing.

THE SUB-MODALITIES OF IMAGERY

The Structural Theory of Emotions states that emotions have an inner structure, organized around experiential imagery. This inner imagery also has a structure in the form of specific sub-modalities, and the feeling energy of an emotion is encoded in these specific sub-modalities.

One of the first structural sub-modalities that encodes feeling energy and felt meaning is spatial. The spatial sub-modality determines where the imagery is seen in a person's inner visual field. It is very common for imagery associated with emotional suffering to appear in one specific position, while imagery associated with happiness appears in a different position. One client, focusing on a phobia of flying noticed that the anxiety appeared as a black patch located infront of her left shoulder. Later, she discovered a strong sense of inner healing energy, which had a pink color and was clearly located in her chest. Needless to say, when these two inner images merged, the intensity of the phobia was greatly reduced and she developed a new inner resource for coping with her fear of flying and other areas of anxiety in her life. Discovering the position of these two emotional energies was an important part of the healing process and made possible through the subtle awareness-investigation of mindfulness. Seeing where various emotions reside allows us to get in touch with our feelings in a very real way that is immediately apparent and real. We can literally reach out and touch them. This is quite different from the abstract and untangible process of thinking about our feelings or trying to understand them.

Whenever we uncover experiential imagery, we always investigate what needs to happen next. You may notice that the image seems to want to change its position and move from one side to the other side, or from top to bottom, or even diagonally. It is useful to follow these inner changes in spatial sub-modalities and see how they affect the quality of feeling. If a threatening image moves from the top to the bottom of your visual screen, does it become more or less threatening? You can experiment and discover what changes lead to the reduction of *dukkha* and what do not by paying very close attention to the associated feeling energy.

Another important spatial sub-modality is the size of the image, which is also related to how close the image is relative to you, as the observer. A large image will be more threatening than a small image. Size is often a key sub-modality in phobias. If a person has a phobia of spiders, it is very likely that his internal representation of a spider will be very large and very close. If the phobia resolves itself spontaneously or after a period of therapy, the internal image will probably have also become substantially smaller and appear at the back of his inner visual field. Like all sub-modalities, any change in structure correlates with a change in the intensity of feeling. When a person says, "It's not such a big problem as it used to be," the words actually reflect changes in in the size of his internal imagery.

Movement is another spatial sub-modality that can encode feelings. Rapid movements are often associated with intense emotional reactions, whereas slow movements generally convey calm and balance. Again, when there is mindfulness, your intuitive feelings will show you what resonates with your present experience and what needs to happen next. All you have to do is be aware and allow these changes to happen.

If you feel overwhelmed or confused, this may be represented internally in the form of spinning imagery. By focusing mindfulness on the spinning image, you may discover certain subtle adjustments that result in the image slowing down to a more comfortable speed, with a corresponding reduction in the feeling of confusion. What is most important is to allow these subtle changes to arise spontaneously, which they will do if given the freedom of mindfulness. We do not have to make the changes happen through deliberate intervention, but simply allow the changes to arise naturally and intuitively from our inner experience of the emotion. These natural, experiential changes will always be more effective than anything we do deliberately. However, it is often useful to experiement with making changes and then be very mindful of the results.

The next group of sub-modalities relates to the detailed structure of the imagery. The mind thinks in pictures, not words and it uses the rich sensory structure of imagery to organize and represent emotional experience. As the expression goes, a single picture is worth a thousand words, and this is because feeling energy can be encoded in the countless variations of color, color intensity, shape, size, texture and movement that make up the structure of an image. These are the structural sub-modalities.

It is not simply the memory of a car accident or a childhood trauma that evokes a painful emotional reaction, but how that image is represented internally. Intense colors produce intense feelings; rapid movements produce feelings of confusion and panic; large or close-up images are likely to produce a feeling of fear; small or far-off images will feel less threatening. Each of these specific sub-modalities is said to *encode* feeling energy, and the variations in these sub-modalities encodes a vast range of different feelings and meanings. Each of these sub-modalities encodes a particular quality of feeling energy and brings this energy together in the form of an emotion. The emotional energy takes on further form as thoughts, beliefs and intentions, which eventually manifests as speech and action. Every habitual emotional reaction has a structure that leads to an outward expression, but this whole process is powered by emotional energy that is encoded in the core experiential imagery.

Awareness of the subtle qualities of experiential imagery is, therefore, very important for facilitating emotional transformation, because any change in these sub-modalities will produce a corresponding change in the intensity and persistence of an emotional reaction. The specific form of the sub-modalities is ultimately what gives power to our beliefs and actions. Understand these specific details and the process of transformation, resolution and healing, will begin to unfold quite naturally. The solutions appear in direct proportion to how thoroughly you investigate the imagery associated with an emotion. The illumination of such specific details is very powerful in the same way that the very act of carefully examining every part of a car engine will reveal the problem that needs to be fixed. The most important action in either case is the response of investigation with mindfulness, because this allows us to see what is *actually* there, and it is this direct knowing which leads to transformation. When you see the loose wire or the broken spring, you immediately know what needs to be done to resolve the situation. If you do not look, then no solutions will appear. In the case of the experiential imagery, every detail that you dicover provides solutions that will lead to healing.

Of course, color is one of the most important sensory sub-modalities and encodes a great deal of feeling energy. The color red is often associated with anger, frustration, lust, and other highly charged emotions. Black often indicates feelings of emptiness and depression, as in the expression, "He is in a black mood." The color blue is often associated with tranquility and a sense of well-being. White is associated with purity and innocence and green is associated with rejuvenation.

Besides the specific color that seems to be associated with the experiential imagery, color intensity also encodes emotional energy. Vivid colors are associated with intense emotional reactions, whereas distant memories often appear indistinct and monochromatic.

Color is usually the first thing that people notice when they focus mindfulness on an emotion, and becoming familiar with these specific colors provides the first tangible contact with the emotion. It is difficult to change an emotion, but experimenting with changing a color is very achievable. *Dukkha* has color and that color can be changed. The conscious awareness of this color is part of the process of opening to the actual deep structure of our suffering, rather than staying stuck at the superficial and abstract level of an emotion. Mindfulness meditation and *vipassana* is, above all, about moving from the level of superficial perception, to the direct awareness of the actual inner sensory structure of our experience. This is the insight that leads to liberation and transformation, not ideas or thinking about *dukkha*. As Krishnamurti said, it is the truth that liberates, not our efforts to be free, and in this case the color, shape, texture, size, position or any of the other sub-modalities are what constitute the actual truth of our experience. This is why experiential imagery can be so powerful for the transformation of *dukkha*.

Besides the spatial and visual sub-modalities, experiential imagery is often associated with other sensory modalities such as sounds, tastes, smells, and temperature. An image may feel cold and clammy or hot and prickly. Very often, experiential imagery will have an auditory component. The inner critic often takes the form of a parent-like figure, sitting, like a raven on our shoulder. Needless to say, discovering *which* shoulder it sits on is one very important detail. You might find that switching shoulders can make a huge difference! Besides position, it is important to investigate the auditory sub-modalities of tone, loudness and the speed of speaking, because these give meaning and encode emotional energy. If you feel intimidated by a parent or authoritarian figure, it is very likely that your inner imagery of that person will not only be very large, towering above you, but that he will speak with a loud, piercing voice. When you ask yourself what needs to change, you may find that reducing the size and position of the parent image and making their voice softer could completely change how you feel. These subtle changes are what you discover quite naturally from your investigation with mindfulness of the *actual* internal experiential structure of your emotions. Through revealing this subtle inner structure through mindful-investigation, you provide specific tools that your psyche can use to heal itself.

Nothing can change if you remain at the superficial and abstract level of perception, but the moment you open the lid and investigate the reality of what is there, you will find that solutions will present themselves in abundance. The key is to look, which is the purposeful application of mindfulness to investigate mental phenomena, and this is the essential nature of *vipassana* meditation. All of the experiential details that you discover are immensely important for the transformation of emotional suffering, and the more you become conscious of the detailed structure of the submodalities, the more things will change in a beneficial direction. Ignorance sustains suffering and one of the specific ways that it does this is by preventing us from knowing the subtle details of the internal structure of our experience. Mindful-investigation, by contrast, allows us to uncover the deeper structure of experience, and it is this direct seeing that leads to transformation.

TYPES OF EXPERIENTIAL IMAGERY

Experiential imagery occurs in a variety of forms depending on the nature of the emotion. Some of the most common types of experiential imagery are Inner Drama, Memory Imagery, Abstract Imagery, and Symbolic Imagery.

Inner Drama

Inner drama is one of the most common forms of internal imagery in which the mind replays an event that has strong associated feelings of pain or pleasure. It could be a recent argument with your partner or child or a difficult encounter with a colleague at work. Emotions like guilt, anger and remorse often involve elaborate inner imagery in which we repeated relive the event over and over again. In a similar way, when we worry about the future we will imagine various scenarios that often include imagery. Such inner dramas can serve a useful function in helping us prepare for the future. However, they are only useful if we can remain objective and have a balanced, non-reactive relationship with the content of the drama.

The best way to work with inner drama is to watch the drama as if projected onto a screen or played out on a stage. You need to remain objective so that you can examine the unfolding imagery with mindfulness, without getting caught up in the drama. As always, the content is not as important as the feeling energy (*vedana*) that empowers it, and as you meditate on the drama, pay careful attention to the feelings that arise. After you make contact with the feeling energy, or felt-sense of the inner drama, you can let go of the contents and stay with the feeling and allow changes to unfold experientially. Eventually, after the process of experiential unfolding has reached a natural conclusion, return your attention to the original inner drama and see if there has been any change in the intensity of the emotion.

We can use inner drama as a way of accessing unresolved emotional reactivity from the past by making it the object of our mindfulness meditation. If we are plagued by regret or anxiety from an unpleasant or traumatic memory, we should not avoid it, but actually make the effort to relate to the memory of the event with mindfulness. This does not mean indulging in the emotion, or thinking about the trauma. Instead, we cultivate a watchful presence with the felt-sense of the emotion and surround it with compassionate space. As always, if you give the emotion the space in which to change, it will respond by changing, and this change will be experienced as changes in the inner drama. We might even experiment by making specific changes in the imagery and then observe, with mindfulness, the results that follow at the feeling level. However, what is generally most important is to simply remain mindful and fully present and allow changes to arise spontaneously from within.

We can also use inner drama as a method of preparing ourselves for the future. It is always a good practice to take the initiative now and prepare the mind to meet the potential difficulties that may unfold in the future. If we don't prepare ourselves, then we will most likely fall into our usual patterns of habitual reactivity and suffer accordingly. We should prepare, and the best way to prepare is to meditate on the specific emotions that are likely to arise, and find a way to resolve this emotional energy beforehand through mindful-investigation. As we contemplate a future scenario, we may discover subtle changes in the sub-modalities of color, size and position that neutralize the anxiety and strengthen our confidence.

In one case, a client complained of extreme anxiety associated with public speaking. Her mouth would become extremely dry and her throat became very tight whenever she imagined speaking in public. With mindfulness meditation, she became very aware of the precise sensations that arose when she imagined giving a speech. When asked what needed to happen next, she was able to use this information to determine exactly what would resolve the dry mouth. She discovered icecream! But not any kind of icecream; it had to be strawberry flavoured icecream. With such subtle attention to these precise experiential details, she was able to imagine eating a specific brand of strawberry icecream as she gave her talk, and this resolved the dry mouth reaction. This is using mindfulness meditation to prepare for the future.

This may seem a long way away from *vipassana* meditation, but *vipassana* is not meant to be an esoteric spiritual practice done by monks in a meditation hall. It is the practice of investigating experience through mindfulness to discover what needs to change in order to bring about the cessation of *dukkha*. Her dry mouth and fear of speaking is her present experience of *dukkha*, and mindfulness meditation on this suffering allowed her to discover precisely what needed to change in the inner *cittasankhara* that created that *dukkha*. Learning to let go of the blind attachment to her anxiety reaction so that she could investigate its inner structure is *anatta* in action. Allowing the *dukkha* to change in the freedom of mindfulness is *anicca* in action. Focusing mindfulness on her *dukkha* is The Path of Mindfulness, and awakening to the Four Noble Truths of suffering, the cause of suffering, the ending of suffering and the path to the end of suffering. This simple, yet very real example fulfils all the requirements of *vipassana* meditation, namely awakening and insight into the three marks of experience: *anicca*, *dukkha* and *anatta*.

Memories

Visual memories are the most familiar form of imagery, but memory images are much more than just a photographic record of events. They can become highly symbolic as they are processed by the psyche. The original memory may change under the influence of other parts of the mind until it no longer represents what actually happened, but takes on a whole different level of emotional meaning.

Some memories are particularly vivid, with a photographic quality that encodes a great deal of emotional energy. Such photographic, or eidetic memories often arise after emotional trauma, and particularly if the individual was unable to process and assimilate the emotions associated with the experience. Not surprisingly, physical, sexual or emotional abuse during childhood can produce intense memories that form the core of future post-traumatic stress, because a child does not have the maturity to process such intense experiences.

Post-traumatic stress may arise from witnessing a traumatic event, such as an accident or from witnessing the extreme violence of war. Such experiences fall outside the normal range and are difficult to process, even as adults. Trauma-induced memories become recurrent, because the underlying emotional energy remains unresolved and unassimilated. Unable to process this emotional energy, the mind becomes highly reactive, generating many layers of secondary reactivity. This secondary reactivity results in the repression of the original unresolved primary reactions and prevents transformation and resolution of the trauma. The repressed emotional energy becomes trapped in the mind, where it continues to generate further reactivity and suffering, which can lead to post-traumatic stress disorder.

Many phobias will also have some form of eidetic imagery that encodes intense emotional energy. A traumatic experience of drowning, being shut up in a closet, or even a frightening encounter with a spider can all generate very intense eidetic imagery that becomes imprinted in the subconscious. When the appropriate stimulus is present, these vivid eidetic images reappear along with the intense associated emotional reactions of fear and terror. When a phobic person sees a spider, it is not the external image of the spider that causes the emotional reaction; the reaction is produced by his internal representation, his subjective inner image of the spider. This will probably be very large and have intense color. These subjective sub-modalities encode emotional energy, and this post-experience processing leads to the intense emotional reactivity of a phobia.

We can work with such traumatic memories during *vipassana* meditation, and cultivate a relationship with the memory image as a primary object for meditation. We do not try to interpret the memory, but simply cultivate mindfulness of the memory image and allow it to unfold and change, experientially. The photographic quality of traumatic memories means that they tend to be very detailed, and it is these vivid details that give emotional intensity to the memory. These sub-modalities are actually much more important than the contents of the memory; they give the memory power to create emotional reactions. Therefore, resolution of a traumatic memory requires that these sub-modalities change. Resolution may lead to a decrease in color intensity or a change in color, or the image may become significantly smaller. Traumatic images are typically very close and "right in your face," so therapeutic change will most likely require that there be more distance between the observer and the image. The contents of the memory may remain the same, but how it is perceived changes and this is what matters.

It is the full conscious experience of the transformation of visual sub-modalities that leads to resolution, and this requires sustained mindfulness. During mindfulness, the details and sub-modalities unfold quite spontaneously under the guidance of *sati-panna*, as the psyche re-processes sensory data into a more stable form. An intense traumatic memory-image is, by definition, very unstable. Psychological Homeostasis will direct the psyche to find a new way of representing this memory that is more energetically stable. It is the freedom and therapeutic space provided by mindfulness that allows the process of inner re-adjustment and re-processing to occur. Habitual reactivity has the opposite effect and prevents conscious awareness of the sub-modalities and internal structure of the emotion, and without this conscious awareness, nothing can change.

Mindfulness Meditation Therapy (MMT) provides a very effective method for treating phobias and post-traumatic stress, because it allows us to discover the inner experiential imagery that lies at the core of these emotional reactions. The first phase of MMT teaches the client to recognize his habitual patterns of reactivity, which is essential, because nothing can change if it remains hidden from conscious awareness.

The next phase of MMT involves forming a relationship, based on mindfulness, with his inner experience of the emotion. Gradually the client learns to stop the secondary reactivity that takes him away from the direct experience of the underlying core emotions. Mindfulness provides a systematic approach for recognizing each and every impulse to react, and as the client becomes skilled in this, he will begin to see the reaction before it overwhelms him. This creates a moment of choice that was not previously available when he was unaware of the reactive process.

Through sustained periods of mindfulness contact, the client experiences more and more of the detailed sub-modalities of the inner traumatic imagery. As this experiential detail is made conscious, the imagery will begin to change under the influence of *satipanna* and the process of Psychological Homeostasis. As the imagery changes, it produces corresponding changes at the feeling level and this can be monitored throughout the mindfulness meditation session. Over time, the traumatic memory will lose its compulsive strength and no longer produce such intense emotional reactions.

It may seem counter-intuitive, but it is the conscious awareness of the details of traumatic imagery that leads to the reduction in the emotional reactivity of extreme anxiety. Although the emotion is encoded in the detailed structure of the traumatic imagery, it is the ignorance of this structure that leads to the emotional reaction. This is analogous to other fear reactions, such as the automatic reaction that might arise when we encounter a snake. When we actually pay attention and observe the detailed reality of the snake, the fear actually subsides and we simply respond to the reality of the situation and move away.

Working with traumatic memories and phobias requires care, so that we do not become overwhelmed by the intense emotional reactions that have developed in reaction to the inner imagery. The best way to work with a painful memory, as with any intense emotion, is by slowly approaching the perimeter of the memory-image and carefully monitoring the level of feeling until you are able to experience the feeling without reacting. In this careful approach, which is greatly facilitated by mindfulness, we are able to find a safe distance in which we can observe the inner traumatic imagery, without being overwhelmed.

The approach of repeated controlled exposure is well recognized as an essential part of the treatment of phobias and traumatic memories. This well tested method is called exposure desensitization and resembles allergy desensitization, where patients are systematically exposed to low doses of allergen over several weeks. Each time we successfully experience traumatic imagery without reacting, we create a new response pathway in the brain, and through repetition this will become the default pathway.

Abstract Imagery

Abstract imagery is quite common and often arises when we focus mindfulness on a general emotional state such as anger, fear or anxiety. Often, what we first notice is one or more patches of color, which later take on a particular shape. The shape may have a specific geometric form, such as a sphere or a cube, or it may have a completely amorphous shape, like a cloud. Whatever the form, the meditator feels that what he is experiencing is significant and resonates with his inner felst-sense of the emotion. Intuitively it feels right, even if rationally it make no sense at all.

In a session of Mindfulness Meditation Therapy, a young man in his late twenties was experiencing intense anxiety and sadness about an upcoming move, away from his home. This anxiety was so intense that it was also causing him to have panic reactions whenever he ventured into unfamiliar public settings, such as a supermarket.

When he focused mindfulness on the felt-sense of this emotion, he noticed a black sphere in the middle of his inner visual field. As he continued to invesigate this abstract image, he furthur noticed that there was a yellow layer on the rim of the black sphere. After furthur mindful-investigation, he was surprised to notice that a second sphere arose, but this was yellow on the inside and black on the outside. As he continued to focus on the unfolding imagery, yet a third object appeared, which he described as "pink and fuzzy."

When asked what needed to happen, all three parts came together, spinning around each other in a swirling dance, eventually merging into one large patch, which lost its solidity and simply evaporated like a cloud of steam. This led to a tremendous upwelling of feelings of inner calm and a new sense of inner strength. When he focused his attention back on the thoughts about the upcoming move, he noticed that the anxiety and sadness had become significantly less intense and he felt better able to meet the challenges that lay ahead.

We continued to work on this new sense of inner strength and calm. Interestingly, the imagery changed yet again into the inner image of a tree. As he focused mindfully on this inner picture, noticing the leaves and branches, his feeling of inner strength and security increased. The feelings were literally encoded in the green leaves and solid branches that could support him. When he was asked to imagine visiting a supermarket, he imagined being there in that crowded and chaotic environment, but now protected by the awareness of his inner tree! He no longer felt the panic and anxiety associated with the unknown.

The conscious experience of these unique changes in the submodalities of his experiential imagery had a dramatic effect on the underlying emotions. None of this experiential imagery could have been predicted and no attempt was made to analyze it. What was important was the *present experience* of this unfolding content and not what it all means. The colors and abstract forms arose intuitively and spontaneously as a result of the non-reactive awareness of *satisampajanna*. It was his intuitive intelligence, or *satipanna*, that directed the sequence of changes that eventually led to the resolution of the emotional complex. It is through this kind of process that the psyche heals itself, through the natural language of experiential imagery.

In another session, a client meditated on the inner felt-sense of depression, which he had been struggling with for years. When he focused on the present felt-sense of his depression, the first thing he noticed was a sense of blackness. This is not uncommon, because black has a symbolic association with depression, as reflected in our language with statements such as: "He is in a black mood." After a few minutes of sustained mindfulness, the amorphous black cloud differentiated into a doughnut shape. When he imagined touching this shape, he noticed that it was rubbery, like a car inner tube. After further mindful-investigation to see what needed to happen next, he noticed that the inner tube began to deflate and as the air escaped, the depression lifted. Through the conscious experience of these changes in the inner structure of his depression, he discovered a way to free the core emotional energy that had become locked up in the mental formation of depression. The imagery provided the means through which this energy could be released and eventually re-assimilated back into the psyche where it could have a more positive effect.

This kind of experiential change is often significantly more effective than trying to understand why we feel depressed, anxious or angry, because when we work with experiential imagery, we are working at a much deeper level of the psyche. Thinking about experience is always one step removed from the actual truth of experience, because thinking is a reaction and not the direct experience of reality. As has been said many times already, it is the truth that liberates, not our efforts to change, and in the cases described above, the truth refers to the actual experience of the concrete inner language of imagery that forms the inner structure of his depression. When we can see this structure, in all its detail, we provide the ideal conditions in which emotional suffering can transform and resolve itself from the inside.

Symbolic Imagery

Perhaps the most familiar kinds of symbolic images are those that arise when we are dreaming. Dreams are internal representations of inner psychological processing and like experiential imagery, they arise spontaneously. The emotional meaning of a dream image is encoded both in the symbolic form of the dream and in the sub-modalities, such as color, shape and size.

Like other forms of experiential imagery, dream imagery can be made a primary object for mindfulness meditation. Traditional dream work usually involves interpretation of the symbolic meaning of dream images in order to shine a light on underlying psychological process. However, in Mindfulness Meditation Therapy, the emphasis is not so much on the contents, as on the process of experiential unfolding of the dream imagery in the present.

If you remain mindful and try not to interfere with the dream imagery, it will typically undergo a process of transformation, guided by our innate intelligence of *satipanna*, and this can lead to profound changes at the emotional level. This way of working with dreams is called Active Imagination and was originally developed by Carl Jung. Active Imagination is not fantasy or visualization, which are products of the thinking mind, but involves allowing dream imagery to unfold in its own way through being mindful of the intuitive feeling energy (*vedana*) that accompanies the imagery. As Jung said,

> A fantasy is more or less your own invention, and remains on the surface of personal things and conscious expectations. But active imagination, as the term denotes, means that the images have a life of their own and that the symbolic events develop according to their own logic - that is, of course, if your conscious reason does not interfere.

The guiding principle in Active Imagination is to be mindful of the intuitive feelings associated with the symbolic imagery and allow changes to unfold in a way can be felt to be meaningful. As always, you let your innate intelligence, or *satipanna* guide the unfolding process and resist trying to make things change according to preconceptions about what is supposed to happen.   Mindfulness helps the process of Active Imagination by allowing us to tune in to our present experience and discover the specific sub-modalities of the dream imagery that encode feeling energy. If you dream of a unicorn, it is not the symbol itself that is as important as the intensity of the white color of its coat, the color of its horn and the position of the beast in your inner visual field. These and other sub-modalities give power to the dream image and it is through sustained mindfulness of these details, that experiential unfolding and transformation will occur. It is the attention to these details that makes the imagination *active*.

Symbolic imagery is not only confined to dreams, and similar dream-like imagery may arise during mindfulness meditation and particularly during Mindfulness Meditation Therapy, where we focus our attention on core emotions. If symboloic imagery arises during meditation, we should form a mindful-relationship with it as an object for meditation, and become familiar with the fine details of the structure of the imagery. We should allow the imagery to change in its own unique way within the field of mindfulness and fully appreciate these changes. As always, such imagery will change and eventually disappear by itself, but if we allow it to change under the direction of our intuitive intelligence, then the resulting change will be beneficial. If we ignore the imagery or react to it with attraction (*lobha*), aversion (*dosa*) or blind belief (*moha*), then the changes that occur will not be in alignment with *sati-panna*, and the opportunity for healing will be lost. As always, mindfulness is the essential factor that allows us to follow the right path.

In one case, a woman complained about feeling completely overwhelmed by too many responsibilities and the continual frustration of things not working out according to expectation. She desperately wanted to find an inner sense of balance and calm to help her cope.

During a session of mindfulness therapy on her feeling of being overwhelmed, she discovered to her amazement that the many frustrations and disappointments took on the form of small, hard billiard balls that appeared on the periphery of her inner visual field. They were moving very chaotically and literally hitting her on the head.

As she continued to observe mindfully, she posed the question: "What do you need from me?" She got a very strong feeling that they needed color. They needed a bright color, not red or orange, but yellow. This bright yellow energy carried a very strong inner sense of calm, strength and freedom for her. This is how she experienced the inner strength that she had lost, and through mindfulness, she was once again able to reconnect with this part of herself. Later, the color took on the form of a large billowing yellow sail on a wooden boat. This symbolic imagery provided her with a way of accessing the inner strength that she already possessed, but had been unable to summon when needed.

Now she was able to bring this "yellow energy" into the scene and imagined taking the billiard balls for a trip in her boat! This gave her the sense of control that she had long been searching for, and could not find by simply talking about her problems. The change came about as a result of her direct experience of this inner experiential imagery, and allowing the imagery to change under the direction of her innate intelligence.   When we maintain a relationship based on mindfulness, solutions present themselves quite naturally. It is not what we do that matters as much as being fully present and open to discover what needs to happen in our present experience. This is allowing the psyche to heal itself, rather than trying to fix things through the distorted activities of the ego, or through endless interpretation and speculation. Experiential and symbolic imagery provide an excellent medium through which the psyche can resolve emotional conflict and trauma at the deep and intuitive level of our emotions. In this process, the psyche essentially learns new pathways for connecting the resources that already exist in the mind, as represented by the yellow sail for solving internal conflict, as symbolized by the billiard balls in the above example. Through mindfulness, the psyche learns how to respond rather than react, and this is the path of liberation of the mind from the constraints and suffering inherent in habitual reactivity, or *samsara*.

19 THE FREE MIND

Ultimately, the purpose of mindfulness practice and *vipassana* meditation is liberation (*vimutti*). This means liberating the mind (*ceto-vimutti*) from all the habitual mental reactivity and ignorance that imprisons our being, and limits our freedom to respond effectively to the demands of life. We also seek to purify the mind through alignment with wisdom-intelligence (*panna-vimutti*) so that we live in harmony with *anicca*, allowing change to manifest under the guidance of our innate intelligence.

Mindfulness facilitates transformation by stopping the proliferation of reactivity that inhibits transformation. The moment we become aware of a reaction as it arises, we gain a moment of freedom to see and experience the truth of the moment, instead of being distracted by reactivity. In this way we overcome *avijja* and begin the process of movement from the superficial surface structure to the deep inner structure of experience.

Mindfulness brings about transformation by allowing intelligent change to unfold without interference from the conditioned ego, because when there is mindfulness there is freedom from the reactive ego. This is freedom from the *knower* of conscious experience. The *knower*, or ego doesn't simply experience phenomena, it *reacts* to phenomena, and reactivity is conditioned by the past, and attachment to this reactivity produces *dukkha*. As we break free from the chains of habitual reactivity, we create the conditions in which *satipanna* can arise and bring about the resolution of *dukkha*. Such transformation with mindfulness always leads towards the resolution of suffering, because the psyche, like any living system will always try to find the most stable state possible, which means freedom from *dukkha*.

In addition to facilitating transformation of *dukkha*, mindfulness also leads to a fundamental shift in the whole psyche, because when there is *satisampajanna*, we transcend the *known* and become the *knowing* itself. We become the container, rather than the contents; the space around mental objects, rather than the objects; the pure awareness of observing, rather than the reactions to the objects observed. From this new perspective, even if reactions arise, we are no longer seduced by them and no longer become them, and if we do not feed reactivity, then it will surely wither away.

As we begin to align with the *knowing* rather than the *known*, we discover the taste of freedom from our habitual reactivity. Reactions may still arise, but we are no longer compelled to become the anger, sadness, fear or other content of the mind. Instead, we find that we begin to relate to these *sankharas* as objects to be observed, without any further reactions of wanting, aversion or deluded identification. Instead of becoming angry when an angry thought arises, we respond with pure awareness that observes the phenomenon of anger. Instead of becoming fearful when a fearful thought arises, we respond to this mental object with *satisampajanna* and simply rest in the pure knowing of fear. Instead of becoming worried because a worrying thought arises, we respond with pure awareness and observe the worry-thought with complete objectivity. This is the universal response of mindfulness, which is the natural response of letting go, or rather, not grasping, and in which there is tremendous spaciousness, compassion and patience.

Through the practice of mindfulness, we transcend the realm of the conditioned habitual patterns of the mind and discover a new freedom and a much more authentic way of being in the world. As we progress in our practice, we discover a new refuge in the unconditioned and unchangeable dimension of existence called the *asankhata dhatu*, which literally means the un-fabricated dimension of existence. If it is not fabricated, then it has no form. If it has no form, then it does not die, and for this reason the transcendence of the habitual reactivity of *samsara* is described as the path to the deathless (*amatapada*).

Unlike an idea, thought or emotion that arises and eventually dies, the pure awareness of those ideas, thoughts and emotions has no *form* in itself, does not depend on conditions, and does not die. *Nibbana* (Skt. *Nirvana*) is the perfection of this transcendence of the conditioned state of mind such that there is no remnant of attachment and conditioned reactivity; it is the state of complete extinction of *lobha*, *dosa* and *moha*. The conditioned world of *samsara* is a world of illusions, and a prison that we create for ourselves through ignorance. However, the Good News is that as conscious human beings, we have the ability to de-construct our prison

242

through awakening to our blind attachments, so that we can step out of our prison into the infinite light of freedom.

Imagine a person who has spent his whole life living in a deep valley. His perceptions of reality are conditioned by what he can see, touch and feel within the confines of that valley. He assumes that the entire world is contained within that valley. Of course, this perception is an illusion, but habitual conditioning and ignorance prevent him from knowing anything different.

One day he decides to climb the valley wall to the top, far above. No one has ever done this before, but something drives him from within to make this jouney. When he reaches the top, something quite remarkable happens: he sees countless valleys and mountains stretching far into the distance. From that very moment of awakening, which could be measured in milliseconds, his entire perception has been changed forever, and he can never turn back to his old belief that the valley is the entire world. No thinking or analysis was required to reach this new perspective; it came about spontaneously as a result of direct seeing and direct knowning. His world was changed forever by simply awakening to the truth of experience as it is. This awakening to reality is profoundly liberating.

Rooted in ignorance, the habitual subjective reactions of *sakayaditthi* create our world by projecting our perceptions onto reality, and this is like being confined to the valley. To follow The Path of Mindfulness and *Dhamma* is to climb the valley walls, driven by an intuitive sense of the innate wisdom-intelligence of *satipanna* that we all possess. The first fuction of *sati* is to bring us into direct contact with the reality of our experience, which happens the moment we become aware of our reactions as they arise. When we are fully present, then we know things as they actually are, which is the pure, undeluded knowing of *satisampajanna*, and with this pure knowing a completely different reality opens up before us. This new vision leads to *satipanna* and we experience a release from the blind acceptance of our reactivity.

This is awakening to not self (*anatta*), in which we see that we are not the contents of our mind and that our essential being transcends anything that can be known or created. As we let go of our reactions, they lose their power and simply become objective phenomena that, like any other *sankharas*, are subject to the laws of

Dhamma: they are impermanent, superficial and not self. Mindfulness practice brings us to the understanding, and more importantly, to the direct living realization that we are not our thoughts, but something much, much more. As the Tibetan meditation master Kalu Rinpoche said,

> We live in illusion and the appearance of things. There
> is a reality. We are that reality. When you understand
> this, you see that you are nothing, and being nothing,
> you are everything. That is all.

The illusion and appearance of things, refers to the surface structure of reality, the transient and superficial thoughts and emotions that arise in the mind. A painful thought arises and we become the pain; a happy thought arises and we become happy. This is living in the illusion (*moha*) and appearance of things.   There is a reality, and this is the totality of our psyche and the unconditioned ground of pure mind living according to *Dhamma*. To see that you are nothing, means that you see that the essential nature of mind is unconditioned pure awareness itself, and this is beyond the thoughts, beliefs and the reactive conditioning that we take to be our personality. This pure awareness can know the limitless variety of thoughts and feelings as they arise, yet the awareness faculty remains unchanged, just as the ocean remains unchanged by the bewildering array of life forms, from plankton to whales, that live in it.

The essential nature of mind is empty of form and described by the Pali word *sunnata*. The analogy of a mirror is often used to describe the nature of Original Mind, because the mirror reflects everything without distinction and without attachment. Actually, Original Mind is neither the mirror nor the things reflected, but the *reflecting* itself, which is empty of all form. This is the nature of the pure direct knowing of things that we call *satisampajanna*, without any hint of reactivity or identification.

When we change from being the contents of our reactive mind to being the knowing of all phenomena, then we discover our inner true nature. There is a verse by Zen master Maezumi Roshi,

In studying ourselves,
we find the harmony that is our total existence.
We do not make harmony.
We do not achieve it or gain it.
It is there all the time.
Here we are, in the midst of this perfect way,
and our practice is simply to realize it and then to actu-
alize it in our everyday life.

This inner essential nature of the mind is our birthright, we are born with it, but we quickly looses sight of this original Buddha mind through the accumulation of blind habitual reactivity, the prison that we call self. Our practice then, is simply to strip away the layers of reactivity, of self, to reveal the pure light within.

BODHICITTA

The mind is always active, continually generating thoughts, emotional reactions and other mental contents. This is its nature, and there is nothing inherently wrong with an active mind, as long as it is balanced with intelligence and wisdom. It is only when we are lacking *panna* that we fall under the spell of this changing content, become attached to it and suffer accordingly.

When we take refuge in the larger dimension of pure awareness, then we are no longer at the mercy of the contents of the mind, and the mind becomes steady and unwavering. As Ajahn Chah, who was one of the most influential meditation teachers of the twentieth century, expressed it,

> The nature of the original mind is unwavering. It is tranquil. We are not tranquil because we are excited over sense objects, and we end up as slaves to the changing mental states that result. So, practice really means searching to find our way back to the original state, the "old thing." It is finding our home, the original mind that does not waiver and change following various phenomena. It is by nature perfectly peaceful; it is something that is already within us.

The practice of mindfulness provides the mechanism for returning our attention to this original state, the "old thing" of pure awareness, which is called Original Mind, or *bodhicitta*. The term *bodhicitta* simply means, "awakened mind," from the root *budhi*, which means "to awaken to experience in the here and now" and *citta*, which means "mind, heart, spirit or state of conscious experience." The word Buddha also comes from the same root and means the awakened one, the one who is awake to the *Dhamma*, or the objective reality of phenomena.

Bodhicitta is the field of consciousness where intuitive awareness (*satisampajanna*) and intuitive wisdom (*satipanna*) come together, unified by the central theme of mindfulness (*sati*). In the very moment when mindfulness arises, reactivity ceases, simply because mindfulness and reactivity are mutually exclusive events. It is in this interval, when there is no reactivity that *bodhicitta* arises. This interval is the unconditioned state of consciousness (*asankhata citta*), in which there is no *atta*, no ego, no self. In that moment of mindfulness the state of *anatta*, or no self, spontaneously comes into existence and there is no longer the subject-object duality created by the attachments and reactivity of the ego mind. What is left is the pure knowing, or *satisampajanna*, which is the original pure, luminous and immeasurable Buddha mind, or *bodhicitta* and the essence of our true self.

Enlightenment or awakening should not be viewed as some abstract state of consciousness, to be achieved in the future after years of practice at the feet of a spritual master. Awakening is actually a living, dynamic, ongoing process that occurs in each and every moment when mindfulness and the clear non-deluded awareness of *satisampajanna* are present. *Bodhicitta* is a natural and direct consequence of mindfulness in action.

The Buddha directs us to follow the path that creates the optimal conditions for discovering enlightenment for ourselves, in the here and now, and this is the path of freedom from the known. To quote the eighth century Tibetan sage, Padmasambhava,

The nature of your mind, which cannot be pinpointed, is innate and original wakefulness. It is important to look into yourself and recognize your nature.

In each moment of mindfulness, we cease to be reactive, because the two are mutually exclusive. The state of *satisampajanna* is the complete opposite of our usual state of *avijja*, in which we are pushed and pulled from one experience to another by the force of reactivity. *Satisampajanna* is the state of "innate and original wakefulness," and is not identified with any of the contents that arise in the mind. This wakefulness is the essence of *bodhicitta*; it is unconditioned (*asankhata*) and not limited by the fabrications of mind (*sankhara*), attachments (*upadana*) or mental reactivity (*kilesas*).

The Path of Mindfulness is the primary route that takes us towards our own true nature. In the words of the Buddha,

Through Bodhi one awakens from the slumber or stupor inflicted upon the mind by the defilements and comprehends the Four Noble Truths.

It is the accumulated habitual reactivity, supported by ignorance and attachment, that dulls the mind into "slumber and stupor," and this obscures the original purity of our innate essence. The heart of the Buddhist path is about removing the *kilesas*, not through willpower and coercion, but through the liberating insight of wisdom-intelligence (*panna*). The path of purification is learning to greet each *kilesa* with *satisampajanna*, rather than further reactivity.

You cannot create *bodhicitta*, but you can remove the obstacles that obscure *bodhicitta* through the practice of mindfulness, and allow *bodhicitta* to arise and be known in each present moment. *Bodhicitta* is always there, but obscured by habitual reactivity, in the same way that an abandoned city becomes completely covered by jungle vines after years of neglect.

Mindfulness practice and *vipassana* meditation are the tools that we use to excavate the lost kingdom of our innate original pure Buddha mind. This is achieved by the careful illumination of each and every obstacle with mindfulness (*sati*) and clear comprehension (*satismpajanna*). Seeing things in their true light allows *satipanna* to arise, and it is this that resolves *dukkha* and transcends *samsara*. When there is *satisampajanna* and *satipanna*, then experience is free to change in an intelligent direction that leads to the cessation of suffering. This is what it means to comprehend the Four Noble Truths, not as psychological concepts, but as a living realization in each moment of consciousness. This natural and intuitive wisdom arises whenever the psyche is free to encounter *dukkha* and realize the natural path that leads to the resolution of *dukkha*. This path is not a path with a beginning and an end, but a path that is to be discovered in *each and every moment* of our living.

SUNNATA

Original Mind, or *bodhicitta* is like the Sky, Ocean or the Earth itself. It is the original ground of all being, the limitless space in which an infinite variety of formations can arise. This spaciousness is the nature of pure *knowing*, which is quite distinct from the contents that can be *known*. The essential nature of Original Mind is the boundless knowing of all mental and sensory phenomena, the pure consciousness that receives all manifestations that have form.

By analogy, the Ocean has an inexhaustible potential to contain any organism ever created, from early life forms, through the age of dinosaurs, to present day ocean life in all its diversity. Throughout history, the Ocean remains the same and unaffected by the contents that arise and disappear. This same analogy applies to the Sky, which is similarly unaffected by the clouds, or birds that fly through it, and which remains unmarked by all these formations. The Earth also gives birth to all manner of formations, from mountains to glaciers and a bewildering variety of life forms, and yet the essence of the Earth remains unchanged. We can look at Earth, Ocean and Sky as having an inexhaustible potential to allow formations to arise, to do their dance, and then to return to the ground of being from which they came.

Original Mind, like the Ocean, Sky and Earth is formless and cannot be equated with any of the contents of mind. It has the quality of pure emptiness, or in more positive terms, pure openness and limitless creative potential. To quote Leonardo Da Vinci,

> Among the great things which are to be
> found among us,
> the Being of Nothingness is the greatest.

Original Mind is the Being of Nothingness. Through mindfulness practice you will naturally become more familiar with the contents of your mind and see how these phenomena arise, do their dance and then pass away. You will gain insight into how thoughts, perceptions and feelings arise and disappear depending on conditions. You will gain insight into how all these phenomena lack permanency (*anicca*) and exist as part of a process; how they are fundamentally unsatisfactory (*dukkha*) and unstable; and how they are essentially impersonal (*anatta*) and beyond your control. The contents of experience are empty phenomena that come and go like bubbles in the ocean. But, what you will also become aware of through mindfulness practice, is the quality of unlimited consciousness that is the "Being of nothingness" that seems to provide a continuity and background to all existence.

This emptiness, or spaciousness is called *sunnata* (Skt. *shunyata*), which is the essence of Original Mind, or *bodhicitta*. The word is derived from the root *sunya*, which means "empty" and the suffix *ta*, meaning "-ness." To say that the essential nature of the mind is emptiness may seem to be a pessimistic view, but in fact the root *su-* conveys the positive concept of good and being at ease, as in the word *sukha*, the Pali word for happiness. *Sunnata* is better translated as the "creative void," or simply the state of complete openness to all phenomena and in which all becomes possible. The great Indian Buddhist, Acharya Asanga described *sunnata* as,

> an aesthetic continuum with all possibilities.

Sunnata actually describes the liberated mind that is open to the real world with all its possibilities; *sunnata* is equivalent to the innate state of freedom that is our birthright. This is in complete contrast to the reactive, conditioned mind of *sankhata citta*, which is closed and restricted to only limited possibilities. To experience the truth of things and to be able to fully engage creatively with life, the mind must be free of conditioning and reactivity. If the mind is cluttered with thoughts, prejudices, views, opinions and habitual emotional reactions, then the mind cannot connect to the "continuum with all possibilities" and will remain imprisoned in *samsara*, the endless round of suffering. Original Mind is un-originated, unconditioned and deathless. If the mind remains free of clinging to the contents of experience, then it is liberated to become the infinite consciousness of pure knowing.

To taste *sunnata* is to taste freedom. To taste emptiness a little brings a little freedom, to taste emptiness a lot brings a lot of freedom, and to taste emptiness continually brings continuous freedom. From this position of freedom we have the flexibility to engage skillfully and wisely with every moment of life, and natural wisdom and intelligence (*panna*) flow in response to this freedom of pure emptiness. As Zen master Suzuki Roshi said,

> If your mind is empty, it is always ready for anything;
> it is open to everything. In the beginner's mind there
> are many possibilities, in the expert"s mind there are
> few.

Original Mind has *sunnata* as its foundation, allowing an infinite capacity for creativity and intelligence as we relate with each and every experience that arises during the day. Through *satipanna*, our actions are purified and much more likely to be skillful and wholesome and in harmony with the needs of the present. This is the *panna* of the "beginner's mind."

The concept of *sunnata* is very closely associated with *anatta*, an equally fundamental concept in Buddhism, which asserts that any phenomena experienced through the senses has no permanent essence, nothing that can be said to be an independent self. The theory of *anatta* is based on the reality of what we can observe in the world, namely that all phenomena are subject to change (*anicca*) and are inherently unsatisfactory (*dukkha*) due to their impermanence and superficiality.   Phenomena arise and pass away according to conditions, but what remains is *sunnata,* the essential substratum of complete openness and complete freedom from changing conditions. *Anatta,* like *sunnata,* is not in any way a negative statement about existence, but a very positive statement that affirms that you are actually much, much more than you can possibly imagine; that you are essentially infinite and cannot be reduced to concepts or labels, or anything that can be given a name.

Sunnata is said to be equivalent to *nibbana*, the extinction of all grasping and attachment. This is why the Buddha taught that,

Sunnata is *Nibbana* and *Nibbana* is *Sunnata*.

Awakening to *sunnata* is actually not that difficult. Every time we respond to experience with mindfulness, then in that very moment there is an opening to *sunnata* and we become *sunnata*. In each moment of mindfulness, we touch *sunnata* and *sunnata* touches us back. When this happens, the mind opens and becomes infinitely expansive. In this relationship with *sunnata*, we allow an intelligent space to arise in which healing, transformation, creativity and wisdom (*panna*) flourish. The heart of the Buddhist Path of Mindfulness is to bring our whole being into alignment with *sunnata* so that we live *nibbana* in each present moment of our life. Living *sunnata* and *nibbana* in each moment allows transformation and transcendence from the fetters that sustain suffering. There is a Zen saying,

Whether sitting or walking,
Silent or talking,
The Essence Itself,
Is always at ease.

Sunnata is the ultimate state of liberation, where our total being is free to respond, without the constraints of the habitual reactivity of our personality (*sakkayaditthi*). *Sunnata* is the antithesis of the conditioned and contracted state of the reactive mind. It is through continuity of practice that we establish and develop this center of balance, this still-point of reference that becomes our refuge and spiritual guide. The essence of *sunnata* is always at ease, a place of stability and well-being, and through mindfulness we can discover this healing presence in each moment of existence.

The more mindful we are, the more we will know *sunnata* and the more we will be at ease and free from suffering. *Sunnata* cannot be defined or created, but it can be known, when there is mindfulness. When there is *sati* there is *sunnata*, and when there is *sunnata* there is *sati*. Mindfulness is the skillful application of awareness that brings us back to the place where we are in touch with *sunnata* and where we are healed by the creative intelligence of this creative void. In each moment of contact through mindfulness, we bring the living presence of *sunnata* into our present experience, and truth and wisdom flower in response.

Sunnata brings an extraordinary calmness and serenity into our being that comes from its extraordinary spaciousness. It is spiritually refreshing, like a cool mountain pool. It nourishes. It heals. It is the essence of the spiritual dimension of our being that transcends all form and all content. The purpose of mindfulness practice is simply to reconnect with *sunnata* so that it becomes our refuge and our source of strength, balance and wisdom. The cultivation of a conscious relationship with *sunnata* provides a strong foundation that allows the development of true equanimity (*upekkha*) as we relate to the chaos and demands of daily life. In the refuge of *sunnata* we are set free from the grip of the reactive ego, and the living death that is *samsara*. *Vipassana* meditation is the primary tool that connects us to the resonating still spaciousness of *sunnata* that is the essence of our being. From this vantage point, we can engage with all that arises in the mind, all the *sankharas*, both pleasant and painful. Connecting with the natural *sunnata* that is our primordial nature helps us be fully present for the afflictive emotions that may arise, whilst remaining steady and non-reactive. *Samadhi* is perfected by *sunnata* and from this secure base we can live without fear. Fear is borne of attachment and identification, the reactions of the ego (*atta*). If there is no attachment (*upadana*), then there is no ego (*anatta*). If *anatta* permeates our conscious relationship with all the ups and downs of life, then we are living the essence of *sunnata* and there will be no place in which *dukkha* can take hold and proliferate.

20 THE PERFECTION OF THE FREE MIND

Bodhicitta arises when the mind lets go of habitual reactivity and conditioning and responds to the experience of the world with *sati-sampajanna* and *satipanna*. This flowering of wisdom and intelligence naturally leads towards the more wholesome qualities of humanity, just as ignorance inevitably leads towards suffering and violence. The awakenned Buddha mind of *bodhicitta* is characterized by ten spiritual perfections called *paramis* that work together to produce wholesome and skillful actions of body, speech and mind. The Path of Mindfulness is a journey that has the perfection of the ten *paramis* as its goal, and in the awakened mind these *paramis* purify our relationships to Self, Other and World. These ten *paramis* are generosity (*dana*); morality (*sila*); renunciation and non-clinging (*nekkhamma*); wisdom-intelligence (*panna*); spiritual energy and vitality (*viriya*); patience (*khanti*); dedication to truth (*sacca*); resolute determination (*adhitthana*); loving-kindness (*metta*); and equanimity (*upekkha*).

At the conventional level of understanding, we can do much to cultivate these ten qualities through the cultivating right thinking, based on the teachings of wise people. However, thinking is always limited to some dgree by reactive conditioning, and what emerges is always slightly unsatisfactory. While we can do much to develop these wholesome qualities through right thinking and right action, we cannot develop them fully by thought or action alone. Therefore, to develop these noble aspirations into *parami*, or spiritual perfections, we must go beyond thinking and the limitations of the fragmented ego.

To go beyond the limitations of the conditioned mind, we need to cultivate *satisampajanna* through the practice of mindfulness in order to develop *satipanna*. It is the non-reactive and objective awareness of mindfulness that allows *satipanna* to arise, and it is this intuitive wisdom-intelligence that will guide us towards the perfection of the *paramis*. Mindfulness places us on a path of learning about the *paramis* from minute to minute, and what emerges will be much more effective than the products of thinking alone. As we free ourselves from compulsive reactivity, we create the right conditions in which the *paramis* will arise and mature in a natural and holistic way from the deepest level of the psyche.

The path for developing these virtues is primarily about removing the obstacles that stand in the way, rather than by trying to create them through thinking and imagination. Rather than forcing ourselves to be truthful, compassionate or generous, we work to remove the obstacles of habitual reactivity that inhibit the natural expression of these qualities. If you unblock the logjam, then the river will flow naturally, and this is how we should approach the perfection of the ten *paramis*. The *paramis* are not abstract ideals, but natural states that flow from the enlightened and awakened mind, the Buddha mind of *bodhicitta*. The seeds of all the *paramis* already reside in our innate nature, but to allow them to germinate and flourish, we must endeavour to remove the rocks and debris of the habitual, conditioned mind.

The mind that is free to change and adapt under the influence of *satipanna*, will naturally move towards the perfection of the *paramis* for the simple reason that they support the path towards the cessation of suffering. Under the guidance of *satipanna* the psyche will always move towards greater stability, well-being and happiness (*sukha*), which is another way of describing the cessation of *dukkha*. This principle of psychological homeostasis, or *satipanna*, not only guides the psyche towards greater stability and equanimity, but also guides our external actions in our personal relationships and in our relationship to the physical and material world. Mindfulness allows us to find peace within, and peace in our world through this natural and organic perfection of the *paramis*.

Before we can perfect these noble virtues in our outer relationships, we must begin by cultivating these qualities in our internal relationship with our own mind. The *paramis* have to become integrated into the whole psyche as we relate to both our personal suffering and our happiness. The path begins when we cultivate generosity, morality, non-attachment, intelligence, effort, patience, truthfulness, determination, loving-kindness and equanimity towards all the ups and downs of our moment-to-moment experience. As we cultivate these virtues in our own life, then we will gain the direct experience that will allow these noble virtues to spread outwards into our relationships with others. Therefore, any work that we undertake to purify our mind and heart is beneficial for all humanity, and working towards our own liberation is also working towards the liberation of all. There is no separtation between the two paths, as so succinctly expressed in the ancient Chinese proverb,

> If there is light in the soul, there will be
> beauty in the person.
> If there is beauty in the person, there will
> be harmony in the house.
> If there is harmony in the house, there will
> be order in the nation.
> If there is order in the nation, there will be
> peace in the world.

The whole process begins by bringing the light of mindfulness into the soul, or psyche. When the mind is purified and liberated from habitual reactivity, blind conditioning and prejudice, then this healing energy naturally flows outwards to bring beauty and harmony externally.

All ten *paramis* depend on each other and work together as a unified force for beneficial change. Above all, the *paramis* are tempered by the four primary colors, the *brahmaviharas*, or sublime abodes that accompany mindfulness. These are *metta, karuna, mudita* and *upekkha*. *Metta* is the courageous response of opening the mind and heart to all that we experience with genuine friendship and love. *Karuna* is compassion for suffering, wherever it arises, internally or externally, and *mudita* is awakening to everything that is wholesome, beneficial and life supporting. *Upekkha* is the perfection of non-reactivity and non-attachment that creates the spaciousness in which *panna* will arise. These four noble qualities are ceveloped through the practice of mindfulness and provide the foundation for the cultivation and perfection of all ten *paramis*.

Mindfulness creates the fertile ground in which the *paramis* will grow by resolving the fundamental defilements of greed, hatred and delusion that prevents the *paramis* from taking root. An angry mind cannot possibly know patience and loving-kindness, because anger is like a black cloud that obscures all. A greedy,

255

clinging mind cannot know generosity and love. A deluded mind that attaches to mental reactivity cannot grow beyond the limits set by reactivity. Therefore, the first job must be to remove these obstacles of *lobha, dosa* and *moha* through the practice of mindfulness. To discover the *paramis* of love, we must first address the hindrance of hatred; to perfect patience, we must meditate of our restlessness; to perfect wisdom, we must apply mindfulness to dispel ignorance. In short, we must have a solid foundation in mindfulness if we are to develop the *paramis* beyond the conventional and superficial level of understanding.

DANA

Dana describes the spirit of generosity and kindness that comes from the heart and is expressed in actions that directly benefit others as well as self. *Dana* is the natural expression of *metta, karuna, mudita* and *upekkha.*

The foundation for true generosity is a pure mind that is not consumed with selfishness, and for this there must be order in the mind and heart (*citta*). A mind that is consumed by the reactivity of greed, hatred and delusion is closed and contracted, and in this state of disorder and conflict it is difficult to cultivate heart-felt generosity. In essence, the greatest gift you can give the world is to liberate your own mind from the grip of greed, hatred and delusion. With freedom from reactivity comes the spaciousness and freedom to discover the natural source of generosity that already exists within the heart. As you develop the direct experience of *dana* within, it will naturally radiate outwards and you will become more inclined to be generous towards others. In the words of the Buddha:

> Thousands of candles can be lit from a single candle, and the life of the candle will not be shortened. Happiness never decreases by being shared.

There is something quite beautiful in the quality of generosity: it brings light and warmth to the hearts of everyone that it touches, and for this reason the Buddha placed *dana* at the center of his teachings.

We may want to be generous or try to be kind, but more often, these creations of the ego-mind are severely limited, especially if our mind is in a state of disorder and suffering. True generosity needs to arise organically from the heart, rather than contrived by the controlling ego, and this requires that we listen internally and externally at a very subtle level, and especially to those reactions that prevent us from naturally expressing generosity and kindness. Mindfulness practice allows us to become aware of the inner fears and emotional contractions that create these obstacles. Through *vipassana* meditation, we can investigate these emotional contractions and allow them to resolve themselves through the actions of *satisampajanna* and *satipanna*. As the obstacles are dissolved through the healing contact of mindfulness, the heart will naturally respond by expanding, and *dana* will flow naturally from this inner expansiveness.

Generosity is a spiritual quality that comes from a heart that is open and exquisitely sensitive to the needs of each moment and this is exactly what we develop through the practice of mindfulness. Then generosity and kindness become elevated to spiritual perfections and the natural outward expression of the liberated mind of *bodhicitta*. The importance of kindness cannot be overemphasised, and the Dalai Lama described Buddhism as the religion of kindness, as in the following passage:

> There is no need for temples, no need for complicated philosophies. My brain and my heart are my temples; my philosophy is kindness.

In all that we do and throughout our practice, we should aim to create the right conditions in which kindness and generosity are dominant. We begin with kindness to ourselves, to our pain and suffering and then allow that attitude to permeate outwards to wherever it is needed. This is one of the signs of a mature practice, where kindness is the dominant feature, inspite of all the conflicts and strife of living in a world in chaos.

Sila

As Rumi, the thirteenth century Persian poet so eloquently expressed it,

> Out beyond ideas of wrongdoing and rightdoing, there
> is a field. I will meet you there.

Sila refers to virtue, morality and ethical conduct, and society depends on various codes and rules designed to promote harmony and cooperation. The Buddha expressed this in the Noble Eightfold Path as the practice of Right Speech, Right Action and Right Livelihood, collectively called *sila*.

However, to reduce *sila* to a set of rules and commandments is to fall into the same old trap of blind attachment to form, to *sankharas*, which is likely to result in more suffering for yourself and others. Attachment to rules and codes is a very powerful force, because it gives the illusion of order and security. However, blind attachment inevitably creates division between the observer and the observed, and this breeds violence. The observer reacts to experience according to his attachment to beliefs about right and wrong, good and bad, moral and amoral. Ideals are fine, but they are always limited, because they are abstract fabrications that are not grounded in the reality of the present moment. This leads to error in the form of assumptions and generalizations conditioned by the past that do not embrace the actual needs of the present.

The perfection of *sila* as a *parami* requires the integration of Right Speech, Action and Livelihood with the wisdom factors (*Panna*) of Right Understanding and Right Thought, in combination with the practice factors (*Samadhi*) of Right Effort, Right Mindfulness and Right Concentration. *Sila* cannot develop as a spiritual *parami* without the guidance of both *Panna* and *Samadhi*.

Blind attachment to ideas about *sila* will inevitably leads to conflict between people with different beliefs. Attachment also creates conflict internally between our different ideals and expectations, which are always at odds with the real world. For this reason, the Buddha warned against blind conformity and attachment to rules and conventions, the form of attachment called *silabbatu-*

padana. In fact, the first stage of the spiritual path of enlighten-ment outlined by the Buddha involves letting go of the three clas-sical fetters of personality-belief, sceptical doubt and attachment to rules and conventions. This does not mean that we should abandon conventions, laws and ethics, but that we should remain open to discover what constitutes right action in the here and now, in real time. This is all that really counts, and everything else is abstract speculation based on ideals and assumptions. Rules and conven-tions can provide a guide, but can never substitute for awakening to the reality of the present moment, which is ever changing and, therefore, requires fresh solutions in every moment.

From the Buddhist point of view, what differentiates moral and amoral actions of body, speech and mind is whether those actions lead to the resolution of *dukkha* and the promotion of stability, well-being and happiness. This is the overall guiding principle that constitutes the first factor of the Noble Eightfold Path, the factor of Right View (*sammaditthi*). True *sila* comes from awakening to the Four Noble Truths in the here and now and this should be our guide in all matters. We must always be open to discover for our-selves what actions lead to order and stability and the resolution of *dukkha* in each present moment, and what actions do not. This means having the flexibility and willingness to engage with the ac-tual details of life as it unfolds in the present, rather than blindly following prescribed rules and dogma dictated to us by family or political and religious authorities.

It stands to reason, therefore, that the first requirement for ethi-cal behavior is awakening to the First Noble Truth of *dukkha*, the state of instability and suffering that arises through blind attach-ment. Simply following rules, while ignoring the underlying con-flicts that exist in society, family or in our own heart is simply a form of repression and *avijja*, and this is not what is meant by the perfection of *sila*, as taught by the Buddha. True morality must, therefore be tempered by mindfulness and wisdom, by *satisampa-janna* and *satipanna*, because only non-conditioned awareness can allow us to discover what is truly appropriate for the needs of the present moment. This is living by the authority of *Dhamma*, rather than by the authority of man-made rules.

259

Virtue, morality and wholesome action provide the cornerstone of the spiritual path to freedom, and *sila* is the outward expression of our spiritual development. The most basic teaching of the Buddha is described in the formula:

> Refrain from doing evil deeds,
> perfect good deeds
> and purify the mind.

From the Buddha's perspective, *sila* is a living process of discovery. *Sila* becomes a *parami* when there is a personal commitment to discovering what constitutes Right Action, Right Speech and Right Livelihood in the ongoing reality of moment-to-moment living, and this requires mindfulness to all that we experience, both internally and externally.

To practice *sila*, requires the cultivation of the two fundamental principles of non-hatred (*abyapada*) and non-violence (*avihimsa* in Pali, or *ahimsa* in Sanskrit). As we resolve each manifestation of reactivity based on hatred and violence, then we open the way for the cultivation of the many manifestations of kindness, generosity, patience, loving-kindness and benevolent action. *Sila* is a path to be cultivated, not through following beliefs, but through awakening to what is wholesome (*kusala*) and what is unwholesome (*akusala*) in each moment. Seen this way, the path that leads to the purification of the mind requires that we greet each mind moment with complete mindfulness and complete absence of reactivity so that we can discover what is wholesome and what is not.

By awakening to what purifies the living present, we set the conditions that will purify the next moment, and the forward momentum of this purifying energy transforms everything in its path. Therefore, we must not only contemplate what is virtuous, but also become very familiar with what is not virtuous. To perfect love, we must open our mind to fully embrace evil, and not resist it with aversion, but greet it with non-reactive mindfulness. Evil feeds on ignorance and aversion, and both reinforce each other. What transforms evil, is the light of awakening through *sati* and the wisdom-intelligence of *satipanna* that directs the resolution of dissonance and *dukkha*. To embrace evil means that we investigate the detailed structure of evil so that no part of it remains outside of conscious awareness. It is in this therapeutic space that the mind is purified, under the direction of *satipanna*.

You cannot solve the problem of evil by fighting it with idealized beliefs and dogma, but rather through the methodical path of attending to each movement of *akusala* mind moments with mindfulness. This is the approach of loving-kindness and compassion, which is the only reliable antidote to evil. By purifying the mind through mindfulness you will discover the true meaning of what it is to do good and to refrain from doing evil in each moment of life. We do not have to rely on others to tell us what to do; far better to awaken to the natural goodness that lies within, which becomes possible once we gain freedom from the mental afflictions to which we have become attached through ignorance.

NEKKHAMMA

Nekkhamma is usually translated as "renunciation," although this does not quite capture the true meaning of the term. The root of the word actually means, "to go forth," and conveys the action of letting go of the conventions and habits of the past to discover something better. The word also conveys the sense of simplifying life and letting go of those things that do not assist us on the path towards liberation.

Nekkhamma means different things depending on the context. For a monk, renunciation begins with giving uo the life of the householder, and giving up worldly possessions and worldly pursuits. However, there is a deeper meaning to *nekkhamma* that can be described as the path of non-attachment and non-clinging. In the words of the well known American Zen teacher, Aitken Roshi,

> Renunciation is not getting rid of the things of this world, but accepting that they pass away.

This is clearly rather different from the common understanding of renunciation in the West as the practice of self-sacrifice. Self-sacrifice and self-denial are only of value if they are accompanied by wisdom (*panna*), and this specifically means that the act of renunciation must lead to greater happiness, greater stability, greater freedom and greater compassion. If it does not, then the act of renunciation becomes little more than another manifestation of the ego trying to control the mind, which is not the path of *Dhamma*.

At the spiritual level of understanding, the perfection of *nekkhamma* means the path of letting go of the familiar habitual reactivity of the self, the ego, that we attach to through ignorance and unawareness. The path to freedom must involve letting go of the familiar habits of the past so that we can transform and grow. This actually requires a great deal of courage, because giving up the familiar can be quite scary. In the words of W.H. Auden,

> We would rather be ruined than changed;
> We would rather die in our dread
> Than climb the cross of the moment
> And let our illusions die.

Therefore, *nekkhamma* must be coupled with the *paramis* of wisdom-intelligence (*panna*), courageous vitality (*viriya*), loving-kindness (*metta*) and great patience (*khanti*).

Renunciation is simply the path of purification of the mind and heart by letting go of anything that corrupts the spirit and perpetuates suffering. When we remove these corruptions, then the mind begins to open, and what is revealed is the natural and innate purity of the awakened mind (*bodhicitta*), and this will naturally purify our actions. As the Buddha said,

> Who so has turned to renunciation,
> turned to non-attachment of the mind,
> is filled with all-embracing love
> and freed from thirsting after life.

Renunciation becomes a skillful and natural response when we awaken to suffering and to the underlying blind attachments that generate suffering. Ultimately, *nekkhamma* is the path of non-attachment (*anupadana*) that comes about when there is truthfulness and mindfulness.

Now it is extremely important to look deeper at what we mean by "letting go" or "giving up." We must ask ourselves who or what is doing the letting go. If the thinking ego-mind is directing the show, with all its beliefs and prejudices, then your actions cease to be *nekkhamma*, but simply the reactivity of the ego trying to control and manipulate the psyche. Learning to let go of a habit is not a matter of thinking, following a belief, or exercising willpower, but comes from opening a space around the underlying attachments through mindfulness. The transformational space of pure knowing, or *satisampajanna* allows *satipanna* to arise and this is what we trust to direct the actions of *nekkhamma*. Then, what results will be a natural and holistic letting go, arising from the greater intuitive dimension of our conscious experience. True letting go and non-attachment happen when there is a relationship based on freedom and full compassionate engagement, which can only happen when the mind is silent and free of thinking, judging and the compulsion to control. In this state of non-reactivity, *nekkhamma* becomes the mind letting go of itself, without the intervention of a controlling ego trying to fix things or trying to manipulate things according to some idea or belief.

PANNA

Panna (Skt. *Prajna*) is derived from the root *na*, which means "to know" and *pa*, which means "completely and thoroughly." It is often translated as wisdom, but this does not quite capture the essence of the term. In the West, we think of wisdom as profound knowledge about something. *Panna* includes such insights, but also describes an active quality of intuitive intelligence that comes from relating to phenomena in the present moment, as they are unfolding. *Panna* is not the fixed wisdom of theories and beliefs, but a living intelligence that continues to evolves in response to the reality of the present moment. Knowledge is static, whereas *panna* is continually changing and adapting to changing conditions.

Perhaps a better translation of *panna* is the wisdom-intelligence that arises from awakening to the objective reality of the present moment. The word *vipassana* also has the roots "*pa*" and "*na*" and is often translated as experiential insight gained through seeing things in their totality, and in fact *vipassana* meditation is the primary means through which we develop *panna*. In addition, *panna* has a very precise and pragmatic meaning in Buddhism, which makes it different from general wisdom knowledge. It refers specifically to the wisdom-intelligence that leads to the resolution of suffering (*dukkhanirodha*), and that promotes happiness and well-being in the living present.

Panna has its foundation in mindfulness, which allows us to awaken to the truth of experience in the here and now. When the pure awareness of mindfulness is established, then wisdom-intelligence can arise, and for this reason *sati* and *panna* are very often combined as *satipanna*. *Satipanna* arises in the very same moment when we establish mindfulness. *Satipanna* is the very active face of *panna* that leads to liberation from reactivity, and the resolution of *dukkha* in the here and now. This is not liberation based on wisdom knowledge; not knowing *about* things; and not psychological insight about your past. True liberation is a living process of direct awakening to the innate and intuitive intelligence of each moment of experience in the present. Ultimately, *panna* means being in complete harmony and alignment with *anicca*, *dukkha* and *anatta* in each present moment.

Anicca informs us that existence is a dynamic process of change and that any system, including the psyche, needs to continually change and readjust to changing conditions. *Anicca* describes the entire process of birth, growth, existence, decline and death. Thoughts and emotions arise, exist for a while and then fade away. To live in alignment with *anicca* means that we establish an equally dynamic relationship with experience, based on mindfulness that allows change to occur under the influence of our intuitive intelligence.

When we live in harmony with *anicca* we become a dynamic living process, in which our intuitive intelligence guides us like a beacon, towards the resolution of *dukkha*, and towards well-being and happiness. This is in stark contrast to a mind that is dominated by habitual reactivity. Such a mind is constrained by its reactivity and unable to respond in skillful ways, and the changes that results will be chaotic and likely to increase instability and disorder. To allow change to flow in an intelligent direction that leads to greater stability, we must be free of reactivity, so that we can discover new responses. Reactivity imprisons the mind like a bird in a cage, and this leads to the death of the inner spirit and much suffering. It is only in the state of complete freedom, that the mind can change and grow in harmony with the innate intelligence of what needs to happen to restore stability and peace.

This brings us to *dukkha*, the second mark of existence, and the symptom of a mind that is not living in harmony with *anicca*, and not allowing inner experience to change and resolve itself under the direction of *satipanna*. Blind attachment and identification with the habitual reactivity of the ego paralyzes the psyche and prevents it from changing in a beneficial direction. Under ideal conditions, the psyche continually moves between states of instability and stability in a dynamic flux around a still center. However, blind reactivity places constraints on this system and prevents the natural movement towards equilibrium. If we are to harmonize with *anicca*, then we must fully harmonize with *dukkha*, and establish a mindfulness-based relationship with whatever is unstable and in conflict in the mind. This is to establish *satisampajanna* and the pure knowing of suffering, that is free from reactivity, judgement and aversion, and from the delusion that keeps us attached to our reactivity. Mindfulness allows us to live in harmony with *dukkha* as it arises in the here and now, and establishes a space around suffering that facilitates healing.

Panna is not simply knowledge about *dukkha*, nor is it insight knowledge about *anicca* that we use to control the unruly mind. *Panna* is much more than such conventional knowledge-based wisdom, and is best defined as the direct and living intelligence that arises from being fully present with *dukkha* with *satisampajanna*. We choose to establish the right conditions in which *dukkha* can change, and change in a beneficial way that leads to its resolution. This is what the Tibetan Buddhists describe as, "the self-liberation that occurs through naked awareness." The path to the resolution of our suffering lies within the suffering itself and is unleashed through mindfulness.

Anatta informs us that there is no permanent self (*atta*) behind our experience, because everything that we experience is in continual flux. The self is a living process and not a static entity and, therefore, the self cannot be defined. Any attempt to define the self is nothing more than a linguistic convention that is both abstract and illusory. Living in harmony with *anatta* means that we do not identify with the subjective reactions of the illusory self, but learn to see them simply as objects that arise in our field of experiene. If a reaction arises and creates *dukkha*, we understand that we are not the hurt, anger, sadness, frustration, fear or any other *sankhara* that has taken form in the mind. Those *sankharas* do not define who we are, but are simply impersonal phenomena that arise and pass away.

Living in harmony with *anatta* means that we cease to attach and identify with our reactions of craving (*lobha*) or with our reactions of aversion (*dosa*). We come to see our true identity as *anatta*, which is free to engage with all experience with wisdom and compassion. Living in harmony with *anatta* is to know freedom from the *knower* and freedom from the *known*. It is the state of non-attachment, in which our identity is as the *knowing* of sensory experiences, and this includes both the *knower* and the *known*, and is completely free from attachment to either.

Living in harmony with *anatta* is simply another way of describing the experience of liberation from the conditioned world of form. It is the experience of freedom in the here and now, in which we are free from all the constructs of the mind that try to tie us down. We become the sky, rather than the objects that fly through the sky; or the ocean, rather than the fish that dwell in its depths. When we are free from the contents, the world of form, thoughts, emotions, beliefs and reactivity, we find that we can relate to all such form with complete presence. When there is complete presence, then and only then can there be complete compassion. Reactivity inhibits presence and limits compassion; mindfulness restores presence and compassion flourishes.

Spiritual transformation is not simply about learning clever ways of fixing our emotional problems, but describes a path of transcending the whole reactive process that produces them. Problems may still arise, but our attitude will be completely different when it is based on *panna*, rather than reactivity and ignorance. When there is *panna*, we stop feeding the secondary reactivity that sustains *dukkha*. With *panna* we open to the therapeutic space of *sunnata* in which transformation of primary reactivity can occur in a natural and holistic way, under the guidance of innate *satipanna*. We let problems resolve themselves in their own way, without the intervention of an observer who reacts with greed, aversion and delusion to the problems of the mind. We allow the psyche to do its own housecleaning and find its own natural equilibrium through psychological homeostasis, without the intervention of an ego that tries to control and manipulate the mind.

When we see things as they really are with *satisampajanna* and remain in a relationship of mindfulness and stillness, we provide the right conditions in which *dukkha* will resolve itself. It is not that *we* make things change by applying psychological insights, but that *satipanna* allows things to change by themselves and we simply witness this change happening. The direction of such experiential transformation is always towards greater energetic stability and homeostasis brought about by the resolution of *dukkha*. When we open our eyes, ignorance evaporates, and without *avijja*, reactivity has no power. If we don't feed reactivity, then the underlying attachments dissolve and wither away, just as a fire burns itself out, if not fed with more fuel. This is the transformation that comes about when there is the spiritual freedom to know *Dhamma*, which means the total freedom of the psyche to know itself, free from the narrow perspective of the controlling ego.

VIRIYA

Viriya is often translated as energy, but with the added quality of vigor and vitality. In fact, these words have the same prefix *vi*, which means "heroic" and "courageous."

Clearly, the perfection of spiritual vitality and life energy is essential for overcoming the powerful forces of *avijja* and *tanha*. Not surprisingly, the lion is often used to symbolize *viriya*, and the resolution to follow the path of liberation is described as "the lion's roar." The importance of *viriya* is repeated many times throughout the Buddha's teachings. It is one of the five spiritual powers needed to bring about freedom, and the third of the seven factors of awakening that describes the stages of liberation and enlightenment.

Viriya refers to the spiritual energy of the psyche that permeates everything and gives meaning to experience, and provides the power behind our actions, good or bad. In many ways, we can look at the psyche as a dynamic energetic system, which is either frozen in place by *avijja*, or released through *panna*. When this energy is free to move where it is needed, when it is needed, then we experience emotional health and harmony.

However, the energy of the psyche frequently becomes trapped in the form of patterns of reactivity based on blind attachments. This trapped energy creates the inner stress that we experience as *dukkha*. In many ways the process of transformation, healing and liberation can be described as the process of releasing trapped energy and restoring freedom so that this energy can move to where its needed. When we describe the perfection of *viriya* as a *parami*, we are referring to the process of restoring complete freedom for this spiritual energy, which is our life essence. Such complete freedom of this essential life energy is a characteristic of the Buddha mind, the awakened and enlightened state of being. To be a fully authentic human being, to be truly alive, it is necessary that there be complete freedom in which *viriya* can move throughout the psyche.

Blind attachment (*upadana*) and the compulsive force of *tanha* consume a great deal of energy. It takes energy to maintain our patterns of habitual reactivity and this drains the psyche, leading to fatigue, depression and apathy. We experience this energy drain as *dukkha*, the suffering caused when emotional energy becomes frozen in the *sankharas* of inner beliefs and emotional reactions. The *sankharas* are the icebergs of the mind that freeze spiritual energy in place and inhibit spiritual or psychological freedom. One of the primary effects of mindfulness practice and *vipassana* meditation is to release this frozen energy so that it becomes free to flow within the psyche as positive energy. Mindfulness is the inner warmth that melts the icebergs of the mind, releasing the water trapped inside. As you dissolve the core attachments through the process of experienitial transformation, energy is released and becomes available for re-integration back into to the psyche. This restores freedom and mobility in the psyche leading to increased vitality, enthusiasm and spiritual aliveness. In the liberated mind, both psychological and spiritual energy unite to form a powerful force that leads to fully authentic action, based on compassion and intelligence.

For the perfection of *viriya*, or life energy, there must be complete order and stability in the psyche and the only way to achieve order and stability is by giving complete attention to disorder and instability. This is another way of describing the First Noble Truth of *dukkha*, which directs us to awaken to suffering, without attachment, aversion or blind acceptance.

Dukkha is disorder, instability and the state in which energy is trapped in the unconscious mind. When we shine mindfulness on this trapped energy, we create the inner freedom that allows it to be released back into the psyche, restoring order and stability. Mindfulness is the process of awakening to *dukkha*, and it is this awakening that leads to transformation. Krishnamurti expresses this beautifully in the following passage:

> Now the very attention you give to a problem is the energy that solves that problem. When you give your complete attention - I mean with everything in you - there is no observer at all. There is only the state of attention, which is total energy, and that total energy is the highest form of intelligence. Naturally that state of mind must be completely silent and that silence, that stillness, comes when there is total attention, not disciplined stillness. That total silence in which there is neither the observer nor the thing observed is the highest form of a religious mind.

Satisampajanna is the stillness of pure awareness, of pure knowing. It is through the relationship of this pure mindful-awareness with the disorder that exists in the mind, that the whole field of the psyche is transformed. This is non-dualistic knowing, without an observer, because there is no one judging, thinking or reacting to the observed. There is no observer, just the pure state of *observing*. In this total silence, which is the creative spaciousness called *sunnata*, the psyche is completely free to receive, and to respond with intelligence and compassion. *Satipanna*, the innate intuitive intelligence arises in this relationship of pure knowing, and directs the whole process of transformation. Therefore, the very action of sustained mindful-awareness is by itself transformational; it is not the observer who transforms disorder into order, but the action of observing. With mindfulness, *satisampajanna* arises, and illuminates the whole field of our inner emotional suffering. This illumination of the truth of *dukkha* allows *satipanna* to arise and orchestrate transformation. Transformation results in the release of *dukkha*-energy from the deep recesses of the mind. The release of this energy revitalizes and nourishes the whole body and psyche. Whenever you direct mindfulness onto an emotional knot or place of inner tension, then in that moment of contact the ego releases its grip and the mind begins to soften and becomes malleable. In this state of freedom, experiential transformation and resolution unfolds quite naturally under the direction of *satipanna*.

The movement of energy from a state of instability and conflict to a state of stability and harmony is a positive experience, accompanied by feelings of happiness and well-being, called *upekkhasukha*, the happiness born from balance and equanimity. The combination of *sati*, *satisampajanna* and *satipanna* will always direct change towards greater stability and happiness, because this is the natural state for the psyche. The psyche will always try to move towards stability if given the freedom to change, provided by *satisampajanna*. In the language of the Buddha, the cycle of liberation through *panna* is called *pannavimutti* and is described as the gate to the deathless (*amatapada*), which is in stark contrast to the cycle of *avijja*, reactivity and *samsara*, which is the gate to endless becoming. The gate to liberation, inner stability and happiness is always open to us, and mindfulness carries us through this gate, into the realm of the deathless and the realm of total freedom.

One of the key factors of the Noble Eightfold Path is Right Effort (*sammavayama*), which is the application of *viriya* in a balanced way to energize all the other factors of the Eightfold Path. However, Right Effort is not the same as willpower, which is a superficial concentration of energy by the ego in an attempt to control the mind. Right Effort must be accompanied by *panna*, which means that effort is applied for the development of the other *paramis* and for the resolution of suffering.

Traditionally, Right Effort means applying energy in four ways. These are the effort to neutalize any underlying unwholesome habitual reactivity from manifesting in the future; neutralizing any negative reactions that have arisen in the present; developing wholesome states as they arise in the present; and cultivating these wholesome states so they will continue to arise in the future. As always, wholesome and positive actions are defined as those which bring an end to *dukkha*, and which liberate the psyche, bringing stability, well-being and happiness for self and others.

KHANTI

Khanti describes the quality of patience, forbearance and endurance that is a necessary part of The Path of Mindfulness. We have a whole lifetime of conditioning to overcome and there are no quick fixes. However, patience is not just endurance, but is also the expression of genuine kindness and love (*metta*) towards yourself and others. As the Chinese philosopher and founder of Taoism, Lao Tzu said,

> I have just three things to teach: simplicity, patience, compassion. These three are your greatest treasures.

Certainly, to follow The Path of Mindfulness requires the courage of a lion and the inexhaustible *viriya*, but this must be balanced with a lightness in the way you walk on the path. If you strive too hard, you may lose the spontaneity and flexibility that are so much a part of The Path of Mindfulness and wisdom. Your journey is not a war against evil, not a battle against the defilements, but a path of opening the heavy curtains of ignorance to let in the light of pure knowing. The spirit of *khanti* is the spirit of tenderness, gentleness and a lightness of being that infuses all aspects of how you relate to the experience of yourself, the experience of other beings and the experience of the physical-material world. The Path of Mindfulness is not intended to be a struggle, but a dance in kindness with life as it is, including all the hardships and challenges.

We need to develop patience, because The Path of Mindfulness is essentially a path of continually encountering failures. Mindfulness practice is analogous to riding a bicycle, which is fundamentally a process of falling and catching yourself before you hit the ground. The art of learning to ride a bicycle involves letting go of the controlling mind, so that you can respond intuitively and intelligently with *satipanna* to each wobble as it arises in the present moment. What leads to success in learning to ride a bicycle is the ability to stay mindful of these wobbles; your intuitive intelligence will do the rest. It is the same way with our progress on The Path of Mindfulness: we practice intuitive awareness, and trust in the wisdom-intelligence that arises in each moment. Mindfulness is the process of catching yourself before you fall into the familiar patterns of habitual reactivity, and with practice, our ability to stay mindful and avoid reactivity becomes quite natural.

The journey can be very frustrating until you realize that this dance with failure is both the path to freedom and the perfection of freedom. Freedom, awakening or enlightenment is not an esoteric state of consciousness, but an ongoing process and dance with life in which you are a conscious participant. It is our nature to wobble, but when we choose to fully engage with all the manifestations of reactivity with mindfulness, kindness and patience, then we are living the Path of Freedom. Through practice, you will experience for yourself these moments of freedom, as you engage mindfully with anxiety, anger or other habitual reactions as they arise. Each moment of mindfulness is a significant event and each change brought about by *satipanna* is a real victory. The dance of mindfulness builds momentum in the same way that a small trickle of water becomes a stream and then grows into a mighty river until it finally reaches its ultimate union with the ocean. All that is required is that you allow the dance to unfold in its own way. Trust in the dance, be patient and greet each movement of life with kindness and an open heart.

SACCA

Ultimately, The Path of Mindfulness is the pursuit of Truth (*sacca*). In the words of the Buddha,

Three things cannot be long hidden: the sun, the moon, and the truth.

There are two levels of truth: the conventional, subjective level of truth, called *sammutti sacca* and the absolute, objective level of truth, called *paramattha sacca*. Concepts, labels, beliefs or any representations produced by the thinking mind are examples of *sammutti sacca*. They have a utility as tools to point to reality, but they are not themselves the reality they represent.

Whatever we experience in the mind is only a superficial representation of the surface structure of phenomena. The reality is hidden in the deep structure, which we rarely see and can never know in its entirety. All that we are left with is a rather unsatisfactory abstraction that is fundamentally wrong, and which depends on ignorance (*avijja*) and not looking too closely at reality. Absolute truth does not exist as an entity, but as a dynamic process that is ever changing. This is the truth of *anicca*, impermanence. Any representation of that process is inherently flawed and unsatisfactory and in conflict with absolute truth. This is the truth of *dukkha*, the suffering that arises from attachment to the unsatisfactory. Truth has no definable identity, which is the truth of *anatta*, that no entity has an existence separate from *anicca* and *dukkha*. These are the three marks of existence that constitute *paramattha sacca*.

The Path of Mindfulness and *vipassana* meditation is a method of progressively letting go of the surface representations of the mind that constitute *sammutti sacca*, so that we can directly experience the objective truth of *paramattha sacca*. Mindfulness stimulates the progression from the superficial to the inner depth; from the gross to the subtle; from the abstract to the specific; or simply, from illusion to reality. When we focus mindfulness on the experience of an object, the conventional level of subjective thinking falls away and we are left with the *knowing* itself, which is *satisampajanna*. It is through this knowing in the present that we encounter *paramattha sacca*. We may never know the ultimate truth of things, and in reality we can never know absolute truth, because it can never be reduced to a form that can be known. What is much more important is that we are committed to the journey towards that ultimate truth, and this journey is essentially one of progressively letting go of untruth, of the known, of ideas and opinions. Truth is not a destination; it is a journey, and mindfulness is the vehicle that takes us on this journey.

As we automatically let go of *sammutti sacca* through mindfulness, we are simultaneously learning to live in harmony with *anicca*, *dukkha* and *anatta*, not as concepts, but as living realities that influences how we relate to experience. Essentially, we allow things to change, without resistance and according to the innate intelligence inherent in the experience. Living *anicca* means allowing this natural process of change to take place. To live in harmony with *dukkha* as a living reality, means that we choose to turn towards our suffering with compassion and mindfulness. To live in harmony with *anatta* means that we choose to relate to our conditioned perceptions, beliefs and emotions as objective phenomena to be known fully through mindfulness, without any clinging to as "I" or "mine."

When the mind is empty of reactivity, which is to be in harmony with *anicca*, *dukkha* and *anatta*, truth is revealed; when the mind is crowded with attachments, which is the nature of the reactive mind, then there is no room for truth. Therefore, to receive truth, we need a mind that is not dominated by attachments and reactivity, and freeing the mind to receive truth is the very purpose of meditation. In the words of Krishnamurti,

> Meditation is freedom from thought and a movement in
> the ecstasy of truth. Meditation is the explosion of intelligence.

Truth is not an entity and cannot be captured and contained in the form of a thought or beliefs. Meditation is the process of letting go of surface appearances and representations, and opening our awareness to the larger dimension of existence.

When we hold on to a thought or belief, the mind becomes dull and contracted; a breeding ground for ignorance and reactivity. When we let go of ideas and beliefs, then what we are left with is an undefinable vastness into which absolute truth can be known. This spaciousness is called *sunnata*, and when we make it our refuge, then the thoughts and beliefs that emerge will be purified and refined like hot metal worked by a blacksmith. In this spaciousness *panna* arises, described by Krishnamurti as the "explosion of intelligence."

Truth and *panna* are one and the same, and they have to be discovered afresh in each moment of living. Neither truth nor wisdom can be held on to as a certainty, because after only a few minutes, that certainty will be out of date and redundant. Therefore, truth is revealed only when the mind is completely open, and when there is *satisampajanna*. The Path of Mindfulness takes us to this place of knowing truth by progressively stripping away the layers of delusion. Truth is what is left behind after all certainties have been abandoned; to know truth, we must emerge from behind the superficial veil of ideation.

Because, truth can never be adequately represented in the form of an idea or belief, we must learn to trust in our own unique and direct experience. In the words of the Buddha,

> Therefore, be ye lamps unto yourselves, be a refuge to yourselves. Hold fast to Truth as a lamp; hold fast to the Truth as a refuge. Look not for a refuge in anyone beside yourselves. And those, who shall be a lamp unto themselves, shall betake themselves to no external refuge, but holding fast to the Truth as their lamp, and holding fast to the Truth as their refuge, they shall reach the topmost height.

The "lamp" refers to the intuitive wisdom-intelligence of *satipanna* that arises when *sati* and *satisampajanna* are present, and the Buddha urges us to take refuge in the pure knowing of experience as it arises in the present. We have to find the Buddha, the "awakened state," in our own experience of the here and now, and this is central to the spiritual path. The Buddha is more than the historical person of Siddhattha Gotama, but points to the truth of the awakened state of knowing that exists at the very center of our being. Taking refuge in the Buddha simply means that we choose to open our mind and heart to receive the reality of existence as it unfolds in our experience. No one can do this for us.

275

Understanding the nature of our experience in terms of relative and absolute truth has tremendous practical implications for working with our emotional suffering, because it immediately alerts us to the illusory nature of first appearances. We feel depressed, anxious, frustrated or angry, and more often than not, we slavishly accept these emotional reactions as true, not realizing that they are only partial abstractions and superficial generalizations that are not real. Such abstractions are very ephemeral like clouds in the sky, and equally impossible to change.

Understanding that what appears in the mind is only relative truth, we choose to let go of this surface structure and begin the path of mindful-investigation into the deep structure of our emotions. As we do this, the delusion of the surface structure falls away and the emotion becomes malleable and begins to differentiate and reveal a rich inner structure. This is equivalent to taking the back off of a Swiss watch and examining the inticate mechanism that is the inner reality of the watch. As we penetrate into the absolute reality of an emotional complex, we successively let go of the superficial surface layers and come to know truth. The solution to our suffering lies in the conscious awareness of the detailed inner structure of emotional suffering (*dukkha*), which is a journey towards absolute truth. It is this journey towards absolute truth that heals, transforms and liberates the spirit and the psyche. This discovery of inner truth is what allows us to "reach the topmost height" of freedom from conditioned existence and *dukkha*.

ADHITTHANA

This *parami* describes the quality of determination and resolution to travel the path of *Dhamma*, The Path of Mindfulness, the path of Truth, compassion and wisdom. The word is derived from *adhi*, meaning "highest" and *stha*, meaning "standing," so *adhitthana* literally meand to excel and be the best that you can be. The perfection of *adhitthana* means never losing sight of the purpose of our practice, which is to perfect all the other *paramis*, so that we are best able to bring an end to suffering, internally and externally, for self and others. To achieve this, we must first liberate our own

276

mind and heart, not just for our own happiness, but so that we can best help others find theirs.

It takes courage and determination to free the mind from the chains of *upadana* and *avijja* and the wold of habitual reactivity that is *samsara*. When the Buddha sat under the Bodhi tree in preparation for meditation, he expressed a tremendous resolve to work towards liberation from *samsara* that should serve as an inspiration to us all.

> In this very seat let my sinews and bones waste away, let all their flesh and blood in my body dry up, but never from this seat will I stir until I have attained supreme Buddhahood.

The Buddha had such strong determination, because he saw the endless suffering that human being inflict upon themselves and each other through ignorance, greed and hatred. The need for purifying the mind and gaining freedom from *samsara* is self-evident and we should endeavor to take up the challenge to make a better world for all.

However, the method to create a better world must be grounded in wisdom and mindfulness. We must build the right foundation within so that our actions are tempered by truth and intelligent insight, rather than blind conviction. Therefore, mindfulness should precede all action; the prayer of mindfulness should be our flag, in which we let in truth and the innate intelligence that arises whenever mindfulness is established.

METTA

Metta is most often translated as loving-kindness, and decribes the positive qualities of friendliness, open-heartedness and goodwill. The word *metta*, or *matri* in Sanskrit, is derived from *mitra*, the word for "sun." Like the sun, *metta* bathes everything with life-giving warmth and brings comfort to all, without discrimination. *Metta* is the energy that heals internally and externally, wherever there is suffering. *Metta* is the outward face of mindfulness, the quality of relationship in which we cherish and hold each experi-

277

ence with affection, just as a mother holds her baby and attends to its every need with complete devotion. When we cultivate mindfulness, we are simultaneously cultivating a caring attitude to every part of our experience, whether arising internally as we encounter our joy and suffering, or externally as we experience the world.

Metta is the smiling face of mindfulness as we greet all that we encounter: pleasant or unpleasant, beautiful or ugly, great or small, right or wrong. *Metta* originates from a solid foundation in mindfulness, where we have developed the confidence that there is space for all and that we need fear nothing; it arises from the vast spaciousness of a mind grounded in the pure knowing of all that arises. *Metta* cannot arise in the mind that clings to anything; it can only arise when consciousness is free and in harmony with *anicca* and *anatta*, and where *dukkha* is welcomed with open arms as a friend in need of our love.

Metta is the universal energy that supports all of the four sublime abodes (*brahmavihara*) of *metta, karuna, mudita* and *upekkha*. *Metta* expresses itself as *kuruna*, or compassion towards suffering, wherever it exists, internally or externally. *Metta* expresses itself as *mudita*, the appreciation of happiness and the conditions that promote happiness both internally and externally. *Metta* expresss itself as *upekkha*, the equanimity, objectivity and non-reactivity that allows us to relate to all that we experience, pleasant or unpleasant, without being overwhelmed or becoming reactive. In the awakened mind of *bodhicitta* these four qualities permeate our relationship with the three primary domains of Self, Other and World. The Buddha described *metta* as follows:

> There, o monks, the monk with a mind full of loving-kindness pervading first one direction, then a second one, then a third one, then the fourth one, just so above, below and all around; and everywhere identifying himself with all, he is pervading the whole world with mind full of loving-kindness, with mind wide, developed, unbounded, free from hate and ill will.

Metta describes the quality of relationship with all dimensions of experience, with anything that enters consciousness, whether arising externally through the physical senses, or internally as thoughts, memories and emotions. *Metta* does not discriminate, but receives all with equal love and care. For this reason *metta*, along with the other *brahmaviharas*, are described as boundless states (*appamanna*) of consciousness. *Metta* does not depend on any conditions or discriminations imposed by the ego, and *metta* has no hidden agendas, wanting nothing in return. *Metta* is, therefore, the expression of true unconditional love, and exists independent of expectations and demands, beliefs or prejudices.

Before we can discover what it is to express this quality of love towards Self, Other and World, the mind must be free to receive, which means that there must be an absence of the reactions of greed, hatred and delusion. Therefore, to develop *metta* we must first develop *sati*, the mindfulness of both the objects of our experience and the subjective reactions of the ego. If we have reactions of greed or hatred and aversion, then we must attend to those reactions, and we must attend to them with *metta* as part of our response of mindfulness. *Metta* cannot be perfected by declaring war on our own imperfections and reactivity. We cannot command the mind to be virtuous and loving. The only effective way to develop *metta* is to apply it equally to *everything* that we encounter in ourselves or in the world. If we fall into the trap of making a discrimination based on preference, then we will cease to have *metta* and will simply be left with another form of conditioned love. *Metta* is unconditional. Our path is to learn to recognize non-*metta*, conditional love, and tease out the underlying aversion, or *dosa*, and attend to that negative feeling with mindfulness and *metta*. Then we will be cultivating *metta* as a *parami* instead of an idealistic exercise in wishful thinking.

If we wish to develop *metta* towards our inner pain, then we must also have *metta* towards our reactions of resistance to that pain. If we wish to cultivate goodwill towards those who have hurt us, then we must also cultivate *metta* towards our reactions of hatred or indifference. If we wish to cultivate *metta* towards the world, then we must have *metta* for our reactions of greed, aversion and delusion in relation to the world. As always, on The Path of Mindfulness, we must start wherever we find ourselves to be and attend to any form of agitation, aversion, clinging or compulsion with mindfulness. This is the reality of the path of awakening: we must *awaken* to things as they are and not as we would like them to be. We all want to be kind, loving beings, but this cannot be achieved by turning away from our inner greed and violence.

Metta towards Self

It is easy to think of *metta* as the expression of love towards others, but *metta* is much more inclusive than this and begins with love, openness and respect towards yourself. In the words of the Buddha,

> You yourself, as much as anybody in the entire universe deserve your love and affection.

Cultivating love and compassion towards the suffering in our own hearts builds a solid foundation from which we can cultivate genuine love for others and for our world. To ignore or dismiss the self in favor of others is not the perfection of *metta*, because to ignore any form of suffering, wherever it occurs, is to cultivate ignorance and division, which are the roots of violence.

We do not like the painful emotions that arise in our mind and we react against them by grasping at something more pleasurable, or we react against them with avoidance and aversion. Both the primary reaction and the secondary reactions against that inner pain contribute to our suffering and, therefore, we must cultivate *metta* towards both sources of *dukkha*. We need to have *metta* for the sadness, the inner fear and all the expressions of the hurt child within, and we must also have *metta* for the anger and resentment that arise in reaction to these core feelings. No part of the equation is to be left out. *Metta* includes the hurt of the abused child and the anger at being abused. *Metta* includes the pain of failure and the reaction of disappointment at failing. The art is in detecting each and every manifestation of primary and secondary reactivity and to respond to each with *metta*, to hold and cherish each within the caring spaciousness of mindfulness.

Metta is indistinguishable from *sati* and cannot exist without mindfulness. Similarly, mindfulness is indistinguishable from *metta* and cannot exist without it. *Metta* is simply directing mindfulness to embrace pain, wherever it exists. It is the compassionate nature of *satipanna* that heals suffering and this depends on *sati*. When *metta* and *sati* co-exist, then we are able to smile at our suffering and care for it in the same way that a mother comforts her child after it has fallen over and grazed a knee or elbow. We need to learn to smile at our inner anxiety and grief and offer that same quality of comforting and love.

Metta towards Others

Metta is often thought of as the deliberate act of cultivating kind thoughts of goodwill and love as a kind of prayer for the well-being and happiness of others. Traditionally, *metta* meditation begins by first directing *metta* towards yourself followed by directing *metta* towards a good friend or member of your family. Next, we cultivate *metta* owards someone less well known to us for whome we have neutral feelings. After this, we undertake the more difficult task of cultivating warm feelings towards someone we dislike and from there we progress to expressing *metta* for those who have done us harm. This is the practice of "loving thine enemy," which is an important teaching in most of the world religions, including Christianity as in the following passage from the Bible:

> Ye have heard that it hath been said: Thou shalt love thy neighbour, and hate thine enemy. But I say unto you, Love your enemies, bless them that curse you, do good to them that hate you, and pray for them which despitefully use you, and persecute you.
>
> Matthew 5:43.

To cultivate love for our enemies does not mean trying to forget the hurt done to us, or pushing away our anger and pain. We may have the purest of intentions and a genuine heart-felt desire to forgive those who have hurt or abused us, but intentions alone are not enough. True forgiveness begins when we are true to ourself, and embrace all of the inner pain and emotional reactivity that exists in our heart and mind. If we wish to perfect *metta* we must face all of our reactions of aversion, hatred and ill will and respond to them with the spaciousness of mindfulness. With mindfulness, comes *satisampajanna*, and this allows us to change from being the hurt and anger, to *knowing* these things as mental objects. The relationship of pure knowing, allows us to dissolve the identification and attachment with our suffering that perpetuates disharmony and conflict. Through *satisampajanna*, we break free of our reactivity, and it is in this state of freedom that *metta* can arise.

It is not the efforts of the thinking mind that leads to forgiveness, but rather the product of extending care and love to embrace *all* suffering, internal and external. To forgive another begins when we make peace with our internal suffering, and create the space in which *metta* can heal internally as well as externally. Then and only then will we be ready to reach out to our enemies and those who have abused us with this same love.

Metta towards the World

Besides our relationship towards Self and Other, *metta* can also purify our relationship with the natural world. With correct mindfulness (*sammasati*), which means that our mindfulness is conditioned by *metta*, we naturally develop a profound sense of care for our environment and the physical world. Mindfulness means that we become fully present and engaged with our world, and this level of direct involvement leads towards intimacy and appreciation. *Metta* brings a natural love and caring that comes from openning our hearts to receive the extraordinary richness of the natural world.

When *avijja* is dominant, we see very little: a fly becomes nothing more than a bug; a stream is simply moving water; a sunset is just the end of another day. But, when we experience the world through the wisdom-eye of mindfulness, then we develop the qualities of *presence* and *engagement* with whatever we are observing. There is a quality of deep involvement and rapure that comes about from being fully tuned in to experience. This is described as *sensory enrichment* and is one of the natural consequences of the practice of mindfulness. A fly becomes a miracle of engineering; a stream becomes a living dance of light and sound; a sunset becomes a symphony of colors that inspires us and nourishes the spirit. Even mundane material possesions such as a car or

282

computer become wonderful gifts that we can appreciate and enjoy to the full when we relate to them with mindfulness. As the thirteenth century Zen master Dogen said,

> Enlightenment is intimacy with all things.

Metta is the expression of this intimacy with all that we encounter through our senses. When our relationship with the World, with physical objects and the natural environment is based on the sensory enrichment that comes from mindfulness, then *metta* naturally shines forth. The more fully we experience the natural world, the more connected we feel. This feeling of connection naturally feeds *metta*, just as ignorance and unawareness feeds hatred and indifference. If you take the time to fully know a fly, a stream or a sunset, with the care and attention of mindfulness, then you will discover the perfection of love in that intimacy. This applies to the physical world; in our relationships with our life-partner, children and friends; and most of all, in our relationship with our inner self. All benefit from the enlightenment of intimacy and love founded on *metta*, which in turn is founded on mindfulness.

Overcoming the obstacles to metta

Metta is the natural state for the awakened mind, the Buddha mind, or *bodhicitta*. The mind purified by mindfulness is able to come into perfect union with Self, Other and World, and it is this seamless union that naturally expresses itself as kindness, friendship and unconditioned love. Love is not a product of belief, idealism or willpower, but is an inner light that shines forth and illuminates all when the obstacles of ignorance and attachment are removed. The path for removing these obstacles is the same path that we have been cultivating all along: The Path of Mindfulness. As the thirteenth century Sufi poet, Rumi expressed it,

> Your task is not to seek for love, but merely to seek and find all the barriers within yourself that you have built against it.

In other words, our path should be to make those very obstacles that separate us from love the focus of our mindfulness practice. These obstacles are the reality of *dukkha* and must be faced directly, not with the heavy hand of the judgemental mind, but with mindfulness and love. These obstacles and defilements are not objects to be destroyed, uprooted, removed and extinguished; they are the unruly parts of our mind that need our love and attention most of all. Although against our habitual conditioning, we must courageously reach out and embrace all these unpleasant parts of our broken mind with mindfulness, and let them heal in the warmth and love of mindfulness.

Another term used interchangeably with *metta* is *adosa*, which means "without hatred." Seen this way, *metta* is what is left behind after all traces of hatred and aversion have been resolved. *Adosa* means *everything other than* hatred, which conveys a very expansive definition of love and one that is not restricted by the corrupted views and opinions of the conditioned mind. *Metta* is the boundless state of love that remains when all other restrictions have been removed. Therefore, to develop love for your enemies requires that you actively search for every reaction of hatred that stains the heart. What is needed is to apply mindfulness at the deepest level to discover and resolve whatever hinders the natural expression of the boundless state of loving-kindness that lies within. In this way we place our attention not on loving-kindness itself, but on the obstacles that prevent us expressing *metta*. If we want to discover *metta*, we must first attend to the enemy of *metta*, which is hatred and aversion based on ignorance. In order for love to develop, we must attend to the ill will, hatred and inner violence that lurk deep within the shadow-side of our personality, and we must illuminate these dark places with mindfulness and investigation, which is *metta*. As we remove each obstacle by facing our *dukkha*, we open the mind to discover the expression of true *metta* in each unfolding present moment. In other words, the path to *metta* begins with the First Noble Truth, which is awakening to the reality of *dukkha*, with mindfulness. Through mindfulness, we create the right conditions and therapeutic space in which *dukkha* can resolve, and as *dukkha* resolves itself then what remains is the ground in which true *metta* can and will arise.

284

Metta is also *alobha,* which means *everything other than* compulsive wanting and blind attachment. *Metta* is unconditional love, free from attachment and expectation, and respects the existence of the other person, or indeed, your own inner self. Love is often confused with attachment and infatuation based on that desire, but love exists only when there is freedom from attachment and bondage. Attachment, or *upadana,* creates division between the observer and the object of love, because attachment generates reactivity. The observer is not free to experience and know the reality and truth of another, but is condemned to react out of habitual conditioning, and sees only his own lifeless creation.

For love to flourish, there must be complete harmonization with *anatta,* the non-attachment to self, so that there is nothing that can obstruct the giving and receiving of love. There must be freedom from attachment and this means freedom from self, or *atta.* This realization of *anatta* happens, not through the action of will power or belief, but through the in the moment awakening of mindfulness. When we surround our compulsive reactions of wanting with the spaciousness of mindfulness, they are rendered harmless, and cease to obstruct the expression of *metta.* When *satisampajanna* arises through mindfulness, then in that very same moment, *atta* becomes *anatta* and reactivity is replaced with the compassionate responsiveness of *metta.* As always, love is not something we create, but a reality that we discover through letting go of *atta,* and that happens when we establish mindfulness.

Above all, *metta* is *amoha,* which means that it is free from delusion and ignorance. *Metta* is not blind love, but love based on the clear perception of reality through *satisampajanna,* coupled with the compassionate wisdom-intelligence of *satipanna.* True love exists when there is complete openness to the reality of life, rather than the shortsighted and distorted perceptions that come from blind idealism and fantasy. In order to discover love, we must let go of all our preconceptions and blind conditioning, and we do this by illuminating these superficial *sankharas* with mindfulness.

We must let go of our expectations and demands. This does not mean abandoning our needs, which is simply another form of reactive aversion, but that we learn to surround our needs with the compassionate space of mindfulness. We need to move away from the superficial first appearance of our likes and dislikes, and investigate the deeper reality of these mind states. In the silence of each moment of mindfulness, in which there is no movement of identification, a space opens up and in this space we discover what is wholesome and skillful. We come to know what supports love, and move in that direction under the guidance of the innate wisdom of *satipanna*. It is only when *satipanna* is free to operate that we can discover how to respond to the needs of each new situation in our relationship with Self, Other or World. Love is a movement in subtlety, a dance based on freedom and careful attention at the intuitive level, and this is brought about by mindfulness and the replacement of ignorance and delusion with clear knowing and *satisampajanna*.

UPEKKHA

Upekkha describes the relationship of equanimity, which is the foundation for the development and perfection of all the other *paramis*. Without balance, we are at the mercy of habitual reactivity and the extremes of indulgence (*lobha*) or aversion (*dosa*), conditioned by ignorance and delusion (*moha*). *Upekkha* is perhaps the single most important quality that is developed through mindfulness practice and *vipassana* meditation. *Upekkha* is the embodiment of freedom and the perfection of objectivity, and it is this combination that allows the wisdom-intelligence of *satipanna* to arise.

As the Buddha described to his son, Rahula, *upekkha* is something to be perfected during meditation:

> Rahula, develop meditation that is like the earth, for then agreeable and disagreeable sensory impressions will not take charge of your mind. Just as when people throw what is clean and unclean on the earth - faeces, urine, saliva, pus, or blood - the earth is not horrified, humiliated or disgusted by it; in the same way, agreeable and disagreeable sensory impressions will not take charge of your mind when you develop meditation like the earth.

The word "equanimity" is a good translation of *upekkha*, being derived from the Latin roots *aequus*, "even" or "equal," and *animus*, "mind" or "spirit." The whole purpose of mindfulness practice is to cultivate freedom from habitual reactivity so that we can fully experience whatever arises in consciousness, whether externally through the physical senses, or internally as thoughts and feelings.

The experiential insight knowledge (*nana*) of non-reactivity in relation to the fabrications that arise in consciousness, the *sankharas*, is called *sankharupekkha-nana*. When there is *sankaharupekkha-nana*, then we can recognize a thought or an emotion as it arises and simply know it as it is, without the compulsion to become identified with it and react. In this way we develop a stability of mind, the inner stability that is called *samadhi* that protects us from being seduced by our habitual patterns of subjective reactivity. *Upekkha* is a fundamental property of *samadhi* that conditions how the mind relates to sense objects and mental objects. It allows us to be conscious of *sankharas*, but not be dominated by them. We can fully experience and engage with pleasant or unpleasant sights, sounds, smells, tastes and body sensations, without reacting with wanting, aversion or delusion. We can experience a thought, idea, belief, emotion, without reacting and becoming lost in the inner stories of our mind. Whether the *sankharas* originate externally or in our minds, we retain our freedom at all times, and this is absolutely essential before we can have any kind of intelligent relationship with any *sankharas*.

Upekkha does not mean indifference, which has a negative, dismissive quality, and is simply a subtle form of reactive aversion (*dosa*). On the contrary, *upekkha* means that we can fully embrace experience with great care and attention, because we have the freedom from the reactivity that prevents us from fully experiencing things. Similarly, *upekkha* does not mean detachment, which is also a subtle form of aversion and lack of engagement. In fact, *upekkha* is the perfection of being fully present and fully engaged with experience. The perfection of being fully present and engaged can only happen when the mind is not reactive, because any hint of wanting, aversion or delusion, will distract attention away from the object of experience. If you react to a pleasant sight with wanting, then the wanting distracts you from the full experience of the pleasant sight. If you react with aversion to something that is painful, then you cannot fully experience and engage with the source of the pain. If you react to fear with anger, then you will experience the anger and not the original fear.

Reactivity results in distraction from the direct experience of phenomena, and this is *avijja*. Any diversion away from direct experience, any manifestation of *avijja* will inhibit beneficial change and prevent the arising of *satipanna*. *Avijja* also leads to the repression of our primary emotional reactions, causing them to become frozen in the dark recesses of the mind. Unseen, these unresolved core emotions will fester and continue to generate *dukkha* and further reactivity, which is the perpetuation of *samsara*. Therefore, the perfection of *upekkha* as a *parami* means the perfection of non-reactivity, and the perfection of the ability to be completely present for any experience, and especially the experience of *dukkha*. With such presence, the mind is free to respond to whatever it experiences, rather than react out of habit and conditioning. If the mind is in pain, then equanimity means being fully present with the pain. If the mind is full of joy, then equanimity means being fully present for the joy. Besides developing *upekkha* internally towards our thoughts, beliefs and emotions, we also cultivate the same attitude externally towards people, events and in fact, anything that we perceive through the senses. The strength of equanimity allows us to maintain balance in a world that is uncertain and changing and to do this with wisdom, patience and compassion.

Equanimity implies the freedom to engage fully with all aspects of life, whether internally or externally, without being compelled to react with greed or aversion. In the language of the Buddha, equanimity exists when there is no clinging to anything as "me" or "mine." *Upekkha* is the embodiment of the Middle Path (*majjhima patipada*) prescribed by the Buddha, and which is a guiding theme in all his teachings. The middle path is the ground of non-reactivity and not being pulled or pushed by the forces of greed or aversion. This becomes possible only when we can be fully present for our experience, because in that moment of complete presence, of *satisampajanna*, there is no ego, no observer, no knower; just the state of pure knowing itself. When we have this solid foundation in the state of pure knowing, then what emerges as actions of thinking, seech and behaviors are purified and balanced by the innate wisdom that exists in the spaciousness of *satisampajanna*. The teachings on the Noble Eightfold Path (*magga*) can be understood as the practice of *upekkha* and *majjhima patipada* in all aspects of moment-to-moment living: views and beliefs, thinking, speaking, action and behavior, livelihood, effort and the practice of mindfulness and concentration. All are perfected by wisdom and equanimity as the antidotes to the corrupting influence of habitual reactivity, greed, hatred and delusion.

The Eight Worldly Winds

The only certainty is that nothing is certain; the only unchanging constant is that everything changes. Nothing can be relied upon, which leads to the inevitable ups and downs of life that are traditionally described as the "eight worldly winds" of changing circumstances (*lokadhamma*). These are:

Pleasure and pain (*sukha* and *dukkha*)
Gain and loss (*labha* and *alabha*)
Fame and defame (*yasa* and *ayasa*)
Praise and blame (*pasamsa* and *ninda*).

Conditions change, and in each moment of change, we are faced with a fundamental choice: we can either react out of habit and *avijja*, which causes suffering; or respond with mindfulness, equanimity and *samadhi*, which allows us to fully engage with change and respond with intelligence and wisdom. At its most fundamental level, *upekkha* exists when we are able to embrace *anicca*, without any trace of resistance, and fully engage in the chaotic dance of life. To resist change is *dukkha*; to avoid change is *dukkha*; to embrace change is the happiness of spiritual and psychological freedom. True spiritual joy is to be found by moving with great intelligence within the realm of change, seeing change as life itself.

The Buddha wanted us to enjoy life to the full and not live consumed by fear and worry, and this is why he taught us to pay very close attention to our attachments and fixations. Through mindfulness, we can tune in to the inner suffering produced by clinging and recognize it when it arises. Through mindfulness, we create the right conditions of freedom that allow the mind to let go of clinging. Finding freedom from wanting and craving is not produced by the thinking mind telling us to let go, but by the letting go that arises spontaneously when there is mindfulness. Mindfulness allows us to both identify and solve the problem simultaneously by illuminating the whole field of *dukkha* and the attachments that feed *dukkha*. When we can see this clearly with *satisampajanna*, then our innate wisdom-intelligence will do the rest, and the letting go happens spontaneously, just as darkness is dispelled immediately in the moment when we switch on a light.

Learning to recognize and resolve our reactions of wanting and aversion, and then resolving the compulsive emotional energy that drives them is an essential part of the art of cultivating *upekkha*. However, there is another primary defilement, or mental affliction, to which we must also attend. This is the reaction of delusion (*moha*) that comes about through the blind identification with our habitual subjective reactions to change. The more we identify with our reactions, the more we put ourselves at the mercy of external conditions and the more we will suffer. The fundamental problem is not pain, loss, failure or criticism, which are an inevitable part of life, but the way we become blindly attached to our conditioned reactions to change. This is what converts the normal pain that comes from loss into the psychological suffering of *dukkha*. Loss, failure and criticism are painful, but the intensity of our suffering is determined entirely by our conditioned negative reactions to pain. We compound the problem and amplify the pain through the proliferation of uncontrolled negative thinking and resistance. We torture ourselves with thoughts of regret such as, "If only this hadn't happened. If only this isn't happening. If only this wouldn't happen." We worry ourselves to death when things don't go to plan. We allow our minds to be wracked with fear and anxiety about the future. We allow ourselves to drown in our sorrow and grief.

All of these negative ruminations are secondary to the event; they are secondary reactions to change. The simple, but hard fact to accept is that there is absolutely no law that says that we have to feel bad when we fail, or feel grief after the loss of something dear to us, or indulge in worry about the future. These reactions are not inevitable, but acquired; they are learned. We have become conditioned to react in these ways and continue to do so through ignorance and enslavement. We do have a choice and we do not have to be victims of our habitual reactivity. The decision to suffer or to end suffering is ultimately ours to make. This is stated in the first principle of the Noble Eightfold Path: Right Understanding (*sammaditthi*), which essentially means not allowing ourselves to be seduced into believing and becoming any of the *sankharas* that arise in the mind, but rather learning to trust in the *asankhatta citta*, the unconditioned and unfabricated reality of pure knowing itself.

The Path of Mindfulness is a path of learning to recognize our conditioned reactions to pleasure and pain, gain and loss, success and failure, praise and blame, and learning to see these habitual tendencies in their true light: as nothing more than learned habitual reactions that have arisen through inattention. We can learn to respond to these *dukkha*-reactions by surrounding them with the spacious quality of mindfulness, in which there is no identification, no blind acceptance and no additional reactivity. Through mindful-equanimity we begin to see our reactions as essentially impersonal objects that we have inadvertently picked up along the way, like barnacles that become attached to the bottom of a ship. Seeing this is awakening to *anatta*, the living relationship to our experience in which such reactions are clearly seen as not "I" and not "mine." Mindfulness practice is about letting go of our trance like identification with suffering, of believing that our suffering is inevitable and beyond our control. As we begin to awaken to the real nature of *dukkha*, as nothing more than the suffering that we produce through our own inattention to experience, we can learn how to let go of our suffering and discover a new way of living, enlightened by freedom, clear seeing and intelligence. Every moment presents us with a fundamental choice in which we can react or respond: reactivity is *atta*; responsivness is *anatta*. The great awakening that happens in each moment of *vipassana* meditation is awakening to *anatta*, welcoming *annica* with open arms, and embracing *dukkha* as the holy messenger that can deliver us from *samsara*.

Upekkha and Equilibrium

Upekkha describes the state of equilibrium in which there is maximum stability, order and harmony in the psyche, not in isolation, but in relationship to whatever arises in our experience. This is the perfection of The Path of Mindfulness and *vipassana* meditation: to develop complete balance and responsiveness to the experience of the inner world of the mind and the external world of other beings and material objects: the three realms of Self, Other and World. We don't meditate to become calm; we don't meditate to brainwash ourselves into being loving persons. We meditate to liberate the mind from the reactivity that causes stress and suffering and that obstructs the natural expression of love, compassion and wisdom.

In the end, it is all about the quality of relationship that we have with our experience, internally and externally, and *vipassana* meditation is the process of refining this relationship until there is complete equanimity in our relationship with all aspects of our experience. As the mind and heart, the psyche, become liberated from reactivity, we discover a spaciousness that allows our whole being to change in a dynamic and intelligent way guided by *panna*. The Path of Mindfulness is the art of relationship: relating to everything that arises in each moment of existence and appreciating everything in its purity. This is the only sure way of purifying right action, right understanding, right morality, and for developing genuine love and compassion.

The great sixth century Chinese Buddhist scholar Seng-ts'an left us with a beautiful poem called *Hsin Hsin Ming*, The Mind of Absolute Trust. In one passage he writes,

> If the eye never sleeps, all illusions will naturally cease.
> If the mind makes no discriminations,
> the ten thousand things are as they are, of single essence.
> To understand the mystery of this One-essence is to be released from all entanglements.
> When all things are seen equally,
> the timeless Self-essence is reached.

The Path of Mindfulness cultivates the eye that never sleeps, the perfection of *sati* and *satisampajanna*. The mind that never sleeps is free from *avijja* and attachment to the illusions of the mind, the *sankharas* created through reactive conditioning. The mind that is free from blind subjective reactivity does not grasp at the superficial discriminations made by the ego. It is free from prejudice and free from the reactions of greed, hatred and delusion that come from blind attachment to distorted beliefs. With the absence of delusional reactivity, we are free to engage with all aspects of life, with "the ten thousand things," and we can engage with them with wisdom and with the balanced perception of *upekkha*. Instead of reacting to phenomena, we respond intelligently to them with *satipanna*, the guiding intelligence that naturally arises when there is complete objectivity and non-reactivity and when we take refuge in the pure knowing of reality as it is, as an unfolding process with great depth and undefinable complexity.

The One-essence of all phenomena is their objective reality; they do not belong to anyone; they arise due to conditions, and pass away as conditions change in the dynamic flow of life. When we can dance in harmony with arising phenomena, without grasping and attaching to what we experience, then we will discover the Self-essence of pure knowing, the unconditioned and deathless consciousness that knows, but is not attached to the known. This is the dance of perfect equanimity and the perfection of the way of *Dhamma* and the Path of Mindfulness and *vipassana* meditation.

The perfection of *upekkha* is to arrive at the end of our journey on The Path of Mindfulness. Now with the perfection of complete balance in how we relate to Self, Other and World, we can begin the journey of living the completely authentic life, free from the constraints and corruptions of habitual conditioned reactivity. Now we can begin to discover the true meaning of compassion and love, and how to act in the world in a way that promotes happiness and peace, and brings an end to suffering and the cause of suffering. This is a journey that has no beginning and no end, and it is a journey that we all take together. The path is clearly marked: it begins by awakening to this moment and then the next. That is the art of The Path of Mindfulness.

GLOSSARY OF PALI TERMS

Adhitthana	Determination, resolve.
Ajahn	Teacher (Thai).
Anapanasati	Mindfulness of breathing as an exercise for developing *samadhi*.
Anatta	Not-self. Whatever we experience does not constitute a permanent self.
Anicca	Impermanence. Everything is in flux as a process of arising and passing away.
Anupadana	Non-attachment.
Avihimsa	Non-harming, non-killing (Skt. *ahimsa*).
Avijja	Ignorance, unawareness. The condition that leads to attachment, mental reactivity and suffering.
Bhavana	Cultivation of the mind (*citta bhavana*) and intuitive wisdom (*panna bhavana*). Another name for meditation.
Bhikkhu	Buddhist monk.
Bodhicitta	Awakened mind-heart. Awakened state of consciousness in which wisdom and compassion manifest.
Citta	Mind, heart, state of consciousness.
Citta sankhara	Mental reaction, mental construct.
Cittanupassana	Contemplation of mind with mindfulness.
Dana	Generosity of spirit.
Dhamma	Objective reality, without any corruption by subjective reactivity; the teachings of the Buddha that point to this reality (Skt. *Dharma*).
dhamma	Objective mental phenomena.
Dhammanupassana	Mindful contemplation of the objective reality of mental phenomena.
Ditthi	Belief, opinion, view.
Dukkha	Suffering and unsatisfactoriness. The inherent instability of conditioned phenomena

	and the mental anguish produced through blind attachment and reactivity.
Kammachanda	Indulging in sensual desire.
Kamma	Action and reaction of body, speech and mind. The theory of cause and effect (Skt. *Karma*).
Khandha	Aggregate, compound formation. All experience and existence is a composite of five aggregates in continual flux: form (*rupa*), feeling (*vedana*), perception (*sanna*), mental formations (*sankhara*) and sense consciousness (*vinnana*).
Khanti	Patience and forbearance.
Kayanupassana	Mindful contemplation of the body.
Kilesa	Mental defilements based on greed (*lobha*), hatred (*dosa*) and delusion (*moha*) that result from reactivity and attachment (Skt. *Klesha*).
Kusala	Wholesome and skillful action that lead towards the cessation of suffering. Opposite is *akusala*.
Lobha	Greed, wanting.
Magga	Path. Generally refers to the Noble Eightfold Path, which is the Fourth Noble Truth.
Mana	Conceit and self-centeredness.
Mara	Personification of *avijja* and *tanha*, the compulsive and seductive forces of ignorance and craving.
Metta	Loving-kindness, with an open heart.
Nama	Mental component of experience and existence.
Nanadassana	Insight and awakening into the Four Noble Truths in the present.
Nekkhamma	Renunciation, letting go of conventions.
Nibbana	The complete liberation from suffering due to mental reactivity (Skt. *Nirvana*).
Nirodha	Cessation of suffering. The Third Noble Truth that can be realized in the present

	moment through the application of mindfulness.
Panna	Wisdom and intuitive intelligence through direct insight and awakening to objective reality in the present (Skt. *Prajna*).
Paramattha sacca	Ultimate, objective truth, independent of an observer (see *sammutti sacca*).
Parami	Spiritual perfections that arise through wisdom and mindfulness. They are generosity, morality, renunciation, wisdom, effort, patience, truthfulness, determination, loving-kindness and equanimity (Skt. *Paramita*).
Paticasamuppada	Dependent origination, with ignorance as foundation, leading to rebirth and suffering.
Piti	Rapture, intense absorption and interest.
Rupa	The physical components of experience and existence, the body.
Sakkayaditthi	Personality. The collection of habitual conditioned subjective reactivity.
Samadhi	Concentration and mental stability that arise from meditation practice.
Samatha	Calm and tranquility that arise from meditation and the release from agitation and mental reactivity. *Samatha* meditation has this as the primary objective.
Sammutti sacca	Conventional truth. The subjective reality of labels, beliefs and language as distinct from ultimate objective reality (*paramattha sacca*).
Sampajanna	Intuitive awareness free from conditioned reactivity. Pure knowing and clear comprehension. See *satisampajanna*.
Samsara	The wheel of existence, perpetual reactivity and suffering due to ignorance and attachment. The word means "perpetual wandering."
Samudaya sacca	The Second Noble Truth of the cause of suffering due to blind attachment.

Sankhara	Conditioned mental formation and the process of mental fabrication based on ignorance. Reactivity.
Sankhata citta	Conditioned mind, reactive mind. The opposite is *asankhata citta*, the unconditioned and non-reactive state of consciousness.
Sanna	Perception and recognition.
Sati	Mindfulness. The mental quality of presence and non-reactivity.
Satipatthana	The establishment of mindfulness in the four domains of experience: body, feelings, mind and *dhammas*.
Satipanna	Intuitive wisdom and intelligence that arise when there is mindfulness.
Satisampajanna	The pure knowing that arises in the present moment when there is mindfulness. Non-delusional awareness and clear comprehension.
Sila	Moral and virtuous actions that lead to the reduction of suffering and promotion of harmony.
Sukha	Happiness. Well-being and ease of mind that arise with the cessation of suffering and mental reactivity.
Sunnata	Emptiness, creative void.
Sutta	A discourse of the Buddha (Skt. *Sutra*).
Tanha	Compulsive-obsessive force of craving based on ignorance that leads to attachment and suffering.
Upadana	Attachment based on obsession and ignorance.
Upekkha	Equanimity. The state of non-reactivity in relation to changing conditions.
Upekkha sukha	The happiness and well-being that arises when there is equanimity.
Vedana	Feeling. The felt-sense and feeling energy that gives meaning and power to experience.
Vedanupassana	The mindful contemplation of feelings.

Vimutti	The liberation of mind (*ceto vimutti*) and liberation through wisdom (*panna vimutti*).
Vinnana	Sense consciousness.
Vipallasa	Perversions and distortions of perception (*sanna vipallasa*), beliefs (*ditthi vipallasa*) and mind (*citta vipallasa*).
Vipassana	Experiential awakening and insight that leads to the cessation of suffering (*dukkhanirodha*). The practice of *vipassana* meditation, or insight meditation leads to this awakening in relation to mental phenomena.
Viriya	Energy, vitality and vigor.

INDEX